CISO Des

A Practical Guide for CISOs

Volume 2

Bill Bonney

Gary Hayslip

Matt Stamper

CISO DRG Joint Venture Publishing

Praise for
CISO Desk Reference Guide
A Practical Guide for CISOs
Volume 2

"This book, and its volume one companion, will provide any CISO, newbie or ragged veteran, the reference material to build and improve their security programs."

Rick Howard
CSO
Palo Alto Networks

~~~~~

"In this, the second instalment of The CISO Desk Reference Guide, Stamper, Hayslip and Bonney team up once again to deliver a seamless continuation of its predecessor. Each author gives us a revealing lens through which to view the remit of a CISO… they challenge the reader to operate to a much higher standard, explaining exactly how to do so. The book's power resides in each author's ability to synthesize and to present this in pragmatic prose, conveying the importance of the role of a CISO."

Jane Frankland
Founder of Cyber Security Capital
Board Advisor ClubCISO, U.K.

~~~~~

"The best disposition I have read on how to, in practical terms, address the cyber talent scarcity issue. We've been talking about the problem for years...the authors give actionable steps for how CISOs can build a "blended capability" program - FTE hiring, cross- and up-skilling existing talent, creating security evangelists across the organization, and leveraging MSSPs for commodity functions. This scarcity of skills is not going away, so it's crucial we take pragmatic steps to address it."

Kirsten Davies
Chief Security Office
Barclays Africa Group Ltd.

~~~~~

"This is how it's done, plain and simple. This is the Rosetta Stone of security, connecting the technology, the business and the people. The devil is in the details, and this book details it in a way that is personal, usable and, above all, practical."

Sam Curry
CSO
Cybereason

~~~~~

"Volume 2 applies the very original and effective Desk Reference approach to more key CISO concerns, from the cybersecurity skills gap to incident response and crisis management."

Stephen Cobb, CISSP
Senior Security Researcher
ESET North America

~~~~~

"This CISO Desk Reference, Volume 2, is by far the best CISO reference available today…. If you are aspiring to become a CISO, this book will help you design a comprehensive security program… If you are currently a CISO, this book will provide you unique guidance about the strategic and operational intricacies of a modern security program!"

Selim Aissi
CISO
Ellie Mae

~~~~~

"The second volume of the CISO Desk Reference Guide is a perfect continuation of the definitive first volume. Volume 2 provides insights, best practices and utility in useful and practical chapters. I am grateful to the authors for generously sharing their years of hard-earned experience and knowledge. They are raising the bar for security professionals everywhere."

Todd Friedman
Chief Information Security Officer
ResMed

~~~~~

"AMAZING! I JUST LOVED THE BOOK! Being a new CISO, I have got to be learning every day... The authors have only emphasised that, promoting continuous learning for the CISOs. They did an amazingly great job."

Magda Lilia Chelly, CISSP, PhD
Managing Director I CISO As A Service
Responsible Cyber Pte. Ltd., Singapore

Copyright © 2018 CISO DRG Joint Venture

CISO DRG Joint Venture Publishing
8895 Towne Centre Drive, Suite 105 #199
San Diego, CA 92122

<www.CISODRG.com>

ISBN 978-0-9977441-4-9

DISCLAIMER: The contents of this book and any additional comments are for informational purposes only and are not intended to be a substitute for professional advice. Your reliance on any information provided by the publisher, its affiliates, content providers, members, employees or comment contributors is solely at your own risk. This publication is sold with the understanding that the publisher is not engaged in rendering professional services. If advice or other expert assistance is required, the services of a competent professional person should be sought.

To contact the authors, write the publisher at the address provided above, "Attention: Author Services."

Cover illustration and original artwork
by Gwendoline Perez

Copy Editing by Nadine Bonney

Contents vii

Acknowledgments

Bill Bonney: I would like first to thank my wife, Nadine, for her loving support and willingness to help us tackle Volume 2. She is my rock, and I cannot imagine doing this without her. I am grateful for the support and camaraderie from my colleagues in the San Diego Information Security community, especially the members of the San Diego CISO Round Table. Thank you also to all the CISOs in the worldwide community who have given us feedback and encouragement as we've published the two volumes that make up the CISO Desk Reference Guide, we hope it makes a difference. And once again, thank you to my partners Gary and Matt for their friendship and collaboration, this has been even more rewarding than I had hoped!

Matt Stamper: Working on a book never happens in a vacuum. You need the support and patience of your family and friends as you work on research, drafting content, refining ideas, and ultimately building a narrative that can be carried throughout the entirety of the work. My wife Lisa and our twin daughters Lauren and Danielle have been supportive throughout this entire process. I am blessed to be Lisa's husband and Danielle's and Lauren's dad. I'm also thankful for the love and support of my mom and my dad who gave me a love of learning. This effort certainly would not have been possible without the patience of my co-authors Bill and Gary. Their friendship and sense of humor have been constant and appreciated. I am also indebted to the broader CISO community for their shared insights and experiences. Equally important, I'd like to acknowledge and thank the San Diego Cyber Center of Excellence (CCOE), the San Diego CISO Round Table, and the San Diego ISACA and InfraGard chapters. The collaboration among San Diego's cyber community is second to none.

Gary Hayslip: I would like to tell my wife of 28 years, Sandi, thank you for your patience and calming influence. Your love and support have allowed me to stay focused as we continue this project. You are my best friend, and I thank you for putting up with my late-night rewrites and rambling debates with Matt and Bill. I often say that cybersecurity can't mature in a box, but as part of a community it will flourish and protect organizations. With that in mind, I'd like to thank the collaborative San Diego cybersecurity community. I am truly grateful for the support and partnership that I have received over the last 20 years. I especially appreciate my friends and colleagues at Peerlyst, ISC2, ISACA, ISSA, OWASP, CCOE, InfraGard, EvoNexus and the CISO Round Table. Each of you in your way contributed to the knowledge and passion that I have today for cybersecurity and the role of CISO. I am honored to count many of you as mentors, friends, and peers. Finally, I want to thank my two co-authors, Bill Bonney and

Matt Stamper. I am happy I listened to your idea over fish tacos and beer. Walking this path together has been amazing. I am honored to count you as friends, and I look forward to continuing this journey together.

The authors wish to thank Gwendoline Perez for all her work in creating original cover art, graphical illustrations and design advice. In addition, Nadine Bonney deserves special appreciation as well for painstakingly combing through our run-on sentences, word usage disasters and our collective under-appreciation for the Chicago Manual of Style. We would once again like to acknowledge our lawyer, Marinda Neumann, for her wise counsel as we set up licensing agreements and trademarks to protect our venture.

Finally, the authors wish to thank the following industry and academic leaders who were kind enough to provide thoughtful review comments that have helped make the CISO Desk Reference Guide a reality.

Thank you to Stephen Cobb, Jane Frankland, Todd Friedman, RADM (Ret) Kenneth D. Slaght, Rick Howard, Sam Curry, Selim Aissi, Kirsten Davies, and Magda Lilia Chelly for your time to review and provide thoughtful feedback.

Preface

Bill Bonney, Gary Hayslip, and Matt Stamper met in the summer of 2014 as members of the very inclusive and collaborative cybersecurity community of San Diego, California. Besides being the eighth largest city in the U.S. and a very welcoming community, San Diego is home to several pockets of technological innovation. These include very successful biotechnology, life sciences, and mobile technology industries; a plethora of defense contractors and aerospace research companies; a blossoming startup community in the Internet of Things (IoT) and Cybersecurity; and a thriving academic environment. San Diego is also home to the fewest number of "Fortune 500" company headquarters, per capita, in the U. S.

The decision to write The CISO Desk Reference Guide, Volumes 1 and 2, came from the shared realization by the authors that the dramatic escalation in cyber threats was not going to peak anytime soon. Cybercrime would continue to move "down the food chain" as more relative economic value is managed via interconnected computer networks. Mid-sized firms in particular, the kinds that make up the local commercial base in San Diego, would come under increasing pressure as targets both for their value and as the supposed "weaker links" in the supplier ecosystem of larger, multinational companies.

Each of the authors has enjoyed over 30 years of success in the Information Technology field, but they have very different backgrounds. It became obvious as they got to know each other by participating on panels and speaking at industry events that these different backgrounds brought diverse and complementary perspectives to the problems the cybersecurity community currently faces. What started as a panel discussion on the role of the modern CISO sparked such a lively audience discussion that the authors began to consider turning this topic into a book for new CISOs and CISOs at mid-size firms in particular.

To allow those different perspectives to come through as obviously in print as they did during interactive sessions, they decided to take a unique approach to writing this book. Instead of dividing up topics or co-authoring each chapter, they decided to have each author write a separate essay about each topic from their unique perspective. While this approach presents minor duplication and an interesting transition in styles from one essay to the next, the authors believe that this tri-perspective take on each topic will provide additional benefits to the reader.

Volume 2 is similar to Volume 1 in that it is structured as a desk reference guide and organized as nine chapters with an introduction, three essays, and a summary for each chapter. The introduction highlights the different perspectives that each author brings to the chapter and sets the tone with the questions that the authors used to frame their thoughts. The summary pulls together five key points and five immediate next steps for the reader and his or her team, making this a practical guide for CISOs. The summary and key action for Chapter 18 is to build your strategic cybersecurity plan.

The order of the essays within each chapter continues to follow the arc of our authors' differing backgrounds and perspectives. Bill Bonney's essays lead off each chapter and provide a high-level perspective that reflects his background in the finance industry and the structured governance that comes with working in a highly regulated industry. Matt Stamper's essays come next, and his perspective on simultaneously providing services to many customers provides insight into a highly programmatic approach. Gary Hayslip's essays finish each chapter and his vast experience in the trenches as a hands-on cyber expert provides the reader with a treasure trove of lists and lessons that they can repeatedly reference.

As a guide written specifically for CISOs, we hope Volume 1 and Volume 2 of the CISO Desk Reference Guide become trusted resources for you, your teams, and your colleagues in the C-suite. The different perspectives can be used as standalone refreshers, and the five immediate next steps for each chapter give the reader a robust set of 85 actions based on roughly 100 years of relevant experience that will help you strengthen your cybersecurity programs. In the conclusion of this book, we provide contact information and encourage you to join the community of CISOs who use these resources. We also encourage you to provide us with feedback about the guidance and our tri-perspective approach to this book. We hope you like it.

Introduction

Throughout Volumes 1 and 2 of the CISO Desk Reference Guide, we have been unfolding the building blocks of a well-designed cybersecurity program. We've held two simultaneous narratives:

- Provide a complete treatment that is risk-aware and standards-based and covers the responsibilities of the CISO from the board's perspective and management's perspective, and from the viewpoint of the CISO as the cyber guardian, chief resilience officer, and the organization's risk management evangelist.
- Provide the material in an instructional manner to allow those who have never been a CISO, especially those who are inheriting a less-mature program or no program at all, to build a program that is grounded in the best practices of those who have already earned their grey hairs. This can also apply to small or medium-sized organizations that don't necessarily have an abundance of organizational resilience.

In Volume 1, we focused the CISO internally, on assessing the state and structure of their program. We started with the basics and laid out our thoughts about how the organization should be structured based on the strengths of the organization, the industry in which it participates, and the needs of management and the board. We walked through regulatory and audit requirements and how these requirements influence where the CISO should focus their attention. And finally, we looked at the data the organization holds, both as custodian for its customers and other stakeholders as well as for its strategic advantage. Armed with an understanding of these basics, we then moved on to governance.

We began the governance discussion with a chapter on third parties, vendors, and suppliers because the ecosystems we build today are so interconnected with partners, and that interconnection creates creases in our cybersecurity defenses and forces us to entrust our data to so many other parties. Then we focused on metrics, reporting and communicating our priorities and status to management and the board to educate the organization and affect the changes we see as critical to creating reasonable cyber resilience.

Then we tied our governance discussion together with a chapter on risk management and cyber insurance because to us, one of the most important governance concepts is how the CISO helps management and the board understand the full scope of risk and the techniques being used to render the risk acceptable to ensure that the organization is a going concern. While no good CISO wants to slow the pace of change, every good CISO recognizes and helps the organization understand that the pace of technology change combined with the expanding network perimeter exposes us to enormous risk.

After we addressed the basics and governance, we began to explore the tactical requirements for any cybersecurity program. We did a deep dive into tools and techniques, both from the perspective of which business processes to prioritize and how to construct a toolkit that would allow the cybersecurity team to meet those needs. The technologies in use at your organization and throughout today's interconnected networks typically don't have a fully defined perimeter. They are designed for the mobile worker and geo-dispersed teams with numerous third-party connections to vendors and trusted partners.

It's these new network infrastructures that exist in the cloud, in shared data centers, and on mobile devices that force CISOs to revisit their strategic plans frequently, so they can implement the cybersecurity program that appropriately addresses and reduces the organization's risks while helping the business unlock opportunity. At the end of Volume 1, in Chapter 9, we looked at how to use cybersecurity policy to provide the framework for the cybersecurity program.

In Volume 2, we flip the focus from assessing to building. In Chapter 10, we look at talent – how to identify, grow, and retain the critical people and people skills so important for a successful cybersecurity program. Now that we had walked the CISO through assessing their program, capturing their inventory of business processes and tools, and aligning their staff, we could begin to describe how to prepare the organization to be the kind of resilient organization we believe will be necessary to be successful in the digital world we compete in today.

We dedicate four chapters in Volume 2 to that resilience. We address education for the staff and the organization, monitoring the health and security of the organization's digital assets, and using threat intelligence to help the organization stay ahead of (or at least keep up with) the changing threat landscape. Finally, we discuss using all of this focus on health, monitoring, and threats to inform the backups and recovery planning that are essential to helping the organization rebound from *any* disrupting event, not just a cyber event.

All of this sets the stage for dealing with the inevitable flood of incidents, large and small. We believe that by treating the small incidents with the same formal process applied to larger incidents, the organization can stay sharp and respond with more agility to the existential threats that are becoming all too common. Key to that preparedness is the communication program that keeps the organization informed and responding as one. And finally, wrapping up the program, we discuss recovery and resuming operations along with a deep dive into what went wrong and what we can learn from the entire episode through an exploration of forensics and the post-mortem process.

Chapter 10 – Finding Talent and Developing Your Team

Introduction

We begin Volume 2 with a discussion about people. As you strive to create a world-class cybersecurity program, you must recognize and address the critical human element. We look at the human element from several different perspectives. We include the technical skills that are required and how to assess them; motivating, inspiring and nurturing the people on your team; and understanding the environmental factors that impact your talent pool and your hiring decisions.

Bill Bonney offers a lot of practical advice on assessing, recruiting, motivating and developing the people on the CISO's team. But he also recommends an honest assessment of the tasks that can realistically be outsourced to third parties and proposes that you look at how technology, specifically artificial intelligence, can help you be more effective in meeting your goals. Bill includes a bit of a call to arms for our industry to address the shortfall of qualified candidates.

Matt Stamper suggests that CISOs should carefully consider how they define each position. It is essential that requirements and job descriptions are realistic and appeal to the people you are trying to attract. Matt also thoughtfully unpacks several factors, both internal and external to the organization, which impact the composition of the talent pool for any particular hire.

Gary Hayslip takes a data-driven approach to workforce planning that acknowledges the fierce competition for talent in the field of cybersecurity and offers practical advice for motivating the people on your team. He continues using data to define a set of metrics to help the CISO determine if the talent on the team is delivering the outcomes that are needed and to help develop the training necessary to close any gaps.

Some of the questions the authors used to frame their thoughts for this chapter include:

- How do CISOs develop their hiring priorities to support the organization and their cybersecurity program effectively?
- What hard and soft skills does the CISO believe their cybersecurity program requires?
- How can I construct a training program that will keep my team's knowledge, skills, and techniques current?
- What metrics can I use to measure the effectiveness of my cybersecurity team's capabilities to provide security services and reduce risk to the organization?

> "CISOs must recognize that they are always recruiting."

I think it's important to put the topics of recruiting, skills, training, and development in the larger context of talent management and the still larger context of the changing workforce demographics and the technical skills shortage that we face in industry – the so-called "War for Talent." My point is not to give the reader comfort that this is a problem faced by many companies across most industrial sectors and throughout the entire world economy because that doesn't absolve us from dealing with the problem, but rather, to draw attention to the true scope of the problem.

In the larger sense, we are dealing with a fundamental transformation of the use of human capital, on par with the industrial revolution. We should keep this in mind when determining how to approach our talent issues. Yes, the short-term tactical advice is always useful. But, planning for the long term can't be ignored and will take a combination of human resource planning, government policy changes, new capacity and new approaches in our education systems, and new technology. These changes will require us to work differently with partners and suppliers to achieve the outcomes we want. We can't rely on the old models of allocated headcount with defined duties and desired skills to just "get the work done."

Talent and the Human Element

Let's first put the topics for this chapter in the larger context of talent management. Talent management as a discipline traditionally includes four pillars: recruitment, learning, performance, and compensation. This chapter is focused on recruitment and learning which is done for an outcome (performance) at a price (compensation). Keep in mind that the purpose of talent management is to create a high-performing, sustainable organization that meets its strategic and operational goals and objectives. The goal we have for talent development is to:

- allow the Information Security team to develop the skills and capabilities to continually adapt to changing business and threat environments, thereby

- help the larger organization identify and manage the risks that threaten its information and operations technology, in order to
- safeguard the organization's data (both generated and entrusted), and
- protect the people and operations from cyber and cyber-kinetic harm, thus
- enabling the organization to compete with less drag and friction.

I think to be successful with how we approach building and developing our team's capabilities we need to consider the human element. Several different works that share some similarities with each other are helpful here. The first is a book called *Drive: The Surprising Truth About What Motivates Us* (Pink 2009) by Daniel H. Pink. The second is a study conducted by Tony Schwartz of The Energy Project along with Christine Porath, an associate professor at Georgetown University's McDonough School of Business. The study is summarized well in an article in the New York Times (Porath 2014). The third is an article in the MIT Sloan Management Review (Gunter K. Stahl 2012) called "Six Principles of Effective Global Talent Management."

What is common to these works is the assertion that the sense of purpose that each person has for their work is more indicative of their engagement and success than their skills. The argument is that affinity is a more important predictor than efficiency.

That is not to say that skills aren't important. On the contrary, one has little chance of being successful without possessing the skills required for the job. But it would be worth your time to review these works. Daniel Pink tells us that by providing our teams with opportunities for autonomy, mastery, and purpose, we are providing the key ingredients to motivate our people. Tony Schwartz and Christine Porath tell us that employees are vastly more satisfied and productive when four of their core needs are met:

- physical, through opportunities to regularly renew and recharge at work;
- emotional, by feeling valued and appreciated for their contributions;
- mental, when they can focus in an absorbed way on their most important tasks and define when and where they get their work done;
- and spiritual, by doing more of what they do best and

---

[1] https://theenergyproject.com/ - referenced November 2016

enjoy most, and by feeling connected to a higher purpose at work.

Gunter Stahl, et al., found that large successful companies adhere to six key principles rather than traditional management best practices focused on maximizing the four pillars listed above. Those key principles are:

- alignment with strategy,
- internal consistency,
- cultural embeddedness,
- management involvement,
- a balance of global and local needs, and
- employer branding through differentiation.

Therefore, I'd like to suggest that we think of the people we work with, who help us achieve our outcomes, as people, not just talent. We would like to hire the best people with the right skills and mindset, help them become even better at what they do, have them share a common set of goals, and have them engaged and happy to be part of our team for the long haul.

Recruitment

With the human element considered, let's turn to the issue of recruitment. I referred at the beginning of this chapter to the "War for Talent" and noted that we are dealing with a fundamental transformation regarding how we deploy human capital. These changes affect different industries in unique ways and the various functions within organizations in very different ways. Three factors I think we need to address are the scarcity of qualified workers, third-party service delivery, and augmentation using artificial intelligence.

Scarcity of Qualified Workers

A significant result of the industrial revolution was the migration of populations from rural to urban centers. This migration was aided by several factors. Among these factors were the ability of manufacturers to expand the capacity of their workforce, the resulting increase in productivity and profitability of doing so, the resulting elasticity of wages, and the relatively low barrier to entry (compared to both the guild system that preceded industrialization and the highly technical skillsets that are required in today's digital workplace). While there were often labor shortages when new factories or industries popped up, the pace of industrial development, the availability of investment capital, and the speed of communications served as natural governing factors.

Still, labor shortages could at times doom businesses or at least temporarily suppress profits. In short, the demand signal was sent, and the response was the arrival of men and women ready to work. Training shifted from years of apprenticeship to mere weeks of classroom or vestibule training, but the key factor was the availability of any person ready and willing to work.

Fast-forward three hundred years, and many of the jobs we need to fill are highly specialized, requiring years of school and what amounts to years of apprenticeship. The demand signal has again been sent, and governments and universities recognize the severe shortages of highly-skilled workers, not just cybersecurity professionals. However, the pace of development in the digital age, the availability of abundant investment capital, and the instantaneous speed of communications serve as accelerators, not governors.

Enough Admiring the Problem. What Are We Going to Do About It?

First, CISOs must recognize that they are always recruiting. Even if there is no unfilled headcount today, the people you meet, the connections you forge, and the network you build will be necessary to create and maintain a pool of talented people for your organization. And while there is a minimum bar for the skills your team will need to be successful, you can only hire for so many of those skills. The cost (in hard cost and opportunity loss) of competing for and hiring fully formed senior security engineers for all positions has already become prohibitive.

Hiring the right team will be a mix of seasoned individuals from outside of the organization along with individuals you nurture. You will use your network, internal and external to your organization, to help you identify and attract both.

You could easily create a laundry list of security domains along with areas of specific process expertise from reviewing the requirements and controls listed in the eight CISSP domains, the 18 security control families from the NIST 800-53 standard, and the 12 PCI-DSS requirements. Add in various processes that have information technology and information security overlap, such as vulnerability management, change management, and mobile device management, along with security-focused activities, services and products such as threat intelligence, forensic analysis, penetration testing, intrusion detection and prevention, and the whole discipline of governance, risk and compliance, and you have a massive set of competencies from which to select job requirements.

It's tempting to reduce this problem to simple analogies such as building a professional sports team. Drafting from the college ranks to fill skill gaps is like hiring workers early in their careers. Using free-agency can fill more senior positions. The minor leagues provide internships. And a deep bench can stand in for succession planning. These analogies can help explain the situation in simple, familiar terms, but they can also seem repetitious and shallow, and the consequences of failure are very different.

When we trivialize talent development by comparing it with building a sports team, we risk treating all professionals the same as members of sports teams – short-term combinations of skills designed to win a trophy. Failing to win a trophy is disappointing to the team and the host city, but teams can be overhauled in a matter of a few years and a trophy in 5 or 10 years, though not ideal, will still be celebrated.

The skills needed to be successful in the modern white-collar workplace (both hard and soft) are not so readily observed, as they are showcased outside of the arena of public spectacle. Employees are afforded many labor protections that professional athletes do not enjoy. And, the consequence of the team's performance is greater than the disappointment in the execution of a billionaire's hobby. And thus, the analogy breaks down.

The few elements of this analogy I do think can add value to our thinking are the youth leagues and skills development programs that exist across all of the major team sports. These programs are available for baseball, football, basketball, hockey, soccer, volleyball, gymnastics and even sports that are more focused on individuals, such as tennis, swimming, ice skating, skiing and golf. In fact, I can't think of any sports that don't have youth leagues and skills development programs, and many include community outreach, traveling ambassadors, senior leagues, and representation in K-12 physical education programs.

While not the only cause for this deep infiltration of sport at every level of our society, one major reason for this is President Kennedy's revitalization of the President's Council on Physical Fitness and Sports.[2] Physical fitness was seen as a critical need for all Americans to maintain a healthy lifestyle, both for their health and the cost to the nation that would most certainly result from the poor health of the population.

I do not mean to trivialize healthcare or the impact of poor health to our lives, but I do think that building a nation that is "cyber healthy" will be crucial to our citizens' financial health and our nation's public safety. I believe that existing programs that invest in STEM (and STEAM) education, hackathons, and other curriculum-based and

---

[2] In 2010, the name was changed to the President's Council on Fitness, Sports, and Nutrition

after-school activities for the K-12 education system are vital to both teach skills and familiarize students and their parents, with cyber hygiene, cyber defense and where the skill and interest surfaces, cyber offense.

Investing for the Long Term

There is widespread recognition that building the skills and competencies needed to improve the overall cybersecurity of critical infrastructure requires national and coordinated attention. NIST's National Initiative for Cybersecurity Education (NICE) is focused directly on addressing this challenge. Special Publication 800-181 outlines the initiative.

NICE offers prescriptive detail regarding seven core security functions, and 33 specialty areas of cybersecurity work. It defines 52 cybersecurity roles while providing the requisite knowledge, skills, abilities, and tasks for each role. NICE thereby helps organizations understand the types of skills and competencies that will be required to support a security program comprehensively.

In the graphics below, the seven core security functions are described, and a sample drill-down is provided. Within each core functional area, NICE provides insights and recommendations on necessary training to adequately address the function. NICE therefore provides the foundation for your cybersecurity staffing program.

Both graphics are courtesy of the National Initiative for Cybersecurity Careers and Studies[3].

---

3 https://niccs.us-cert.gov/workforce-development/cyber-security-workforce-framework#

Analyze
Performs highly-specialized review and evaluation of incoming cybersecurity information to determine its usefulness for intelligence.

Collect and Operate
Provides specialized denial and deception operations and collection of cybersecurity information that may be used to develop intelligence.

Investigate
Investigates cybersecurity events or crimes related to information technology (IT) systems, networks, and digital evidence.

Operate and Maintain
Provides the support, administration, and maintenance necessary to ensure effective and efficient information technology (IT) sytem performance and security.

Oversee and Govern
Provides leadership, management, direction, or development and advocacy so the organization may effectively conduct cybersecurity work.

Protect and Defend
Identifies, analyzes, and mitigates threats to internal information technology (IT) systems and/or networks.

Securely Provision
Conceptualizes, designs, procures and/or builds and secure information (IT) systems, with responsibility for aspects of system and/or network development.

Figure 10.1 The NICE Cybersecurity Workforce Framework

All-Source Analysis
Analyzes threat information from multiple sources, disciplines, and agencies across the Intelligence Community. Synthesizes and places intelligence information in context; draws insights about the possible implications.

Below are the roles for this Specialty Area. Click each role to see the KSAs (Knowledge, Skills, and Abilities) and Tasks.

All-Source Analyst
(AN-ASA-001)

Analyzes data/information from one or multiple sources to conduct preparation of the environment, respond to requests for information, and submit intelligence collection and production requirements in support of planning and operations.

⊕ Abilities

⊕ Knowledge

⊕ Skills

⊕ Tasks

Related Courses
Security+ (SYO-501) Certification Training
CyberVista
Online, Instructor-Led, Online, Self-Paced

Security+ SY0-501 Certification Training
Web of Security, LLC
Online, Instructor-Led

EC-Council Certified Ethical Hacker v9 Certification Training
Web of Security, LLC
Online, Instructor-Led

Protecting Your Organization from Insider Threats
Georgia Tech Professional Education
Classroom

Certified Expert Fusion Analyst (CEFA)
Lunarline Inc.
Online, Self-Paced

Show More Courses

Figure 10.2 Detailed Description of Analyst Position

With the NICE skills framework, educational organizations across the nation, including K-12 schools, trade schools, community colleges, technical institutes, and universities can design programs to provide the critical training our workforce needs.

Helping the cyber workforce become productive is another gap that we must fill. The traditional model of graduating four-year degreed individuals from colleges and universities will not, by itself, overcome the worker deficit we face. On-the-job experience, in the form of internships and apprentice programs, is another vital source of learning that is necessary to allow newly trained workers to put their skills to use quickly.

Internships are excellent supplements for the typical four-year program that help the student step out of the classroom and spend critical time in the field at a variety of organizations, seeing real-world events unfold in real time. Apprenticeship programs allow a broader set of experiences that can help trainees use additional avenues to gain the skills they need. These include students who are not following the four-year degree path, workers reentering the workforce, military personnel who are transitioning into the commercial workforce, and unlocking other sources of specialists that are currently under-utilized. A critical insight is that just as the total number of seats in four-year degree programs is not adequate to provide all the cybersecurity workers we will need, and the traditional four-year program is simply not required for many of the entry-level positions that currently go unfilled.

One final recommendation about some of these novel approaches to training the cyber workforce of tomorrow is to look to cyber ranges as an option worth exploring. Cyber ranges can help you train new workers on current methods and help keep your existing workforce up-to-date. Think of cyber ranges as simulators, but under live fire. In order to train our pilot workforce without crashing real planes, we built and deployed flight simulators. Cyber-ranges scenarios are real, but with coaches and highly-skilled experts available as backup.

Hiring Who You Need

Coming back now to your immediate hiring decisions. While it's difficult to hire individuals with a mastery of the complete list of skills and experience across each of the relevant domains, senior security engineers and security architects should have a fundamental knowledge of all of them. How can you possibly determine whether the more senior people you are hiring have the right level of broad mastery? Some rely on certifications, but I challenge how effective that is. I see a lot of value in certifications; they set an effective minimum bar in many areas, they come with an ongoing requirement for continuing education that in theory keeps people in constant learning mode, and they provide a shorthand for assessing, in aggregate, the skill level of a department.

The latter is the most perilous, though. In any population of certificate holders, just given a normal bell curve of capability, there will be some people who barely met the proficiency requirements. It is not statistically impossible to have a larger than normal collection of people on the left side of the bell. Also, the minimum bar I spoke of is just that, a minimum. It gives a reasonable assurance of familiarity with general concepts, but unfortunately, there is not enough assurance that the familiarity comes along with experiential knowledge.

So, while certifications have their purpose, we can't solely rely on them for determining the technical fit for new hires. What other tools do we have? A lot of time and energy have gone into interviewing techniques that will both root out the hard skills (have the candidate take a coding test or configure a firewall rule) and soft skills (subject the candidate to team interviews with each team member tasked with assessing certain key soft skills such as communication skills, problem solving, managing up, and team dynamics). There are several systems out there. One of the more popular ones is the "STAR" Technique: situation, task, action, result. It's so popular that interview candidates also use it to prepare to talk to you.

None of this is ground-breaking, and chances are good your Human Resource department will have a favorite rating system that you can adapt to the hard and soft skills that you want to test for in your screening. But most of the last two paragraphs assumes that you have a pool of reasonable candidates to start from, and your job is to screen for a fit for your team. I do happen to agree that these techniques are valuable. However, I have always found the greater challenge to be finding the reasonable pool of candidates in the first place.

That is why I said that even if there is no unfilled headcount today, the people you meet, the connections you forge, and the network you build will be necessary to create and maintain a pool of talented people for your organization. You want to make sure you always know who you would try to recruit to your organization if you should have a position open. Every interaction you have in your local security community is a recruiting event. Every meeting, every talk, every conference, every happy hour.

I'm going to put the cart before the horse to share a brief thought. The single most important recruiting tool you have is your team. If team members are motivated, work as a team, win more often than they lose, celebrate their wins, pick each other up when they are down, and care about the company they work for, others will want to come work for you too. I know that doesn't help a lot when you are building a new team, but there is some element of that statement that you can leverage in practically any situation. They will help make your team an attractive place to be before there is a position available.

It is also important to pay attention to social tools such as LinkedIn and Twitter as well as any blogs or security forums you participate in. Make sure your profiles are up to date and that they show a positive image of you and your role. The same should be true for the people on your team. Just as companies use social tools to vet candidates, we all use social tools to vet the companies and teams we want to join. When we see a limited profile, we might believe them to be insular and two-dimensional. That may not always be accurate but underestimate the subconscious signals we pull from social tools at your own peril.

Chapter 10 Key Point and Action Item 1

It is essential to recognize that the CISO, and the entire Information Security team, are continually recruiting. Every opportunity to interact with your community is an opportunity to assess and impress the people that can help you succeed.

You should identify formal and informal networking activities offered by your community to make sure you have an appropriate presence at these events. Remember to include your team as recruiting is often most effective at the peer level. Also, include a thorough review of social media profiles and activities.

Practical Steps to Take

How do you know what is right for your organization? Before posting a job description on a job board, make an objective assessment of your team. Determine where you are strong and where you should make improvements. Prioritize the capabilities you need to add or shore up. Ground that priority assessment in the reality of the outcomes you need to deliver. Extending the process and tool inventory we recommended in Chapter 8 to include the people responsible for your process outcomes is a great way to start.

It's important to have a good understanding of how you stand across the skills that are important to you. If you are a newly-hired CISO yourself or are building a new team or significantly expanding capacity, this skills assessment is vital not just for making hiring decisions, but also to define staff development needs. What I have found helpful is to rank each of your people across the skills you need using a 6-point scale (remember to include the soft skills in this ranking):

- 0=no capability
- 1=beginner
- 2=capable of executing with coaching or oversight
- 3=adequate to the task
- 4=capable of assessing, executing, and directing projects on their own
- 5=expert/teacher

You'll notice in looking at the values 0-5 that there is not a linear degree of skill ranking. Rather, these labels identify a skill level that defines suitability to task. The value of using numbers (you can substitute letters A-F if you like) is that sorting and grouping become easier as you are assessing many skills over a large group of people.

The table below shows a simple grid layout for capturing the rankings in a way that I have found to be very helpful for decision making.

Person	Role	Skill	Current Capability	Ideal Capability	Action
Alice L. Glass	Current Role	Skill 1	3	3	None
Alice L. Glass	Current Role	Skill 2	2	3	Training
John B. Good	Current Role	Skill 1	2	3	Training
John B. Good	Current Role	Skill 2	4	3	Mentor
None		Skill 3	0	3	Partner
None		Skill 4	0	4	Hire

Figure 10.3 Skills Ranking Matrix

Focusing on the current capability alone could be useful for performance management, but only in the sense that you are identifying who possesses the skills that are most difficult to replace. Focusing on the ideal capability allows you to set a bar of competence supporting the outcomes you identified for your key processes. Capturing both the current capability and the ideal capability allows you to identify both those areas where you have no coverage and where you have inadequate coverage, in a single inventory. You can then use this for prioritizing hiring decisions and development opportunities. These two activities should always be connected.

Tracking the improvement in current capability over time allows you to track the progress of members of your team. Tracking the delta between current capability and ideal capability over time allows you to track your progress in improving your organization's ability to address the goals of talent management identified at the beginning of this chapter.

Third-Party Service Delivery

Now that you have identified your key processes and assessed your existing team's ability to produce the outcomes you want, you can work with your management peers and agree on where you will need to add security specialists to ensure the right level of protection for your key business processes. Do not assume that every security gap you find must be filled by a security professional on your team. Ask yourself three questions about each potential position you want to create:

1. Is the best way to address this gap for my company to hire a person or to contract the service from a trusted vendor?
2. Is this job best filled or only filled by a security professional with specialized skills?
3. With my limited budget, is this a priority for me to hire as opposed to another department?

For question 1, the decision is whether it makes sense to outsource this function. Most executives at this point have learned to avoid the temptation to turn outsourcing into a purely economic decision. Certainly, there were instances in the past when there were overwhelming cost advantages to outsourcing some functions and failing to consider that option could potentially put your firm at a competitive disadvantage. That is rarely the case now as the cost of labor arbitrage has largely dissipated. Still, many executives in the past made the erroneous assumption that these decisions were made for purely economic reasons and that was rarely the case.

An exercise I have found helpful in deciding which functions I might safely outsource if that seems to be the right option is to use a model such as this one adapted from Geoffrey Moore's model of mission-critical core versus context from his book *Dealing with Darwin: How Great Companies Innovate at Every Phase of Their Evolution* (Moore 2005).

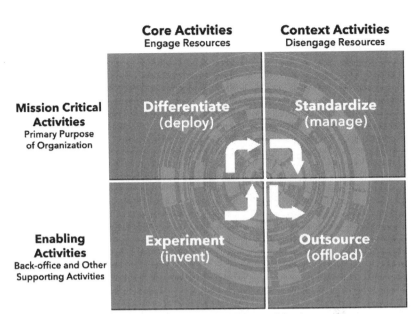

	Core Activities Engage Resources	**Context Activities** Disengage Resources
Mission Critical Activities Primary Purpose of Organization	**Differentiate** (deploy)	**Standardize** (manage)
Enabling Activities Back-office and Other Supporting Activities	**Experiment** (invent)	**Outsource** (offload)

Figure 10.4 Core Versus Context Matrix

Using this matrix to group functions into mission-critical vs. enabling and core vs. context allows me to easily see what I can safely offload, either by outsourcing or by engaging another department. This combined with the skills inventory and ranking described provides a powerful assessment of where and how to invest in the right talent for your organization. While this exercise was developed by Moore to address whole organizations and how they allocate money and management, along with time and energy, as in Chapter 8 when I suggested using horizon planning for building your toolset, I think it is extremely useful to adapt business tools to your purposes. They are valuable tools, they get you thinking strategically, and they also keep you thinking like a business executive, and that's key to making decisions that are best for the business.

Economics is a factor, but so too, and often more important, are reducing management oversight burden, utilizing specialized skillsets that are difficult to acquire and difficult to maintain, and taking advantage of pools of talent and graduating expertise that a single individual cannot bring to an organization. These reasons are quite valid and should guide you in your choice to outsource or not. While the pure labor arbitrage has mostly disappeared, there is a recognized concentration of specific skills within companies and regions.

Although this concentration may eventually dissipate, security firms are hiring to create a competitive advantage much like investment banks have done in the past. This is forcing some companies to move or expand into regions (domestic and international) that have acquired these concentrations of specific skills.[4] For those companies who are not large enough to use their national or global footprint to their advantage, it may be cost prohibitive to staff some functions internally.

Let's assume you have asked and answered question 1. As a result, you have decided that you can't hire someone external to the organization, through contracting or third-party engagement, and you've gone through the exercises to determine that this is a priority function to fill. The core versus context exercise should now help you decide whether this is a core function of your organization as well. If you are not out to build the biggest group, but instead want to build

---

[4] The willingness of companies to do this, along with the natural concentrations that occur due to the gravitational pull of educational institutions and the labor force concentrations that occur because of previously successful companies and their offshoots, create competitive advantages that are exploited by regional planning commissions much like tax breaks and infrastructure construction.

the group best suited for the task at hand, the best answer might be to locate this function in a central operations team that provides services throughout the company. If the task doesn't require a security background, the function probably doesn't belong in your department.

Now that you have decided to hire, I'm going to refer you to Matt and Gary's essays for this chapter. You will find detailed treatments on skillsets, competencies, recruiting techniques, job descriptions, and other valuable material. To conclude my contribution, I'd like to come back to a statement I made a few pages back.

Augmentation Using Artificial Intelligence

I listed three factors that I think we need to address and so far, we have covered two: the scarcity of qualified workers and the need to effectively engage third parties to get all the work done. I have suggested some tools that can help you determine where your gaps are, and which gaps to fill first. The scarcity of qualified workers is the issue that gets brought up more by CISOs we talk to than any other. I don't get the feeling this problem is going to go away. And that brings us to the final factor: augmentation using artificial intelligence.

We are just starting to use artificial intelligence to solve real problems. Initially, this is limited to behavior analysis, anomaly detection, and predictive analytics. Using weak artificial intelligence and structured machine learning, we can detect patterns, establish baselines for normal activity, and detect anomalies within those behavior patterns. Using predictive analytics, we are getting better at guessing which of these deviations from normal are dangerous and which are merely new benign behaviors. As we develop and then learn how to apply strong, or general artificial intelligence, I believe there is an increasing role for AI in cybersecurity. It is practically mandated because of the exploding number of devices trading gigantic volumes of traffic and storing enormous amounts of data.

I do not advocate the haphazard application of AI or throwing money at every early-stage AI-enhanced cybersecurity tool that hits your radar. I think there is way too much hype in this field. But I do think that a key part of your strategy should be to seek the best guidance you can find and invest in promising AI approaches in the tools you deploy and in the people that you seek. Learn how to integrate data sciences and business intelligence, along with your AI-enhanced tools. Every function, at some point in the future, will be enhanced by artificial intelligence. My advice is to start planning for that by adding in hiring competencies and experimenting with various AI approaches to see how they might fit into your organization, now and in the future.

> "Cybersecurity is still an ascent and rapidly developing field in which job titles and role descriptions vary from organization to organization and sector to sector."
>
> (NIST)

Is there a cyber-skills shortage? Your answer likely reflects several considerations, many of which are not directly related to cybersecurity. We need to recast and reframe this question.

The dramatic increase in cyber-focused degrees reflects a demand signal in the economy. Universities across the country have created cyber programs to address the cyber-skills shortage "crisis." [5] However, our industry has also contributed to this current "skills shortage" by being imprecise with our requirements and by not segmenting cyber skills into better, more clearly defined categories.

I had the opportunity to assist San Diego's Cyber Center of Excellence (CCOE) with some analysis related to open cyber positions in the San Diego region. The objective of my review was to determine what companies and organizations were actively seeking in their prospective candidates (essentially which skills and competencies they were recruiting) and evaluate this required skills inventory against the curricula of some regional universities and colleges that had cyber programs.

The context was similar to what other regions are conveying, that industry "struggles" to find cyber talent and the universities are wondering why so many of their graduates are having a tough time finding a position that purportedly matches their studies. As part of my research and analysis, I reviewed many open security positions and created a skills inventory. I then assessed the curricula from the universities to see if there was a gap. My goal was to answer the question, "Are we training new entrants to our profession with the wrong set of skills?"

Cyber Is So Broad

What I found was both encouraging and challenging. The good news is that the universities have re-tooled to focus on the nation's cyber challenge. The challenge is that cyber encompasses a broad range of

---

[5] http://www.cyberdegrees.org/listings/top-schools/

disciplines, from DevOps (DevSecOps) at one end of the continuum to regulatory compliance at the other. Essentially, all industries are recruiting positions or roles that have an overly expansive set of requirements. A good number of the job postings looked for individuals with highly technical skills that also had in-depth working knowledge of industry regulations and compliance. These are highly disparate skill sets. Someone who looks at the security implications of software code is rarely also well-versed on the regulatory requirements of HIPAA and HITECH.

There is some valuable context in more traditional IT where job functions are frequently segmented, especially in larger organizations (e.g., unique positions for the database, storage, backup, network, Unix/Linux, and Windows administrators). For many posted security positions, there tends to be an expectation that the security personnel should have *full stack* knowledge. Full stack knowledge would include experience with applications, databases, operating systems, hypervisors, networks (LAN/WAN/IP), backup and storage services, cloud services, and coding. Only then do we add knowledge of security practices. We also expect our security professionals to know not only security domains but also the nuance of regulatory and compliance disciplines. Effectively, our expectations of our security personnel are overly ambitious.

Chapter 10 Key Point and Action Item 3

Cybersecurity is simultaneously a broad, very technical and relatively new field. As the CISO, you need to ensure that the roles you define are well matched to your objectives and to the technology your organization is using.

You should work with your human resources partner to calibrate job roles, banding, salary and title and validate that you have appropriately reflected this in any posted job openings.

There is a similar dynamic for our colleagues in the legal profession. Many attorneys know state, federal, municipal, and civil law, and also have in-depth domain knowledge in biology, chemistry, physics, engineering, and computer science disciplines. Typically, attorneys that have this combination of domain knowledge work in intellectual property law and are some of the most highly compensated professionals in any profession. We see something similar within the cybersecurity profession, namely the CISOs that have strong full-stack knowledge of IT infrastructure, broad and extensive security knowledge, and vast industry experience or regulatory knowledge. These CISOs are some of the highest paid individuals in our profession and justifiably so.

Given the preceding, our "skills" shortage could be a product of how we are defining our roles (overly-expansive expectations concerning required competencies and industry knowledge) as well as the many "non-security" factors noted below.

My perspective is that the cyber-skills shortage is the product of many variables, often having little to do with actual cybersecurity functions. Certain organizations readily attract, recruit, and retain highly-talented security staff. Other organizations have cybersecurity positions that remain open, at least from the perspective of the hiring manager, in perpetuity. What is the cause of this dynamic?

Key Variables that Impact Recruiting Cyber Talent

Let's look at some of the variables that impact an organization's ability to recruit security talent.

- **Geographic Location**: The talent war extends beyond company-specific considerations to include regional and national dynamics. Here in my hometown of San Diego, several non-profit organizations are focused on attracting cyber talent to the city. As an example, the San Diego Cyber Center of Excellence (CCOE) focuses on championing the economic impact of cyber for the greater San Diego region. While San Diego has a healthy and vibrant cyber community, our numbers are a fraction of those in Silicon Valley. Companies in our region compete against larger, well-known companies in the San Francisco Bay Area for cyber talent. This competition for talent is playing out in other industries and across multiple geographies, both nationally and internationally.

  This dynamic is ugly for organizations that are outside of large metropolitan areas. Large metropolitan areas have a more extensive pool of candidates to select from, including recent graduates from well-known universities and colleges in the same area. Organizations operating in less populous, even rural, communities should anticipate a more challenging recruiting environment.

  Demographics are not on the side of smaller companies in smaller markets. We need help from our colleagues in human resources to sell a less hectic lifestyle, lower costs of living, and other benefits to attract cyber talent.

Regional economic development corporations also have an essential role in ensuring that big-city advantages do not create cyber deserts in rural America, and for that matter, other non-metropolitan areas throughout the world. CISOs who confront "cyber deserts" will need to be proactive with their recruiting efforts by engaging regional advocacy groups such as chambers of commerce and economic development agencies and highlighting the unique opportunities their specific program offers ideal candidates.

Recruiting managers and CISOs should be well versed in their geographic pros and cons. Think creatively about these dynamics and how your organization can cast its specific geographic challenges in a positive light. As a case in point, I previously worked with a company that had its headquarters in the foothills of the Yosemite national park. They were able to attract good IT talent by "selling" the outdoor lifestyle their location offered.

- **Organizational Size and Maturity:** Here is a quintessential catch-22. Larger organizations typically have more mature operations. Generally, they have overcome the "going concern" dynamic and are focused on executing their strategy. Larger organizations also have more mature governance models and structures, including independent directors on the board, internal audit functions, and appropriate separation of duties. Frequently, these organizations are also staid and frankly perceived as boring. The perception they face is that they are slower to react to changing market conditions, slower to adapt to or adopt new technologies, and highly risk-averse. Larger companies are, however, precisely the organizations that are most capable of hiring skilled cybersecurity professionals (e.g., security analysts, security architects, security managers, SOC technicians and the like).

In contrast, smaller organizations, because they appear to be more innovative, move faster, have less hierarchical reporting structures, work with "cooler" technology, and offer significant upside with options and the allure of an IPO, tend to be very attractive to cyber professionals. Who isn't attracted to that shiny object? Smaller organizations, however, are typically less focused on

---

[6] Few of us really think about the downside of smaller companies, e.g. loss of funding, patent battles, technology obsolescence impacting a smaller, narrower product line, that make them riskier under certain circumstances.

security (because they are focused on keeping the lights on or executing against an ambitious growth plan) and do not have the resources required to hire expensive security talent.

These overly generalized points serve to highlight that the organization's size and maturity will have a significant impact on the ability to attract and retain security talent. You and your colleagues in HR will need to be aware of these dynamics and build a strategy to mitigate obstacles to your recruiting efforts.

- **Budget**: It's amazing what supply and demand can do. Tighten the supply while demand is increasing, and you'll see a commensurate increase in costs – in our case wage inflation, which is currently occurring in the cybersecurity job market. Anecdotally, there are too many open positions for the number of qualified individuals available to fill these roles, driving salaries for cybersecurity professionals upward. As economics teaches us, eventually supply and demand meet to create an equilibrium point where the supply equals the demand.

The labor market communicates these demand signals to prospective applicants and universities alike. The result is that individuals working in lower-paid professions effectively re-tool their skills to become qualified for higher-paying jobs. Universities and colleges also respond by building programs to address the labor shortage. The cybersecurity marketplace is experiencing this now. Schools are developing programs focused on cybersecurity and many skilled individuals in other disciplines, many of which have lower salary expectations than cybersecurity, are "certifying" their way into the profession.

An organization's budget will have a critical role in attracting cybersecurity talent. As noted above, cybersecurity professionals are earning premiums over other IT roles. Organizations will need to anticipate paying more to attract cyber talent. How much more, however, reflects the organization's specific context (risk tolerance, industry, profitability, etc.). There are salary benchmarks that can be used to determine if the projected salary and benefits packages are in line with the market.[7] Longer term, we should expect the "cyber" premium to

---

[7] Robert Half's Salary Guide is cited for specific markets and roles.

decline as more qualified individuals enter the profession and more cyber work is automated.[8]

- **Reporting Relationships:** To whom any professional reports and where their "manager" fits within the overall organization are important considerations. If a prospective employee is applying for a job reporting to a CISO who is buried within the organizational chart, he or she can infer that security is not a top priority for the company. When the applicant is reporting to a security organization where the CISO is a valued member of the executive team who facilitates and supports organizational strategy, there's likely to be more interest. CISOs who have limited organizational visibility and gravitas are likely to be those CISOs who are most challenged when recruiting, including "funding" poorly understood and valued security programs.

  If you are a CISO who faces this dynamic, this may be an opportunity to recast your position within the organization. To recruit and staff up correctly – essentially helping the organization mitigate risk – you may need more visibility within the company and the industry. While a separate area of discussion, you should align your security program with the organization's strategy and mission. It is a step in the right direction.

- **Risk Appetite:** CISOs are well served to align staffing levels and the competencies of their team with the organization's overall risk appetite. If the current security program is inadequate to address these requirements, the CISO can highlight this dynamic to advocate for new positions and training for his or her team. As CISOs, it's imperative that we translate cyber risk into business risk. Certain cyber risks, if realized, could impact the organization financially, harm its reputation and its operations, and even expose it to existential risk. Converting cyber risk into business risk allows executive management to make a reasoned determination about what security resources should be deployed to mitigate cyber risk.

  Ultimately, as CISOs we are not in a position to make this call. Our job, however, is to help our colleagues in executive management determine what should influence

---

[8] This is a critically-important topic for our industry. Having highly-paid individuals doing overly manual work is not sustainable.

the organization's overall risk appetite. If we fail to express this in terms that are accessible to the business, we can anticipate that building our security program will be more challenging than it should be.

- **Corporate Culture and Industry:** It's no accident that General Electric (GE) launched an advertising campaign in 2016 to recast their business from a "staid" manufacturer to that of an innovative developer of software focused on industrial and machine automation. The ads show recent hires all telling their friends and family that GE's new software business is on the cutting edge. The point is that GE, like so many traditional "brick and mortar" companies, is now competing against fast-paced, early-stage [insert platitude here] companies vying for the same talent. Mobile, web, social media, and other "economy 2.0" companies are attractive. Do you know how the marketplace perceives your company? Does the organization need to refresh its image to be more attractive to prospective applicants? If so, you'll need to be innovative in your approach to recruiting cyber talent to your organization.

- **Job Title:** There has been a lot of debate on terminology in our industry. The language we use to describe our jobs, the infrastructure and information we protect, and even our profession varies dramatically from company to company. I used to think that the difference between "Information Security" and "Cybersecurity" reflected a difference without a distinction. The reality was that I was wrong. How we define things matters. Applicants unfamiliar with antique jargon may never see job descriptions that emphasize yesterday's terminology.

  How we describe our work reflects our employment history, the vendors we've used, and the industry in which we operate. Hiring managers and CISOs should be aware of these unintentional biases and question whether the job titles they're using are hiding great jobs from prospective candidates. Stated differently, are you hiring an information security manager or a cybersecurity manager? Know the difference. It may have a considerable impact on the effectiveness of your recruiting efforts.

- **Skills and Experience Requested:** As hiring managers, we've all been guilty of drafting a job description that represents the ideal candidate. Effectively, we write job descriptions for candidates that just do not exist. As a result, essential positions are left unfilled, waiting for that ideal candidate to appear. We also frequently don't invest the time to work with our colleagues in HR to accurately define the role and help them recruit.

Organizations would be well-served by being more realistic about the types of skills they need to fulfill the role as well as the number of years of experience required. Can specific less-critical skills be acquired while on the job? If so, great. Adjust your job postings accordingly. Do you require all the certifications listed to do the job correctly? If not, offer to sponsor certifications and find an alternative way to validate whether the candidate has the skills that purportedly come with the certification.

- **Industry Counts:** Adapt your security recruiting efforts to your industry. Specific industries require unique competencies rarely found in candidates who have never worked in that field. If this is the case, make sure that your recruiting efforts target the social media sites, publications, and industry associations that the industry-knowledgeable personnel frequent. Some industries require more in-depth background checks, notably within law enforcement and the defense sector.

Other industries have less rigorous background requirements but are focused on unique techniques and tools of the trade (e.g., software platforms and applications). The bottom line is that your industry influences your ability to find and retain security talent. Know these characteristics and make sure that you adapt your security program and recruiting efforts to them.

Given the extreme business reliance on technology in the digital era, you as the CISO need to be aware of the unique environmental conditions that drive the concentration of the talent you will need to address your business risk, as well as the factors that create unique challenges and opportunities in attracting that talent.

You should conduct a review of the environmental factors that affect your industry, your organization and the specific talent you need to attract, and then develop a strategy to highlight your opportunities and overcome your challenges.

There is a cyber-talent shortage. Like other labor shortages, supply and demand signals will ultimately result in equilibrium where supply roughly meets demand. Until then, CISOs and their organizations should recognize how the factors described above will affect their ability to build their security teams. Ultimately, as CISOs, it's our unique interactions with our current teams and prospective employees that will have the most impact on our ability to address this cyber shortage. Helping our staff meet their professional objectives, mentoring new entrants to the profession, and raising awareness of good cyber practices within our organizations will all help address this shortage.

CISOs and How They Build, Manage and Keep Their Teams – Hayslip

> "The CISO's goal is to be a strategic business partner and have their security team viewed as a valuable corporate asset."

In the first volume of the *CISO Desk Reference Guide*, we discussed how the position of Chief Information Security Officer (CISO), though relatively new for many organizations, is one of technical complexity that is not for the faint of heart. We also discussed how this dynamic position is the leading cybersecurity expert for the organization and makes decisions that impact all aspects of the organization and its ability to conduct business. Some of these decisions will involve technology; however, many of them will also involve non-technical issues such as interpreting regulations, establishing new policies, or influencing employee/corporate culture.

To meet these requirements and be the effective cybersecurity leader that companies require, the CISO will need to rely on a core asset – his or her cybersecurity team. The teams the CISO leads are a critical element of his or her strategy for implementing a security program. How the CISO finds talent, builds teams, identifies required skillsets, and implements a security training program are core competencies a CISO must learn and develop in order to be successful.

There are several questions whose answers will be fundamental in determining the CISO's ability to provide a qualified cybersecurity team, which is crucial to protecting the business and its operations.

Obviously, the CISO's goal is to be viewed as a strategic business partner and have his or her program viewed as a value-added corporate asset. The CISO doesn't want to be viewed as just another checkbox on a compliance requirement scorecard. So, let's approach this discussion with an honest intensity about how we can assist CISOs in creating, managing, mentoring, and retaining their world-class security teams.

"Talent" is defined as the capacity for achievement or success; a group of persons with special ability; or a special natural ability or aptitude. The reason I remind us of the definition of talent is that this chapter will be about how we, as CISOs, recruit the talent we need for our teams, how we manage and inspire that talent, and how we train and retain that talent. We know from the news that there is a shortage of cybersecurity talent. This means that the individuals who have the skills and experience our organization is looking for will typically receive multiple employment offers and, in all actuality, will control most employment discussions. This is why it's imperative that before the business starts the search for cybersecurity talent, the business understands what skills, experience, and certifications are currently in-house and then proceed to fill any identified gaps. This leads us to our first question: *"How do CISOs develop their hiring priorities to support the organization and the cybersecurity program effectively?"*

Workforce Planning

The answer to the first question is honestly a factor of workforce planning, which in its simplest terms is a systematic approach that helps an organization to (Kristina Dorville 2014):

1. Determine current and future human capital requirements (demand);
2. Identify current human capital capabilities (supply); and
3. Design and implement strategies to transition the current workforce to the desired future workforce.

An organization can use this approach to inventory its current cyber professionals. This methodology identifies and quantifies the current workload and workforce requirements unique to the organization that these cyber professionals serve and then analyzes the skills and talent needed to fill any identified gaps in workforce capability. Much of this process is explained in detail in documents that can be found on the Department of Homeland Security's Cybersecurity Workforce Development website (Department of Homeland Security 2017).

I use many of these documents because I like to follow a framework approach for how I would identify and create a skill-set inventory and gap analysis of my current cybersecurity teams. To begin this process, I would request a list of the organization's current cybersecurity positions from the human resources department. As the CISO, I should have this information already. However, I have found that sometimes what I have may be different than what human resources believes is current. I want this list so that I know all of the positions that are within the scope of my security program.

I would also request copies of all cybersecurity job descriptions so that I can verify that the skill sets, and competencies listed in the job requirements are still current. I need this data, so I can establish a baseline for what skill sets my teams should currently possess. Next, I would conduct an inventory of all current work processes and technologies used by my teams, basically asking the question, "What services do we currently provide internally and externally to our customers?"

I would then meet with my team members and selected stakeholders to identify the skill sets currently required for each identified work process and technology. Once these skills have been documented, I would have each team member rank themselves on their experience for the selected skill sets.

Now as you can guess, many people tend to overrate themselves. Therefore, I take these ratings and then add what I have seen and experienced, and the average is the score I will use until I have enough data to effectively rate their knowledge and experience. With this completed, I now have a current state skill set inventory for the organization's cybersecurity workforce. I know what skill sets we advertised for when we filled our positions, I know what work processes and services we currently provide to stakeholders, and I know what technologies we currently use to manage and enforce our selected security controls.

However, nothing in the field of cybersecurity is static. I know I can expect change, and with it, new requirements that will necessitate a reevaluation of the skill sets my teams presently have. These new requirements will drive the need for new training, new equipment (applications and technology), or new personnel. I must also take into account my organization's requirements. As a CISO, it is critical that I am continually aware of my company's goals, strategic plans, and current business operations. Because my teams provide services to the business stakeholders, changes in organizational plans can impact requirements and drive the creation of new ones.

This leads to the production of a skill set gap analysis document. It is a comparison of the current cybersecurity workforce skill set inventory that is now analyzed and compared to the organization's future state plans. This comparison, more often than not, may require you to make changes to meet your organization's goals.

As a case in point, I worked for an organization in the past that made a strategic decision to become Payment Card Industry (PCI) certified. This was a strategic decision based on the fact that over 50% of the internal departments wanted to accept credit cards as a method of payment to allow external partners to purchase services from the organization. This organizational requirement, to meet PCI compliance, would change our current skill set portfolio and would require the implementation of new services and technologies.

I bring this case up to illustrate the point that when you are hiring new staff you will find that your priorities will be dictated by skill sets you currently lack that were identified in your cybersecurity workforce skill set inventory. You will also find that your priorities will be tied to new requirements identified by your organization and its enterprise strategic goals. These priorities will be documented in the skills requirements section of the job description for new positions that you want to hire, and they also will be documented as possible new training requirements, which we will discuss later. Now that we understand where we get our priorities when we are sourcing talent, let's look at how we find it.

Fierce Competition for Talent

We know that cybersecurity incidents are not only increasing in number, they are also becoming progressively more destructive. It is evident that our adversaries are improving their technologies, sharing intelligence, and training their teams to attack with a specific purpose. In fact, in CSO's 2017 U.S. State of Cybercrime Survey (CSO 2017), 76% of respondents said they are more concerned about cybersecurity threats this year than in the previous 12 months. It's this concern and the rising threats to organizations that are creating a critical shortfall in qualified cybersecurity talent.

Burning Glass Technologies documented this shortfall in their Cybersecurity Jobs 2015 report (Restuccia 2015). In essence, the report documents how cybersecurity job demand is growing across all sectors of the economy. Some sectors that manage consumer data are seeing a substantial increase, such as Finance (+137% over the last five years), Health Care (+121%), and Retail Trade (+89%). Because of this stiff competition for talent, you need to understand that any out-of-date sourcing and recruiting practices your human resources department is using will be ineffective in this dynamic environment.

There are several methods I would suggest for successfully sourcing quality candidates:

- Make sure your organization's social/professional pages on LinkedIn, Twitter, and Facebook are updated and display the correct information for the position you are trying to fill. However, remember that this is only part of the social media approach you will need to use because the cybersecurity talent you are looking for tends to be more guarded with their use of social media. They understand the dangers of an online presence, so you will need to go to forums, web sites, and discussion groups which are specific to cybersecurity to begin a discussion.

- Look internally within your information technology department and other stakeholder departments for candidates that might be a fit for the position. Especially if the position is entry level, you may find a candidate that with some training, mentoring, and experience, will grow into the team member you need for this position.

- When sourcing to fill a position, especially a critical position, ask yourself whether the requirement for a college degree is actually necessary. I have had some CISOs argue vehemently that a college degree is required, but I have also heard the opposite argument that experience and skills matter more. Is it possible to take both approaches? I have successfully specified either a college degree and five years' experience or ten years' documented experience with certifications and no degree as a sourcing requirement for a senior security analyst position. Be flexible if you can. You don't want to miss out on good talent that can really help your teams.

- Speak to your human resources department and ask if they are able to use a third party that specializes in recruiting cybersecurity talent. Just posting the position on a job board may not give you a good pool of prospects for building your security teams or adding new personnel due to a critical new business requirement. Be willing to ask for help and reach out to your peers in the community for leads or retain a service that can assist you in finding qualified talent.

- Be active in the cybersecurity community. As a CISO, are you writing articles, making presentations, attending conferences, or joining professional organizations? Basically, are you visible in the cybersecurity community at large? When you post an open position, most candidates will do research not only on the organization but on you as the CISO. They will want to know more about you and whether from a professional career standpoint it would be a good move to work for you. You set the tone in the cybersecurity community for how candidates view your organization, so be active and let them know your company is an innovative place to grow their career.

- My last point is that it's not always about the money. As plainly stated in the ESG-ISSA State of Cyber Security Professional Careers report (ESG & ISSA 2016), many cybersecurity professionals are attracted to their position because they want to use their skills to protect and defend an organization. Many others are interested in learning new skills, getting the chance to be a part of innovative teams, or working on cutting edge projects. So as a CISO who is sourcing to fill a position, use some of these motivations to advertise why cybersecurity professionals should come work for you.

What Skills Do We Need to Succeed?

To begin the discussion on our second question, we first need to establish whether you have an executive charter for your security program. The reason I ask is that a charter establishes why the CISO and the security program exist. It will typically spell out what strategic objectives are under your purview and what authority, if any, you may have to protect the organization in times of crisis. Some charters have specific mission statements listing programs and policies that are accountable to the cybersecurity team. This charter provides you with a path to understand what policies, processes, and assets you have direct ownership of and which ones your program has indirect influence over.

With this information from the charter, you and your teams can start breaking down the policies and processes to identify what knowledge, skill sets, and experience will be required to meet the charter's objectives. You will find many of the required skill sets will be in categories, like soft skills, general network infrastructure skills, basic security skills, etc. Once you have these strategic categories, you will be on the path to identifying the skill sets that are necessary for your teams to be successful. So, with this context let's look at our second question: *"What hard and soft skills does the CISO believe their cybersecurity program requires?"*

In our first question, we created the cybersecurity workforce skill set inventory to help you gain visibility into skill sets your team lacked or ones that were currently immature. This information enabled you to set priorities on which ones were critical for the business and helped fine tune the candidates under review for open positions. However, for you to create this inventory, you will need the document I describe in the previous paragraph, a skill set matrix. This skill set matrix is developed by taking all of the business processes the security team is responsible for and grouping them into categories. Once you have these categories established, with the subcomponent processes in each, you can break down each work process and identify "what skill sets do we need to do this work?"

In answering this question, you and your teams will dissect each skill set and identify its sub-components, like knowledge, professional certifications, secondary training, and breadth of experience required to effectively provide the process or service under review to your company. As you can guess, many of these identified skill sets will also be tied to the technologies the organization is using or the compliance requirements the company must meet because of its chosen business environment and industry.

One critical note in doing this review: it will allow you to also develop a gap analysis of what skills your current teams may be lacking. This information will be beneficial when you are reviewing candidates because you will want to select a new team member that is not only a good fit for the team but brings skills that will improve its performance.

To be effective in the above process, group the requirements together and break them into two overall categories, for example (these are for illustrative purposes only – your security objectives, architecture, and requirements may vary):

1. Technical Categories
    a. Manage SIEM solution
        i. Knowledge of Python scripting to create queries
        ii. Training on the selected SIEM technology
        iii. Experience with data flows
        iv. Knowledge of network architecture
    b. Manage PCI DSS program
    c. Manage AV and Anti-Malware platform
    d. Manage Firewalls
    e. Manage Identity and Authentication platforms
    f. Manage GRC platform
2. Non-Technical Categories
    a. Provide risk-management oversight on IT projects
    b. Interface with Help Desk and Service Desk personnel to answer security questions
    c. Provide security reports with metrics and status of security-related projects
    d. Create and manage policies on security controls and frameworks used by the organization
    e. Manage the PCI compliance documentation of the organization's third-party partners

Once you have the requirements in this type of format, you can begin to break down what is required for a specific process, such as managing an SIEM solution or providing risk-management oversight of ongoing projects. Do not be surprised if as you make these lists and break them down into their subcomponents you find that a required skill set, or training requirement is needed across multiple processes. That is fine, just move forward and focus on creating this matrix to understand what the underlying hard skill requirements are for you and your team to get work done and provide the services that are outlined in your team's executive charter.

You should also note that as you build this matrix, you will identify soft skills that will be required by your staff to be successful. Many of these skills are needed because you work closely together in teams in a dynamic, fast-paced environment. You are also modeled after a service organization, which means you have to deal with people. You have to answer questions, assist with projects, advise stakeholders on issues, and deal with problems. To me, these soft skills are just as important as the technical ones. Some of the soft skills that I look for in candidates include:

1. Ability to communicate effectively – both in writing and verbally.
2. Team skills – We operate in teams, so it is essential that we are able to work together effectively.
3. Integrity – Due to the nature of security work, we must know we can absolutely trust our personnel.
4. Willingness to ask for help – Cybersecurity is a field where it is impossible to know everything. We must be willing to ask for help and collaborate.
5. Ability to cope with stress – With constant moving threats, this field is not for the faint of heart. To work in this field, one must be able to prioritize and deal with stress.
6. Critical thinking skills – the ability to assess issues, look at the data provided, and decide on a course of action.
7. Time management – Many times, while working in teams or by oneself, the individual will be under a time line requirement.
8. Willingness to admit they are wrong – if you make a mistake own it, learn from it, move on and get back to work.
9. Passionate about the field – Typically you see this in their career progression, for example continued education on new technologies or involvement in the cybersecurity community.
10. Systems thinking – The ability to look at networks, security suites, and enterprise architectures as a collection of systems with intricate parts that feed one another is critical for troubleshooting and project management.

At this point in our discussion, we have the security skill set matrix developed from the requirements and processes contained in your security programs charter. We also have the current cybersecurity workforce skill set inventory that lists your team's current skill set gaps; plus, we have prioritized the gaps based on input from our organization's strategic business goals. From these two datasets, we are now able to create a plan of action for how we will develop the job descriptions we want to source. We will list those skill sets, required experience, knowledge of specific technologies, and professional certifications in the job descriptions we plan to advertise.

From the current skill set inventory, we know which skills are deemed critical, and we will highlight these as mandatory for applicants applying for the advertised position. From the list of soft skills above, we have created a conceptual framework to evaluate candidates for "team fit." We want to make sure that not only do they meet the technical requirements for the job, but that they will also fit into the team culture and be able to work with team members and be effective.

As a CISO, the above process is what I have used numerous times to understand the organizational requirements for my team and provide insight into the security services my team is expected to manage and provide to our customers. Time and again, this knowledge has proven useful in identifying the services that were immature and assisting me in remediating the issue through new training for staff, hiring of new personnel, or review of the service to verify its validity to the team's overall mission.

Motivating Cybersecurity Professionals

In the aforementioned ESG-ISSA State of Cyber Security Professional Careers report, researchers spoke with cybersecurity practitioners from all over the world. They asked them questions about their career in cybersecurity, the health of the cybersecurity field as they viewed it, and why they worked as a CISO or Senior Cybersecurity Professional. In this document one of the more fascinating views into why people work in this field was the question of job satisfaction. The top five answers are as follows:

1. Competitive compensation
2. Working with an organizational culture that supports cybersecurity
3. Business management's commitment to cybersecurity
4. Ability to work with highly skilled, talented people
5. Organization provides support and incentives to enable staff to receive training and improve skills

It is the final two factors that I want to talk more about. As security professionals, we want to serve and protect our organizations. We want to work with talented people and improve our skill sets, whether through classroom training, online training, or training exercises. It is this view of what about their job satisfies security professionals that leads us to our third question:

"How can I construct a training program that will keep my team's knowledge, skills, and techniques current?"

In the previous questions under discussion, we created a security skill set matrix and a current inventory of the cybersecurity workforce's skill sets. Part of creating this inventory was to have the security staff rank themselves on their level of knowledge or competency for each specific skill set under review. When you have your team complete their skill assessment, you now have a matrix showing you specific areas within your staff that need to be addressed.

In the past, as a leader of multiple teams, the way I would handle this is to break out the processes and the component skill sets that belonged to each team on a spreadsheet. I would then list the team members' names along the left side and the specific skill sets at the top. I would transfer their assessment grades to the spreadsheet after I reviewed them to ensure they were accurate. The following are three pictures of skills matrix questionnaires and skill set inventory documents. As the CISO for a U.S. Navy command, I used these documents to track training for over 40 information technology personnel.

NAME: _____	INFORMATION ASSURANCE SUPPORT TECHNICIAN (DoD 8570 IAM II)					
CODE:						
SKILLSETS / COURSEWORK / CERTIFICATIONS						
SKILLSETS	C	B	A	N/A	COST	NOTES:
DIACAP/Certification and Accredication						
NPCI Network Audit Process						
CCRI Network Audit Process						
Web Sense Config. Instal. Management						
Incident Response Procedures						
Classified Spillage Procedures						
I/A Training						
IAVA/STIG/CTO Compliance						
Retina / Hercules Administration						
Symantec Server Administration						
TCP/IP Troubleshooting						
Network Troubleshooting						
Network Monitoring / Penetration Testing						
Windows 2008 Server Administration						
Windows 2016 Server Administration						
Active Directory Management						
Share Drive Management						
Cisco Routers / Switches Administration						

Figure 10.5 Example of a Skills Matrix Questionnaire

As the CISO for a U.S. Navy command, one of my jobs was to manage the training and professional certifications for multiple information technology teams and ensure they met the Department of Defense 8570.01-M baseline certification requirement (DISA 2016). To assist me with identifying what training and certification my staff would require, I sat down with my teams and we identified each skill set that we felt was required for a specific class of jobs within our department.

From the above document, which was for my network engineering team, they would rank themselves for each skill set as an:

- "A" – Expert, can work independently to solve complex problems
- "B" – Competent, can resolve routine technical problems with occasional assistance
- "C" – Minimal Experience, may have some basic training and could assist others

I would take these assessments and review the ratings with each staff member to verify why they believed they should be rated at a specific level and identify areas for improvement. Once these were completed, I would then transfer them to an overall skill set inventory spreadsheet where I would track the maturity of skill sets and the completion of professional training and certifications. This skill set inventory document would look as follows:

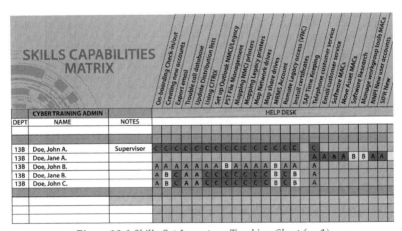

Figure 10.6 Skills Set Inventory Tracking Sheet (ex 1)

From these documents, I had a current inventory of my staff's level of ability to perform their jobs based on their current skill set maturity. This provided me a foundation to create an evolving list of training that my staff required to conduct business and protect our organization.

I would group personnel with skill sets that were labeled "C" as junior to mid-level technicians and we would sit down together as partners and discuss training options to help them increase their knowledge and be a more effective technician or analyst. As a rule of thumb, once a staff member's skill set grades transitioned to all "A" or "B" rankings, demonstrating that they had reached a level of maturity, I would start to include attending professional development conferences or seminars as part of their training curriculum.

My goal was to use this evolving list of skill sets to identify the training my staff needed for specific technologies or competencies within their unique field and also mature them enough to attempt a professional certification as proof of their hard work and dedication.

As we finish this question, we have covered how the CISO would create a skill set matrix to list what unique skills are required for his or her teams. The team members themselves evaluated their experience and competence with regard to these identified skill sets. With that information, the CISO created a current skill set inventory for the organization's cybersecurity staff. This inventory provided insight into what skills personnel will need training for to upgrade their competencies and also identified services that may require new personnel. Now that the CISO has put the time and effort into building this part of their security program, how do they know that it's benefiting the organization?

How Do We Know We're Effective?

This leads to our final discussion point, where the CISO will have to defend their requirement to continually assess, train, and educate security staff. The CISO must know the answer to this question or their program could face significant impact on its ability to perform critical services promptly and retain experienced team members. This critical question is as follows: *"What metrics can I use to measure the effectiveness of my cybersecurity team's capabilities to provide security services and reduce risk to the organization?"*

To honestly answer this question, I believe a CISO must look at the effectiveness of their team in providing cybersecurity and risk management services to the organization. To do this correctly, the CISO must identify their team's services, required technologies, and supporting skill sets. The CISO should also provide training to junior team members to improve their level of knowledge and competence, and from this investment, the organization should see an improvement in services to departmental stakeholders.

Of course, this improvement may not be immediate. Even with training, a competent analyst or technician will still need to employ the new skills they have learned, and gain experience from this new knowledge. What the CISO must do to effectively make a case for continued training funds is use metrics to establish a service baseline. With this baseline, they can over time show a progression in improvement in services and reduction in risk to business operations.

The way I have approached this issue is to keep track of the number of trouble tickets my teams managed and the times for resolution. I also used metrics from the Center for Internet Security (CIS) Benchmarks (CIS 2016) so that I could track data on how my team performed on the following services:

- Complete configuration changes
- Complete maintenance on critical infrastructure (Firewall, IPS, Server)
- Mean Time to Incident Discovery
- Incident Rate Time of Completion (initial report to completion)
- Percentage of Incidents Detected by Internal Controls
- Mean Time between Security Incidents
- Mean Time to Recovery

Obviously, there are numerous types of metrics that a CISO can use to track whether their team is effective. One last tool I would recommend that is easy to create and extremely useful is an online customer service survey. I look at my security program as a service-providing team that has customers in all of my organization's departments. I want to understand from my customers what they expect from my teams, what problems they are having, whether they understand what services we provide, and if so how well we are providing them.

These surveys allow me to evangelize cybersecurity to my stakeholders and find out what they need to be successful for their business. They also help me identify areas for improvement that may require training, and as a team we can set improvement goals. Then over time, I can track if we are meeting or exceeding our service goals and use these numbers plus the previous metrics to make the case that my team is effective and is of strategic value to the organization.

Highly-skilled individuals are motivated more by a sense of purpose and opportunity to grow than they are by salary and traditional benefits. As the CISO, you need to make sure that your team is effective in delivering on its objectives and that your people continue to grow and develop.

You should align the metrics you routinely track to your organization's goals and to the capability to deliver on those goals so that growth and development of personnel are a standard aspect of your continual improvement effort.

In conclusion, much of the services, required skill sets, and job positions that you will manage will be based on the needs of the organization. However, even with that in mind, the CISO must remember that the technology environments we operate in are dynamic and subject to business-impacting changes.

It will be incumbent upon you to understand the strategic goals of the company and your stakeholder community, so you can continually assess the services you provide to reduce risk and minimize the impact on business operations. You will need to manage your team's professional development and ensure they are trained and knowledgeable, so they can not only meet the threats currently facing the organization but also provide quality security and risk management services to your customers for the future.

To do this effectively, educate yourself on new threats and technologies, evangelize and make a case for educating your teams, and educate your executive staff on why a trained cybersecurity team is a valuable, risk-reducing resource for the company.

Summary

For Chapter 10, we began our discussion by asking these four questions:

- How do CISOs develop their hiring priorities to support the organization and their cybersecurity program effectively?
- What hard and soft skills does the CISO believe their cybersecurity program requires?
- How can I construct a training program that will keep my team's knowledge, skills, and techniques current?
- What metrics can I use to measure the effectiveness of my cybersecurity team's capabilities to provide security services and reduce risk to the organization?

Each of the authors provided their point of view, exploring the organization's talent requirements, and internal and external factors that shape the talent pool. They also provided multiple examples of tools that can be used to assess and develop the people that are so critical to the success of your program.

In closing, we leave you with these five key points and next steps:

1. It is essential to recognize that the CISO, and the entire Information Security team, are continually recruiting. Every opportunity to interact with your community is an opportunity to assess and impress the people that can help you succeed. **You should identify formal and informal networking activities offered by your community to make sure you have an appropriate presence at these events. Remember to include your team as recruiting is often most effective at the peer level. Also, include a thorough review of social media profiles and activities.**

2. Given the depth and breadth of knowledge that a cybersecurity team must possess, it is impossible to acquire and maintain a staff that can do everything. Various third parties have virtual monopolies on specific expertise. **You should conduct a gap analysis of the cybersecurity capabilities your organization requires versus what your team can realistically provide. With this in hand, create a plan of action to fill the gaps**

through hiring, training, and outsourcing to third-party providers.

3. Cybersecurity is simultaneously a broad, very technical and relatively new field. As the CISO, you need to ensure that the roles you define are well matched to your objectives and to the technology your organization is using. **You should work with your human resources partner to calibrate job roles, banding, salary and title and validate that you have appropriately reflected this in any posted job openings.**

4. Given the extreme business reliance on technology in the digital era, you as the CISO need to be aware of the unique environmental conditions that drive the concentration of the talent you will need to address your business risk, as well as the factors that create unique challenges and opportunities in attracting that talent. **You should conduct a review of the environmental factors that affect your industry, your organization and the specific talent you need to attract, and then develop a strategy to highlight your opportunities and overcome your challenges.**

5. Highly-skilled individuals are motivated more by a sense of purpose and opportunity to grow than they are by salary and traditional benefits. As the CISO, you need to make sure that your team is effective in delivering on its objectives and that your people continue to grow and develop. **You should align the metrics you routinely track to your organization's goals and to the capability to deliver on those goals so that growth and development of personnel are a standard aspect of your continual improvement effort.**

As Matt pointed out, while there is currently a cyber-talent shortage, it is up to us to make the short-term decisions and long-term investments to help our organizations address risk and build the talent pool for the future.

Chapter 11 – Cyber Awareness Training: It Takes an Organization

Introduction

Educating your workforce about cybersecurity through an awareness program is a foundational requirement that all cybersecurity standards share. So why don't we have a very well-educated workforce when it comes to cybersecurity? Perhaps too many organizations, when they recognize the need for a cybersecurity awareness program, treat it like a change management effort; roll it out just in time and then add it to the corporate training curriculum. We know that's not effective.

Bill begins this chapter by recalling that there have been other large-scale societal changes that have required massive, sustained awareness programs. He outlines the commonalities between these programs and allows the reader to draw inferences that will help put their program into context and set it up for success.

Matt continues the discussion by showing how each member of the executive team must buy in and be part of the solution. Education and awareness are about people, and specifically, the role each of us plays and how that role is personal to every one of us and through us becomes personal for each organization.

Gary then shows us how important it is to measure what we do, and more importantly, to build a habit of learning from each breach and changing the training content so that it evolves as our threat environment evolves. Tying our metrics to our awareness program is a powerful concept and will help any team be more successful by focusing on continual improvement.

The authors would like to pose some important questions to think about as you read this chapter:

- What are the "lessons learned" from industry data breaches that can be used to reduce our organization's risk exposure to these adverse events?
- How successful is training our staff in actually preventing breaches versus having the right software and hardware in place?
- Does our organization have a culture of cybersecurity awareness and do we have a program to educate our staff?
- What is our Incident Response Plan and how do we train staff, stakeholders and partners on how to use this plan?

Education – Bonney

"The final measure of success is the strategic focus of the CISO. Successful CISOs will be improving employee education and enhancing their communications and collaboration capabilities so that they can drive systemic change in the enterprise."

The Carrot and the Stick

First, the carrot: one of the most important duties of a CISO is that of change agent, especially when it comes to online cyber hygiene. The sad reality is that while Advanced Persistent Threats (APTs) get a lot of attention, most successful breaches are initiated by relatively unsophisticated attacks. It's a matter of economics. Why would a hacker spend a lot of money and time on an APT when they can pay little or no money and get quick results using phishing or drive-by attacks (i.e., seeding commonly visited sites with malware so that anyone who browses to the infected page is themselves infected)?

It has become a cliché: "Your employees are your first line of defense." Security professionals and standards writers agree, of course. NIST 800-53, ISO 27001, and PCI-DSS all devote portions of their standards to training and awareness. Also, attack post-mortem analysis and employee response testing show that companies with new employee security training programs experience less than 25% of the losses of firms without new employee security training programs.[9]

And now the stick: while PCI-DSS is a standard, to be PCI certified, you need to pass a PCI-DSS audit. Additionally, the following regulations all require a security and awareness training program:

- HIPAA (for healthcare)
- GLBA (for banking)
- The Texas Health Privacy Law
- 201 CMR 17.01 (the Massachusetts data privacy law)
- 23 NYCRR Part 500 (The New York Cyber Security

---

[9] http://www.pwc.com/us/en/increasing-it-effectiveness/publications/2014-us-state-of-cybercrime.html in part states that companies without security training for new employees spent an average of $683,000 per year for cyber incidences and companies with security training for new employees spent an average of $162,000 per year for cyber incidences. Annual savings were roughly 77%.

Requirements for the financial services industry)
- FISMA (the Federal Information Security Management Act)
- The EU-US Safe Harbor requirements (along with its successor, the EU-US Privacy Shield)
- Canada's Personal Information Protection and Electronic Documents Act (PIPEDA)

OK, so it's a good idea to have a company-wide education program that focuses on cyber awareness and security training. But how do you do it, and what works? Don't most people just nod their way through mandatory training? Well, yes, and the main reason, in my opinion, has less to do with it being tedious and overlong (though that doesn't help) and more to do with the fact that it is a corporate training program detached from every other goal the company might have. It's lumped together with workplace harassment training and anti-bribery training and the new-hire classic: "how to log onto your new expense reporting system in 20 easy steps."

I am not suggesting that security training must be snappy and quick, or indistinguishable from sketch comedy. Best practice has advanced from the timed lessons that prohibit quick clicks and require a minimum think time per module to ensure the employee had ample time to absorb the material they aren't reading. Best practice is now a series of short, to-the-point vignettes focused on key messages. And in many cases, this training is delivered automatically right after an issue has occurred. In other words, if I click an inappropriate site or click on a link in a phishing email, many of the systems are sending immediate training modules to the user for message reinforcement.

But more importantly, the cyber education and awareness program needs to align with corporate mission. Cyber hygiene needs to be important, practiced, and taught by every executive, starting with the CEO. That means you need to get the members of the C-suite signed up and evangelizing before you can have an effective cyber-awareness training program.

Awareness, Self-Defense and a Shared Sense of Purpose

We addressed the issues of working together with senior leadership in Chapter 6 of Volume 1, so I won't spend much time on it here. Suffice it to say it is the necessary first step. Once this foundation is in place, you can start to address awareness first, then self-defense, and then a sense of unity of purpose and shared outcomes.

For awareness, try to focus on the reality of the threat, the depth of the ecosystem supporting the bad actors, and the objectives of the cybercriminals. Try not to focus too much on fear, uncertainty, and doubt (FUD). FUD seems on the surface to be a shortcut right to hyper-awareness of the challenges we face. But it often has the opposite effect as it makes the problem appear unsolvable. FUD creates a sense of hopelessness that leads to paralysis. It is usually sufficient to explain the motives briefly and frame the consequences in business outcomes (direct fraud, damage to the brand, IP theft, business disruption) in roughly the same terms as you would to your leadership colleagues.

After you have established awareness, it's time to teach self-defense. Keep it simple: don't click, don't open, and don't reuse. There are more advanced concepts we can try to explain, but most successful attacks gain entry through enticing workers to click on links they should not click, open files they should not open, and by exploiting shared or reused passwords. We're not aiming for perfection at this stage, just trying to reduce the harmful behavior to the point that your tools give you a fighting chance.

Finally, once the awareness and self-defense programs are rolled out and measured as effective, it's time to move on to coordinated behaviors and establishing a sense of unity of purpose and shared outcomes.

Historical Role Models

During World War II, several phrases became famous as part of home front propaganda. These included: "Loose Lips Might Sink Ships" (shortened to: "Loose Lips Sink Ships"), "Defense on The Sea Begins on The Shore," and "Defense in The Field Begins in The Factory." Without getting into the particular behaviors being encouraged, the more significant point was that everyone had a role to play in the effort to protect troops and ships. Spies and sympathizers were everywhere.

The general theme of civil defense is that civilians have a role in defending themselves, fending for themselves, and acting in a way that, at the very least, allows the public safety workforce the ability to focus more on the crisis at hand and less on the immediate safety of the civilian population. In the best of circumstances, civilians provide direct aid.

Another example is a coordinated and ongoing program to reduce accidents on the factory floor through awareness, training, and feedback loops that implement suggestions for safety improvement from the workforce. And a fourth example is the all-out effort during the mid-twentieth century to eradicate many infectious diseases through immunization programs. In February 2015 (Bonney 2015), I published an article on user responsibility that had this to say about immunization:

"Though there are some on the fringe, most people agree to have their children vaccinated. Many believe they are acting in their own best interests or the interests of their child. But they are also acting in the best interest of their community. Witness the outbreak of measles at Disneyland in January 2015 for an example of what happens when too many unvaccinated children flock together. To fight infectious disease, the CDC does its part; they fund research, they act as a center of excellence for best practice and drive information sharing. The pharmaceutical companies do their part; they develop vaccines. Hospitals treat those who are sick, train medical personnel to respond to outbreaks, and often also administer the vaccines themselves. But for the whole program to work, the parents, the "users" if you will, must play their part. It takes 90-95% vaccination coverage to prevent outbreaks. As of 2013, according to the CDC, 90.8% to 94.1% of U.S. children have been vaccinated for the various legacy childhood diseases. So, while the measles outbreak is a concern, it is so far under control."

Each of these examples shares these key attributes:

- There is a coordinated effort required amongst both leadership and the population (or workforce)
- Diligence is demonstrated over an extended period
- An ecosystem that includes messaging, material, and roles and responsibilities is developed and rolled out
- The issue is of sufficient magnitude, and failure has personal, relatable consequence

I believe we are at the point in the ongoing struggle against cybercrime that you can make the argument within your organization for a sufficient parallel to one of these programs and mobilize your company in the right direction. If you operate in an industry that is part of the United States Critical Infrastructure, you might consider joining the FBI's InfraGard program, which is designed to connect the public and private sector for coordinated effort and intelligence, shared educational resources, and preparedness training.

Let's put this in context. I am not suggesting that you need to have the equivalent of the Manhattan Project operating within your organization to stamp out cybercrime as we know it. What I am suggesting is that you consider how the programs I used as examples succeeded, think about how the four attributes I listed above would apply to your organization, and execute accordingly. How would you coordinate between senior leadership and the workforce? What level of staffing and support do you need to provide to allow the program to prosper over the long haul? Who do you work with, internally and externally, to craft messages and utilize collateral to bring the right information to your employees in a way they can consume and act on?

Chapter 11 Key Point and Action Item 1

You need to align your cyber awareness education program needs with the organization's goals for the program to be effective. While a great many cyber-related regulations mandate cyber awareness training, your job as the CISO is to try to help the organization avoid the trap of administering the program as just another compliance activity.

You should evaluate and adjust your existing cyber awareness education program to ensure that the messaging and any calls to action are visibly linked to organizational objectives, so your workforce sees the immediate relevance of the training.

How do you relate the consequences of poor cyber hygiene to your employees so that they take it personally, without scaring them into paralysis?

As with any communication plan designed to effect real change within your organization, the program needs to be thought out, you must get buy-in among your peers, and the program needs to be rolled out with sufficient gravitas. If you are lucky enough to inherit a training program, assess it against the four attributes noted above and make sure it has the impact you'd expect.

To measure the effectiveness of your program, look at the click-through rate on phishing (test this by targeting your workforce), look at the number of systems being infected with malware over a given period, validate password strength and change frequency in central identity stores, and engage your workforce in an ongoing dialog.

You'll know your education program is working when different departments are reaching out to you because they have detected behaviors that are harbingers of imminent compromise, when departments report success and failure for cyber awareness on their own, and when your peers are sharing best practices about what has worked for them and what hasn't. If you continue to get feedback about how confusing, unnecessary, and ineffective your cyber awareness training is, you still have work to do.

The Critical Role of Security Awareness with Executive Management – Stamper

> "Securing information is the ethical and legal responsibility of the organizations with which individuals entrust their personal information."
>
> (California's 2016 Breach Report)

Doesn't Every Executive Value Cyber?

Who doesn't love the technical side of cybersecurity? With thousands of innovative cyber tools hitting the market each year, it would be easy to lull us all into believing that the security of our organizations is just a toolset or adjusted configuration setting away. Oh, that it was that simple.

Before becoming a CISO, I helped organizations comply with the requirements of the Sarbanes-Oxley Act (SOX). Our company would help management address the state of the organization's internal controls over financial reporting (ICFR). I was responsible for assessing IT General Controls (ITGCs) in the context of financially material business applications. Our process began with a risk assessment of the organization's financial statements to determine the materiality of business processes and capture control detail about the applications (think ERP, CRM, and other systems) that supported material business processes. With this context, we'd evaluate and assess the design and operational effectiveness of controls. Our goal was to determine what level of assurance or confidence the organization had that its financial statements were accurate, complete, and valid.

We had two types of customers. The first and rarest were those that were genuinely interested in establishing good governance practices and sound controls over their processes such that ultimately their financial reporting was free from material weaknesses or significant deficiencies. The more common group consisted of those executives that merely asked that we "make them compliant." It was in this group that the quality of financial reporting was most suspect, and no matter how much we worked to implement, document, and ultimately transfer good governance practices to the organization, we knew that given the lack of "ownership" the governance practices would not stick. The simple reason: there was no accountability or commitment to good governance.

Embarrassingly, we would call executives from this second group "walking material weaknesses." They put their organization's standing with financial markets, regulators, and other critical constituencies at risk because they did not value governance. Or, as I'll discuss below, no one explained the linkages between good governance and financial performance for their organization in a way that resonated with how they saw their role within the organization. It was like we were speaking the wrong language to this second group. It was not that they desired poor governance and ineffective controls. It was, more accurately, that no one showed this group of executives how good governance and internal control could facilitate and underpin their organizational strategy. The failure was on us...we did not communicate in a manner that was effective.

As CISOs, we see similar issues within our organizations. Some organizations take security awareness and security training very seriously and are committed to excellent security practices. Others only pay lip service to security training and education. The consequences for the latter include increased regulatory oversight[10] and brand damage resulting from high-profile breaches. Awareness must start with executive management. It's imperative that you help your colleagues in the C-suite understand the risks and consequences of security practices that are inadequate or incomplete. How you address this one function may have more bearing on your security program than any selected tool or security configuration. Similar to the challenges with SOX described above, leaders of organizations that do not currently value security the way we would hope may simply lack the context required to change their approach.

It's About the People

Now back to the opening of this chapter. Cybersecurity, while reliant upon technology, is ultimately about people. Good security practices require engaged and informed stakeholders, be they the board of directors, executives, or frontline employees. One of the most critical components of the CISO role is to help drive this engagement. Behaviors that bypass the best technologies can happen without awareness, an understanding of the acceptable use of organizational assets, and the investment in the training of our teams. One need not look any further than how the best "preventive" technologies deployed are easily circumvented by well-crafted phishing emails that entice employees and executives to expose their organization's network to bad actors. People count. It is obvious why cyber education and security awareness training are so necessary.

---

[10] Please reference Chapter 1 in Volume 1 of the CISO Desk Reference Guide for a discussion on the role of the FTC.

I considered focusing this chapter on how the CISO can facilitate security education and security awareness training with his or her staff and employees in general. But instead, I'd like to address how the CISO can and should invest time to ensure that senior management, the board of directors, and executive colleagues are informed about cybersecurity in the context of their organizations. The goal of this engagement is a more open dialogue on cyber risk and cyber resiliency.

As someone who loves the technical side of cybersecurity, it's easy to fall into the trap of communicating the value of cybersecurity in purely technical terms. Years ago, I remember asking for budget to license a vulnerability management tool and conveyed my request based on the technical merits of the selected scanner. My colleagues looked like deer in headlights. To say that I misread my audience would have been an understatement. I quickly adjusted my communication to focus on the business impact of proper vulnerability management. It was a mistake I did not let happen again.

What I learned from this simple request is that the majority of our colleagues outside of cybersecurity or IT frankly don't care about the technical intricacies of what we do. What they do care about, and justifiably so, is how secure and resilient the organization is. Cybersecurity for them is a more nuanced form of risk management. What are the risks and exposures of the organization based on its current staffing levels and competencies, its lines of business, and the technical controls in place to prevent cyber-attacks and breaches from occurring? More precisely, what are the impacts to the organization if (frankly, when) an incident occurs, and what is the right level of control to mitigate these risks to a business-acceptable degree? The CISO has to translate technical risk, vulnerabilities, and insights about the threat landscape into the language of enterprise risk management that executives use and understand.

Use the Language of Business

Those CISOs who excel at this translation from technical to business-focused risk are frequently those that have their security programs well received by their colleagues, executive management, and ultimately, and ideally, the board of directors. There are some relatively simple, pragmatic steps that CISOs can take to "train" their executive colleagues and the board on cybersecurity practices and why good security hygiene ultimately drives a resilient organization, an organization better positioned to meet its strategic objectives.

First and foremost, the CISO should know and thoroughly understand the objectives, strategy, and mission of their organization. Equally important, the CISO should capture and inventory the unique strategy or objectives of colleagues and their respective departments within the organization. Know how your counterparts are measured. Know their motivations and goals. Know the context of their functions in the broader context of the overall organization. Understand how their line-of-business or executive function facilitates the organization's overall strategy. This knowledge is invaluable. This background and context is the foundation of proper security awareness training directed at senior members of the organization.

With this detail, you can build an informal business impact analysis that links cyber risks to these various constituencies and their objectives. Stated more directly, and as an example, your colleague, the Vice President of Sales, is focused on achieving a top-line revenue target of 20% year-over-year growth. In speaking with her, you learn that the focus of the sales team is meeting sales quotas by developing a more personal knowledge of your organization's clients and prospects.

As part of their effort, and unbeknownst to you before your discussion, the sales organization has re-configured their customer relationship management (CRM) software to incorporate several new fields that help profile critical contacts within both client and prospective client organizations. As you review her objectives and her proposed strategy to meet this target, you learn that the re-configuration of the CRM includes capturing highly sensitive detail on prospects and existing clients. She will record details about hobbies, birthdays of their children and spouses, and their favorite wine. Exposure of this data in a breach or through an inadvertent employee error would create severe "reputational damage" to the organization.

Knowing how the Vice President of Sales' objectives translate into a high-risk strategy that could expose the organization to significant regulatory and reputational risk offers an opportunity to raise cybersecurity awareness. Your job is to help educate your colleague on the potential business risks associated with these field changes and open a dialogue on the best approach to mitigate or reduce this risk. These risks, however, are not owned by you and your security program.

These are business risks, owned by your colleagues. Your goal is to help them understand the implications of the risk in the context of the organization's overall risk appetite and strategy and, more specifically, your colleague's objectives. The risk treatment, including security practices that you and your team will offer, is ultimately a business decision. Your role is to help define the risk pattern, provide options to address the risk that are financially sound – who wants to spend $100,000 to address a $10,000 risk? – and then help the organization meet its strategic priorities.

Addressing Risk with Rigor

CISOs who have grown comfortable in communicating with their line of business colleagues and senior executives can translate security and privacy risks into business and enterprise risk as second nature. They know the priorities of their colleagues, are well versed on the goals of their organization, and they can readily position their security program as an enabler of these priorities under the best of circumstances, or as insurance should something go awry.

CISOs are well served by establishing periodic meetings with colleagues with a business-focused agenda. The meetings should seek to capture detail and confirm your understanding of the following:

- Your colleagues' core initiatives and the plans they have to achieve these objectives
- Any changes to systems or information that may be used to achieve these objectives
- Any material vendors and suppliers who are engaged in the initiative
- Other dependencies that could impact the initiative
- Timing and other constraints on the effort

Effectively, your goal in meeting with colleagues is to ask, "What is it that I don't know that I should know about your department and its objectives so that I can help you achieve these goals?" This information will support the CISO's evaluation of the cyber risk for his or her colleagues. With this detail, the CISO will be in a position to make recommendations to facilitate the effort and highlight areas of potential risk that could impact the success of the initiative. In this context, the CISO becomes a partner to senior executives within the organization, functioning as a risk officer with a nuanced and valued perspective related to technology and digital risk for the organization.

Beyond establishing a standing agenda to understand and support organizational initiatives, you need to develop a framework for dealing with risk treatment when you know that your colleague's approach would put the organization at risk. Pre-establishing a "let's agree to disagree" conflict resolution framework is extremely valuable. Determine with your colleagues how to address these scenarios and delineate who within the organization should make these risk decisions when you and your colleague "respectfully disagree."

Chapter 11 Key Point and Action Item 3

A unified plan will only be effective if each senior leader recognizes the value and is fully engaged in solving cyber awareness problems that represent specific threats to their line of business.

You should work with your peers and senior leadership to make sure they are informed about cybersecurity in the context of their organization. The goal of their engagement is an open dialog on cyber risk and cyber resilience that aligns the various elements of the cyber awareness education program to the needs of the organization.

Let's return to this chapter's theme of security awareness training and overall security education. The byproduct of these discussions with colleagues is a valuable education for the CISO. You have a better sense of what's important to the organization, the newly-launched key initiatives, what systems, applications, vendors, and other relevant detail related to the initiative come into scope. It is also helpful as cyber training and awareness for the CISO's colleagues. The CISO's colleagues and executive management benefit from the CISO's insights on cyber risk, especially related to digital technology. Ultimately, this collaboration creates an informed organization, one that is more resilient and better prepared to manage cyber risk.

There's another audience that is critical to this process, namely the board of directors. Boards have become increasingly concerned with cyber risk. High-profile breaches (notably the massive breach at Equifax), lawsuits directed at specific board members, and personal experiences with malware and spear phishing are all driving their desire to understand how prepared their organizations are to address a cyber-attack. As we've noted, boards do not like to be surprised. They share this trait with CISOs. Frankly, no senior executive likes surprises.

The work done by the CISO and his or her colleagues in looking at organizational priorities and initiatives, evaluating risk, and understanding the materiality of the efforts for the organization serves as a solid foundation when the CISO is asked to present to the board on the preparedness of the organization. Instead of being blindsided by a new project that introduces significant risk, the CISO enters this presentation with the knowledge that he or she has been proactively engaged with business colleagues, evaluating cyber risk, and making recommendations to bring that risk within acceptable business parameters.

Equally important, the discussions with other senior executives have translated technical risk into enterprise risk expressed in business terms. When presenting to the board, the CISO becomes a valued business leader, one versed in technical risk and with a strong working knowledge of the risks the organization faces and how these can be mitigated. The CISO is effectively the board's trusted advisor on digital strategy.

This chapter has highlighted the pivotal role the CISO plays in evangelizing good cybersecurity practices by translating highly technical risk into business-accessible terms. CISOs who are proactively engaged with their colleagues, capturing priorities and initiatives, understanding the risks associated with these efforts, and looking for organizationally-acceptable mitigations for this risk become valued members of the executive team. Their ability to pivot between technical and business risk makes them an invaluable resource for the resilient organization.

How CISOs Use Cyber Hygiene to Protect and Educate Their Organization – Hayslip

"In cyber hygiene, a missing patch is equivalent to an open door."

In today's fast-moving threat environment, consumers and organizations rely on their enterprise network environments for so many aspects of their daily lives without fully understanding the threats they face. It is this acute reliance on networked systems that demonstrates the need to be proactive and vigilant in protecting against cyber threats. To be as secure and successful as possible, we as security professionals need to follow a concept called cyber hygiene – that is, making sure we are protecting and maintaining these networked systems and computing devices appropriately and using cybersecurity best practices as a daily guide, not as an afterthought.

As the CISO, it will be your responsibility to architect a cybersecurity program that assures the organization follows proper cyber hygiene and manages all known risks. As you can imagine, this can be a daunting task. However, industry frameworks have documented these cyber hygiene processes and industry sectors around the globe have adopted them for their use.

Common Sense Hygiene

Cyber hygiene, for many seasoned technology professionals, is basic common sense. We've learned lessons from significant failures and reconstructed scenarios to understand better how to deploy technology-based services securely. These practical ideas for systems implementation and maintenance of systems are foundational to frameworks such as NIST SP800-53, ISO 27001/27002, and CIS Critical Security Controls. As CISO, you will also find there are other cyber hygiene related frameworks and methodologies used by technology professionals of which you should be aware.

Examples of disciplines that you will interact with as a CISO are IT Service Delivery and Software Development; both use security and risk-based frameworks such as ITIL or OWASP to deliver services and code securely. What all of these various frameworks mean to you is that there are structured methodologies that your organization can use to understand current technology risk, remediate known issues, and manage the residual risk as a mature strategic process.

As we look at the questions for this chapter, we'll see how they relate to cyber hygiene principles and how cyber hygiene can be used to influence organizational behavior. We will review how these concepts and methodologies affect how we should learn from our mistakes, how we should train our staff to fight cyber intrusions, how we teach employees to be cyber aware, and how we prepare our teams to respond to cyber incidents. In essence, you need to get these necessary digital hygiene steps established as your foundation; bake them into your cybersecurity program as fundamental processes.

Without this level of maturity, a lack of cyber hygiene will negatively impact your ability to provide "Cyber as a Service" to your company. You will be too busy remediating the constant flow of risks caused by immature cyber practices. These threats will lead to a recurring battle caused by a lack cyber hygiene that will impact your security program and its effectiveness in protecting your organization.

Learning from Mistakes

As we begin, it is valuable to review and understand the idea of "lessons learned." Critical in many processes is the concept of permitting mistakes but learning from them. There are five steps in this learning process:

- *Recognize Mistakes* – Have a policy/methodology in place to review projects, maintenance, workflows, and events – the key here is to recognize abnormalities.
- *Observe What Works* – Have a policy/methodology in place to observe and document what works for the organization. Don't forget that what works for one company may not work for another.
- *Document, Document, Document* – In both steps above you and the organization must document what is happening so you can review these lessons learned and get better.
- *Share Your Findings* – Learn from mistakes, share what you find as best practices, and incorporate what other companies are doing to better themselves and reduce their risk exposure.
- *Make Changes, Improve Yourself* – Incorporate all of the information available, and be willing to try innovation through continuous improvement. Embrace change as a strategic process like cyber hygiene.

As you can see, lessons learned is a lifecycle process of continuously reviewing problems and seeking improvement. To be successful as a CISO you must continually assess what happens in your community and how it will impact your program and your business. You should review what happens to organizations within your industry vertical, what happens to your fellow CISOs and their responses to adversity, and across the cybersecurity community how vendors and government entities respond to new technologies and emerging threats.

Chapter 11 Key Point and Action Item 4

Continual learning and continual improvement are essential elements of success. Best practices such as formalizing a review of lessons learned from every breach can also play a vital role in your cyber awareness program.

You should establish a formal process to absorb lessons learned from each breach and ensure that the resulting improvements include making appropriate updates to your cyber awareness program and communicating them.

All of these views will provide education and insight into changes you may need to incorporate in protecting your company. Which brings us to our first question for discussion: _"What are the "lessons learned" from industry data breaches that can be used to reduce our organization's risk exposure to these adverse events?"_

Who Is Being Disrupted?

Companies around the world are implementing new technologies such as mobility solutions, social media solutions, cloud computing, converged networks, business intelligence and analytics at increasingly breakneck speeds to increase competitiveness and capture market share in today's digital economy. However, with each new technology a company incorporates into its enterprise portfolio, gaps in security controls, doorways that attackers can and will exploit, are introduced. A progressively sophisticated array of new tools is now abusing these weaknesses, and it is becoming harder to detect. This abuse is having an increasing impact on an organization's ability to conduct business.

The challenge organizations face with incorporating disruptive technologies is that security for these new solutions is usually an afterthought. Now add the deployment of these new technologies within an infrastructure that is often not up to today's cybersecurity standards, and you will have some significant complications.

To face these escalating dilemmas with new technologies and disparate legacy systems, you must assess the hygiene of your cybersecurity controls and the resiliency of your security processes. In February 2016, the Attorney General's Office for the State of California released the California Data Breach Report (Harris 2016). This report analyzed the data breaches reported between 2012 and 2015 in the State of California. In 2012, 131 incidents involved 2.6 million citizens' records. However, in 2015, a mere three years later, there were 178 breaches reported with over 24 million citizens' records impacted.

Now keep in mind, these are the reported data breaches. Many believe the real number is much higher. Also noteworthy were the types of breaches that were prevalent in specific industries. Breaches caused by intentional intrusions into systems by unauthorized outsiders, so-called "malware and hacking," made up the largest number of breaches (54%) and the largest number of records (90%) in this period. The report also notes that specific business sectors tend to have breach types that are more common to them. Case in point, "malware and hacking" breaches seemed to be more prevalent in the retail sector while "physical" breaches (theft or loss of unencrypted data on an electronic device) were more common in the healthcare sector.

I mention this report because I believe that you should continuously review material like this and others like the Verizon Data Breach Report (Verizon 2016) to understand the impact of breaches on organizations like yours. You must understand the methods being used by cybercriminals to attack businesses and why the cyber actors want access to your data. This insight will assist you in making educated changes to your security program that will be intentionally focused on reducing the risk exposure from these new threats. These reports will also provide you with information that will help you explain new evolving threats to your company's executive leadership team and educate them on the importance of cybersecurity hygiene.

While the California report is more focused on a specific region, the Verizon report gives you greater insight into what is happening across the cybersecurity community in all sectors around the world. Please note, each report mentions, and the California report specifically calls out that following industry best practices for "cyber hygiene" could have prevented or reduced the impact of many of the breaches studied. The California report recommends the implementation of relevant security controls. The specific framework it recommends at minimum is the Center for Internet Security's (CIS) Top 20 Controls (Center for Internet Security 2015). The report also suggests that an organization's cybersecurity processes should follow a standard, repeatable cyber hygiene process. That recommendation is again from the Center for Internet Security's (CIS), Cyber Hygiene Campaign (CIS 2015).

The CIS Cyber Hygiene Campaign is a straightforward methodology to follow. It consists of five steps: "Count, Configure, Control, Patch, and Repeat" (CIS 2015). Brief descriptions of each step and their underlying components are as follows:

1. *Count* – you can't protect an asset if you don't know it's there. Conduct an inventory to identify authorized and unauthorized assets, accounts, and programs. Every item or asset has potential vulnerabilities that might expose you to risk. The business needs of the identified assets will drive prioritization and remediation of those risks.

2. *Configure* – you should have a configuration management program with a configuration management database (CMDB). Configure assets based on secure baseline configurations such as CIS Security Benchmarks (Center for Internet Security 2016). After establishing baseline configurations, the organization should develop a formal change management program and a process to monitor all IT assets for unauthorized changes continuously.

3. *Control* – this hygiene concept addresses account and access management. Do you have a plan for the roles and responsibilities of the various accounts your business has and do you manage the identities/credentials of authorized assets and users? Do you have training in place for employees on protecting their credentials – e.g., protecting against phishing attacks (Ryan Stark 2015), and are you logging all access activities and continuously monitoring them?

4. *Patch* –– this process concerns appropriate patching that fixes vulnerabilities identified in third-party software. It also addresses security flaws in applications your organization relies upon on a daily basis. The timely patching of security issues is critical to maintaining a resilient network environment. Unapplied patches are a heavily-cited reason for many large-scale data breaches. Missing a patch equates to an open door. You must have a program in place to continually scan for these issues, and when patches are available, be sure to test before deploying.

5. *Repeat* – make sure your hygiene processes are mature, established, and followed, and that you are continuously monitoring them for improvement.

As we finish the analysis on our first question, I want to emphasize that lessons learned review should be a continuous part of your review process as a CISO. I continuously read articles and reports about the cybersecurity community and recent breaches. I then relate my findings and how I believe these threats may impact my security program and organization to my staff and executive leadership. I think this knowledge provides strategic awareness of the digital landscape we must compete in and how we should safely navigate the new and treacherous issues our threat intelligence sources identify. A little paranoia never hurt anyone.

However, even with a continuous review of lessons learned and the deployment of security controls and mature cyber hygiene processes, you will still have a significant issue that you must manage. This major problem is something I call the "human element dilemma." This issue consists of three groups that you will need to manage, and each has their own dynamic needs and requirements.

The first group is the staff on your teams and their ability to implement your vision of cybersecurity. The second group is the stakeholders in your business and their awareness of cybercrime. The final group is your teams and stakeholders who need to respond together, as a team, in crisis conditions during an active breach incident. Our second question for review, applied to the "human element dilemma," is *"How successful is training our staff in actually preventing breaches versus having the right hardware and software in place?"*

Does Training Really Work?

This question gets asked many times when I deal with executive staff who don't understand that cybersecurity is a continuous lifecycle. It is the "one-and-done" mentality that all the cybersecurity team needs is a piece of equipment and everything is good; we are now secure.

This view, that cybersecurity is a technology issue that IT Departments or Information Security Departments should solve, is incorrect! Cybersecurity is an enterprise-wide opportunity for an organization to understand the risks it took on by selecting the technologies used to conduct its business. I believe that cyber touches all business processes at one level or another, which is why from my viewpoint it needs to be accepted as a strategic asset that must be supported and leveraged.

If upon review of any cyber incident the business finds missing patches, misconfigured equipment, incorrectly followed policies, or that staff members were unable to recognize that an intrusion was underway – this information should be viewed as an opportunity to improve, not a reason to remove. It is this opportunity that I believe provides the answer to our question above, whether we should train our staff or buy equipment; it should be a hybrid of both based on business needs.

In the Cisco 2016 Annual Security Report (CISCO Security 2016), 92% of the enterprises that responded to the report employed dedicated security personnel. 82% of the respondents have a formal, annually reviewed organization-wide security strategy. From those numbers, it looks like companies are actively addressing cybersecurity as a corporate issue. The problem is the same report found that only 41% of the respondents are increasing the training required by security staff. This demonstrates a fundamental disconnect because companies think they can build an impenetrable wall of security technologies and be 100% safe.

Unfortunately, we have to work with third-party vendors and mobile solutions and cloud-based applications, so our data never stays inside that impenetrable box. I believe that you will need to train your personnel not just on the theory and practical knowledge of cybersecurity, you will need to educate them on the use of your selected technologies to protect the company's strategic assets. You will need to teach them how to mitigate and remediate damage when attacks occur, because they are inevitable.

In fact, as you read this chapter, your organization is being attacked. What this should mean is when you review technology solutions that are to be a part of your security suite, you must factor in how you will maintain them and the required training. I have found at times that I wanted a specific technology, but my staff did not have the technical competence to manage it. You must understand your staff's level of knowledge and experience, so you can factor in what training they require or reach out to a trusted partner for staff augmentation.

With insight into your team's cybersecurity capabilities, you should proceed to set up a training schedule prioritizing the specific skills they need immediately, with a secondary level of training once you've validated that they have learned the critical skills. From a cyber hygiene perspective, I would continuously track my personnel's skill sets. I would have them assist in evaluating the requirements for their specific jobs, (e.g., Security Analyst, Security Architect, Security Operations Analyst), and then have them assess themselves on their maturity for those skills. I would do this periodically to track if they were getting better after training, and I would observe the metrics we collected on how quickly and efficiently they managed and resolved security tickets and incidents.

As a CISO, I would pay for each of my staff to have access to online training that they could do at their desks or from home, and I would schedule at least one formal class (a vendor class or a cybersecurity course) and one conference for them to attend per year. I believe this exposure gives them a more strategic view of how cyber provides value to the company and their part in the process. So to answer our question, for the CISO and his or her staff to be successful and the organization to be resilient we must continuously conduct training.

Now understand this doesn't mean we train our people and do not upgrade our equipment. With the ever-changing threat landscape and the new destructive attack methodologies, we are now seeing it is critical that we continuously review our IT assets and keep them upgraded to meet the new challenges. We just need to remember that when we source new technology, we need to include training in the costs, so our teams can be effective in using that technology to protect the organization.

From the cyber hygiene perspective of managing the human element of cybersecurity staffs, it is imperative for the CISO to understand his or her team's limitations. Evaluate technical experience, knowledge, and soft skills; then draft a training program that incorporates the current technology in the security suite and the skillsets the team members need to be competent security professionals. However, there is the second group of the "human element dilemma" that CISOs must manage and this one is just as important and extremely impactful in organizations.

This element is the organization itself, the stakeholders in all of the various departments the CISO and his or her teams serve. Do you know if your employees are aware of their responsibility concerning cybersecurity and protecting the business and its technology assets? Do they even understand that business processes they have been performing for years may pose an existential risk to the company? These questions will frame our next discussion, *"Does our organization have a culture of cybersecurity awareness and do we have a program to educate our staff?"*

Organizational Cyber-Awareness Is Fundamental

To begin this discussion, we need to understand that every data breach report or cybersecurity best practice policy I have read recommends training stakeholders. In the State of California Data Breach Report (Harris 2016), the Cisco Data Breach Report (CISCO Security, 2016), and the Verizon Data Breach Reports (Verizon 2016), all three recommend training as a core strategic process that organizations should provide to their staff. One of the primary breach types in every report is that of the inside actor: the employee who makes an unintentional mistake, who clicks on that web link or attachment, or the employee who sabotages the company for personal reasons.

This is why I believe organizations need to invest in a cybersecurity awareness program that trains their employees on basic cyber hygiene principles. People (employees, users) are the weakest link in protecting a company's digital assets. As humans we make mistakes, we bypass processes, we create workarounds that in the short term help us with work but open the organization up to enormous risk. Our employees are a soft target. They are the easiest doorway targeted by hackers through phishing, malware, social media-borne attacks, and social engineering. So, if we wanted to implement a cybersecurity awareness training program, how would that look?

There is a framework that you can use to get started. The NIST Special Publication 800-50 (Wilson and Hash, Joan 2003) is one document that you can use to build a cybersecurity awareness training program. Understand that championing a cybersecurity awareness training program for your organization must be an ongoing, continuous process of learning that is meaningful to stakeholders and delivers measurable benefits to the organization.

The objectives of your program should be to communicate the risks and vulnerabilities facing the organization, show them the tools they can use to minimize these risks and vulnerabilities, and describe the organization's policies and procedures with regards to security and risk management. This training provides the opportunity to hold an organization-wide discussion on risk. It helps bring cybersecurity out of the server room and enables your stakeholders to see that cybersecurity is everyone's responsibility. Finally, it allows you to evangelize that having a cyber-risk-aware business culture is right for the organization.

Now understand, this isn't just purchasing some software and having your employees take the training. You should be putting together a formal training program that may encompass a software package and that includes other types of training, including informal training. Informal training can be such processes as knowledge sharing between teams, presentations to your stakeholders' departments on critical subjects, or roundtable discussions with executive staff and management to answer questions. I have found that as you set up your training program, you will want to provide basic cybersecurity awareness training that all personnel should take. Then, you will also want to put in place specific training for different management roles or positions that handle sensitive data such as data with compliance requirements.

An example of this is an organization that manages payment card information (PCI). Employees who work with payment card data would take the basic cybersecurity awareness training required for all personnel, plus they would take a second set of training that is specific to PCI to meet compliance requirements. As you can see, your cybersecurity awareness program will have multiple levels that will require more in-depth training depending on the roles of the employee. When sourcing a training package for your learning management system make sure it meets the needs of each of your identified audiences within the organization. An excellent example of this is the following illustration from the PCI Security Awareness Program Training Manual (PCI Security Standards Council 2014).

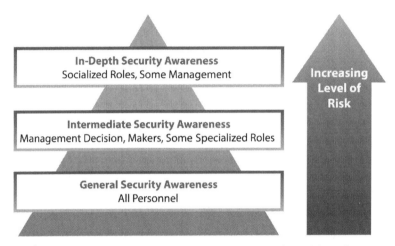

Figure 11.1 PCI Security Awareness Program Training Manual

As you can see from the illustration, each employee's role will have different training requirements based on their job responsibilities. I have managed training programs that had specific training modules for cybersecurity awareness, data privacy awareness, and cybersecurity for managers, and then compliance training for HIPAA and audit requirements. The list of training types can be quite extensive, so talk with your stakeholders and make sure you have an updated list to focus your training program to meet their needs.

Now that I have made the case that you need to have this program for your organization and have given you some ideas on putting it together, the next question is how often should you require the training and how would you measure its success? You will find across all industries that doing annual basic cybersecurity awareness training is standard. I have spoken with people who build training programs, and they estimate that completing awareness training has an impact on workers and is retained for about 90 to 180 days.

After three months' time people start to forget, so you need to include informal training methodologies such as sending out reminders and videos of best practices and visiting departments to present on key points. You want to keep cybersecurity top of mind and make it a repeatable part of the organizational culture.

You also want to collect metrics showing the number of user-related cyber incidents later in the year, after training has faded but before the next annual training, and then the number of incidents after companywide training has been conducted. Earlier in my career, I witnessed a 30-40% reduction in incidents through the use of informal training with trusted agents in my organization's departments. These trusted agents would provide timely reminders to stakeholders about security issues, and through this simple process I was able to keep awareness of security issues going for months after formal companywide training.

This type of continued awareness provides value to the organization. In my example, we estimated that each time one of our employees' machines was infected we would lose two days of productivity while our contracted help desk reimaged the asset and recovered the impacted employee's lost data. This downtime was estimated to cost about $600 per incident in lost productivity. So, if before security awareness training you average 40 assets per month that get infected, and after training you see that reduced to 24 assets infected per month, that is a substantial behavioral shift due to training. It is also saving the business $9,600 per month or $115,200 annually, and with those numbers you can state that your training program is providing impactful value to the business.

Chapter 11 Key Point and Action Item 5

We've discussed metrics at length in both volumes of the CISO Desk Reference Guide. Given that your cyber awareness education program is vital to achieve cyber resilience, some metrics you collect will directly measure the effectiveness of your cyber awareness program (such as familiarity with messaging) or indirectly measure its effectiveness (such as click-through rates on phishing campaigns).

You should review the metrics you track and identify the metrics that indirectly measure your program, typically identified as behaviors that you wish to limit or encourage within your workforce. These might include clicking on links and changing passwords. You should also make sure you have appropriate metrics that directly track the effectiveness of your program, such as familiarity with messaging and cost of recovery from incidents directly related to user activity, such as virus infections via click-through.

Cybersecurity awareness training for the organization is considered to be a basic component of cyber hygiene – it just makes common sense that organizations in a digital world should educate their employees, so they are able to work without putting the company's enterprise assets at risk.

How Do You respond in a Crisis?

We come to our final discussion as we analyze the third group in the "human element dilemma" that keeps CISOs up at night. This final part of the cyber hygiene puzzle is also considered to be a core policy or program that every organization should have in place. As a CISO in today's digital economy, there is only one event that I can guarantee will happen and will impact my organization: a data breach. The final piece of the "human element dilemma" that CISOs will own is how their teams and designated stakeholders respond in time of crisis. The final question under discussion: *"What is our Incident Response Plan and how do we train staff, stakeholders, and partners on how to use this plan?"*

An active incident response event is what organizations would call having a very bad day. I view incident response as "The mitigation of an incident that involves the violation of security policies and recommended practices – i.e., security controls." The incident response program is the strategic asset the CISO creates to coordinate the organization's response to emerging threats and mitigate incidents. Like all good things in cybersecurity, incident response is a lifecycle. The following depiction is from the NIST Special Publication 800-61, Computer Security Incident Handling Guide (National Institute of Standards and Technology SP800-61 2012).

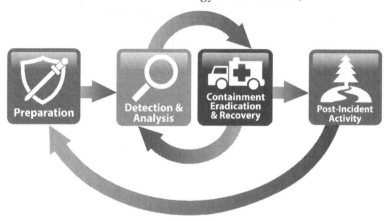

Figure 11.2 Incident Handling Process Flow

I think this guide does an excellent job demonstrating that incident response is a continuous process. It consists of training, continuous scanning and monitoring, containment and remediation, and finally post-incident activity; which we would call "lessons learned" – now where have we heard that term before? As a CISO, you will be responsible for establishing an incident response program. This will require you to create the organization's incident response policy, incident response plan, and a set of incident response procedures.

These documents will start at the executive level with an overall description of incident response, how it applies to the organization, and the structure of the incident response team. Succeeding documents will get more in-depth and provide details on implementing the incident response program and team members' direct responsibilities. As I stated above, the NIST document (National Institute of Standards and Technology SP800-61 2012) is an excellent reference to use in creating your program and establishing it with an industry-tested framework.

Incident Response Policy – This is a high-level document tailored to the organization and its business requirements. This policy document will have critical components such as a statement from management regarding the purpose, objective, and scope of the policy and outlining who it applies to and under what circumstances. You can also expect the policy to define the types of incidents that it applies to and the organizational structure under which it will operate. The policy will also include some form of reporting/communication checklist. Its primary purpose is to give a high-level definition of why the company has an incident response program and how to manage incident response.

Incident Response Plan – In this document you will outline the mission of the incident response program. There should be a statement of support from senior management. This is critical because in time of crisis, the incident response program will reach across all organizational boundaries and you will want that sponsorship to get things completed quickly. You should also have a communications matrix and a RACI matrix as part of the plan. The matrix provides a framework for who is responsible for what components of the program and should also include a checklist for how communications will work.

I periodically update the matrices in my plan because people frequently change positions. You want to have the correct names and phone numbers available. Understand that these contacts will not always be within your organization because you will have third-party entities you will need to contact in the event of a significant data breach. One last component of this plan is you should have some metrics to measure the effectiveness of the plan and a description of how this program fits into the overall organization. I have seen the Incident Response Plan be a sub-component of the company's broader Business Continuity Plan.

Just remember that the purpose of the Incident Response Plan is to provide a guide on how the incident response program will be implemented in the organization and a methodology to determine its effectiveness.

Incident Response Procedures – The organization's mission heavily influences this final component of the incident response program. Incident response procedures include the strategies for implementing the Incident Response Plan and the roles and responsibilities designated for internal teams and those that will require a third party. In these documents, we put together operating procedures that delineate how we respond to specific incidents.

What I have done in the past is use a RACI matrix and break down incident types into categories with workflows for each incident type, and document specific techniques, procedures, checklists, and forms that should be followed by the incident response teams. As you and your teams create these Standard Operation Procedures (SOPs), they should be comprehensive. Make sure they include step by step instructions on how the team members should respond.

In the incident type RACI matrix that you create, note which SOPs should be followed to help teams react quickly with the correct checklists, tools, forms, etc. These SOPs should be tested annually at a minimum and updated to reflect changes based on industry best practice. Having these procedures and testing them should minimize the time to respond and the impact of breaches of your company's enterprise IT assets.

As you finish creating your procedures for how your Incident Response Program will operate, you will need to train the teams on how to use them and continuously review what assets and incident scenarios you are targeting with your procedures. As a CISO, I recommend training your organization on a semi-annual basis using tabletop training exercises.

In these exercises I would select a specific breach type and walk my stakeholders and team members through the process of how we would respond, who we would contact, and what procedures we would use. Then I would make it interesting by stating that this is happening at 2:00 AM on a Saturday – then we game out how we would respond. I would also highly recommend doing an incident training exercise at least annually, but this time include all of your third-party contacts to verify that they know how to respond, and they have their procedures, and note any changes to your procedures at the end of the exercise.

An example of why this is critical: I had an incident where a company that was supposed to provide forensic services in case of an emergency was acquired by another company and was no longer available. By testing your program, you can keep your processes current so that you can respond quickly, and the incident will have less impact on your company.

As we finish this discussion, there is one last point I want to make. There are several incident response frameworks, standards, and guidelines that you can use to map out the steps in architecting your program. I used NIST as an example. However, there are other standards and documents that I have used as references because I continually update my program. Here are several to start with:

1. *NIST Special Publication 800-61*, Computer Security Incident Handling Guide (National Institute of Standards and Technology SP800-61 2012)
2. *ISO/IEC 20735*, Security Incident Management (International Organization for Standardization 2016)
3. *SANS*, Incident Handler's Handbook (Wright 2011)
4. *State of New York*, Cyber Incident Response Standard (State of New York, Office of Information Technology Services 2016)

I believe it is evident that cyber hygiene practices support and enhance all business processes and security programs that you will manage, and that for your program to be efficient, training will be required. As a CISO, your cybersecurity program and the risk management services you provide to the business will continually change and mature over time.

As the threats the organization faces develop, the technologies you use get upgraded, and the community and business environment you operate in react to new opportunities; all of these scenarios will require you to adapt and upgrade your program. I believe the regular review of lessons learned is critical for the CISO, as a senior technology leader, to be successful within an organization. The knowledge gained provides context for the strategic processes the CISO must put in place to reduce risk and protect his or her company.

Some of these processes will be the training program created to mentor and lead cybersecurity staff, the cybersecurity awareness program created to evangelize and educate company stakeholders, and finally the incident response program, designed to identify specific procedures to be followed when the company is in crisis.

As the leader of these programs, using training to continually improve these individual efforts will pay off in your staff's readiness to manage incidents, your stakeholder's appreciation for the value of cybersecurity, and your organization's improved capabilities to respond to cyber incidents. All of these lead to a more stable, competitive, resilient organization. To do this well, you must leverage education to reduce the impact of the "human element dilemma" on your company. In closing, train hard, train like you plan to fight so you will be prepared, take care of your staff, and include your stakeholders so they know they are part of your team.

Summary

For Chapter 11, we began our discussion by asking these four questions:

- What are the "lessons learned" from industry data breaches that can be used to reduce our organization's risk exposure to these adverse events?
- How successful is training our staff in actually preventing breaches versus having the right software and hardware in place?
- Does our organization have a culture of cybersecurity awareness and do we have a program to educate our staff?
- What is our Incident Response Plan and how do we train staff, stakeholders and partners on how to use this plan?

Several consistent themes emerged, including the requirement to align the cyber awareness program to the organization's business objectives, the need to measure direct and indirect performance and the value of using these measurements to make continual improvements to your awareness program.

In closing, we would like to leave you with these five key points and next steps:

1. You need to align your cyber awareness education program needs with the organization's goals for the program to be effective. While a great many cyber-related regulations mandate cyber awareness training, your job as the CISO is to try to help the organization avoid the trap of administering the program as just another compliance activity. **You should evaluate and adjust your existing cyber awareness education program to ensure that the messaging and any calls to action are visibly linked to organizational objectives, so your workforce sees the immediate relevance of the training.**

2. We are at a point in the ongoing struggle against cybercrime where every organization must recognize the threat and take sustained action to ensure its survival. **You should work with your peers and senior leadership to create a unified plan with consistent support across the entire organization. Coordinate the efforts and**

include messaging, materials, and well-defined roles and responsibilities in the ecosystem. Communicate messaging and roles broadly, and continually reinforce them.

3. A unified plan will only be effective if each senior leader recognizes the value and is fully engaged in solving cyber awareness problems that represent specific threats to their line of business. **You should work with your peers and senior leadership to make sure they are informed about cybersecurity in the context of their organization. The goal of their engagement is an open dialog on cyber risk and cyber resilience that aligns the various elements of the cyber awareness education program to the needs of the organization.**

4. Continual learning and continual improvement are essential elements of success. Best practices such as formalizing a review of lessons learned from every breach can also play a vital role in your cyber awareness program. **You should establish a formal process to absorb lessons learned from each breach and ensure that the resulting improvements include making appropriate updates to your cyber awareness program and communicating them.**

5. We've discussed metrics at length in both volumes of the CISO Desk Reference Guide. Given that your cyber awareness education program is vital to achieve cyber resilience, some metrics you collect will directly measure the effectiveness of your cyber awareness program (such as familiarity with messaging) or indirectly measure its effectiveness (such as click-through rates on phishing campaigns). **You should review the metrics you track and identify the metrics that indirectly measure your program, typically identified as behaviors that you wish to limit or encourage within your workforce. These might include clicking on links and changing passwords. You should also make sure you have appropriate metrics that directly track the effectiveness of your program, such as familiarity with messaging and cost of recovery from incidents directly related to user activity, such as virus infections via click-through.**

As Bill mentioned, you'll know your education program is working when different departments are reaching out to you because they have detected behaviors that are harbingers of imminent compromise, when departments report success and failure for cyber awareness on their own, and when your peers are sharing best practices about what has worked for them and what hasn't.

Chapter 12 – Monitoring Your Environment

Introduction

Networks are noisy. From heartbeats to probing, from legitimate database extracts to covert data exfiltration, from sensor telemetry to malware infusions, there is an enormous amount of traffic on your network. Without a strategic and diligent approach, It is difficult to know how much of your traffic is appropriate. Long gone are the days when volume alone was the biggest hint that you were under attack.

Bill starts the discussion by reminding us just how much the network and the devices on the network have changed. In the last decade, we have seen not just an explosion in data volume, but a significant change in control as to how the network and the applications and devices on it are acquired, deployed and exploited for business utility. Bill also highlights the need to look at a wide range of activities to successfully monitor the organization's infrastructure.

Matt reminds us that monitoring involves more than just checking the flashing lights for activity and sniffing packets. His advice for program monitoring shows us the broad range of health indicators that the CISO must be concerned with and how important it is to be integrated with the lines of business to know what matters to the entire organization.

Gary emphasizes the need for continued diligence through scanning, monitoring, and remediation before addressing the critical requirement for having a deep understanding of the health and security of your applications. To end this chapter, he brings the discussion back to one of our favorite topics: metrics.

Some of the questions the authors used to frame their thoughts for this chapter include:

- As a CISO, what frameworks, security controls, or processes would you recommend to continuously monitor your organization to prevent or mitigate a data breach?
- What framework and/or processes should a CISO use to remediate vulnerabilities and search for malware in their organization's application portfolio?
- Your organization experiences numerous unauthorized attempts to breach its enterprise networks. What metrics are important to your enterprise cybersecurity program to enable it to see these attempts?

> "They will use the easiest method possible to gain access but will stop at nothing to get in."

Needle in a Haystack

The goal for most hackers is to remain invisible for as long as possible. The reasons vary, but the key ones are to afford the hackers the time to sufficiently map the infrastructure and identify the highest-value assets for maximum lifetime value and to allow them to come back to the target to cause additional mayhem. There are exceptions such as ransomware, a strain of malware that maliciously encrypts the data on a target device without the owner's permission and then holds the decryption key for ransom. Another exception is a false flag operation where noisy cybercriminals attempt to attribute the attack to a rival. But this is rarely the case.

In general, hackers aren't likely to rattle around in your network with tons of pop-up messages and chat requests, and your tools, unfortunately, don't come with a "Spot the Hacker" button. You're going to have to find them, and the goal of this chapter is to give you some advice on how to do that over the long haul.

In addition to the cybercriminal's stealth, it is essential to understand that the firewall that promised a thick, hard shell to protect the soft, chewy center no longer (if it ever did) offers the protection that it once was theoretically intended to provide. Almost immediately after deploying firewalls, organizations started poking holes in them. Some are small holes – using a single port between two specific hosts over a well-controlled route, limited to a single protocol, allowed only for white-listed processes, fully authenticated, at a particular time of day. Some are big, gaping, Grand Canyon size holes – how secure does "Permit IP Any Any" seem to you?

Most large organizations have so many rules permitting specific traffic that they require special analysis tools to tell them what traffic they are in fact allowing. Hundreds of thousands to millions of firewall rules is not an uncommon number for huge networks. We can't call them firewalls anymore; they are more like gateways.

Another critical mindset to understand is that cybercriminals are very economically motivated. That seems evident, as they are often looking for something to steal that can be sold immediately on the dark web, but it also means they will not spend money on a tool they don't need. If a non-targeted phishing campaign works, they won't invest the time or money to build a spear-phishing campaign. In the same vein, if garden-variety malware works, they won't bother with an APT (advanced persistent threat). Regardless of how they get in, though, they'll want to be as stealthy as possible, which means removing their tracks as best they can. There are some who are experienced nation state-caliber actors and some who are using an exploit kit for the first time.

Also, the networks that organizations began to deploy in the '70s, '80s, and '90s no longer completely define the attack surface. With the introduction of cloud services, the network has no hard boundary. It started with SaaS (Software as a Service) in the late '90s (then known as Application Service Providers – ASPs) and now includes software-configurable infrastructure (known as Infrastructure as a Service - IaaS). We've also added the ability to consume entire, preconfigured services in various public, private, hybrid, and community cloud deployment models (known as Platform as a Service - PaaS).

And finally, personal digital assistants such as the Simon Personal Communicator, followed by devices running the Palm OS, the Blackberry OS, and the Windows CE/Pocket PC set the stage for BYOD (Bring Your Own Device). What started in the mid-'90s with the forerunners to the smartphone began to explode in 2007 with the introduction of the Apple iPhone and then arrived in earnest as a substantial security concern in 2008 with the advent of the Android mobile operating system. Non-curated marketplaces then became significant sources for app delivery and would then soon drive, along with Apple's curated market, a pivotal shift toward individuals choosing how and where to use their IT.

This evolution of small devices is also significant as a precursor to the significance of the Internet of Things (IoT). As sensor devices dropped in price, communications options multiplied, and the device footprint shrank, the number of endpoints to defend has increased by such a factor as to change the approach we must take to protect our network. What worked when you could quickly inventory the entire server base in person will not work at the scale of the IoT.

We Can No Longer Rely on the Castle and Moat Defense

So, thanks to the history lesson, we now know we have semi-permeable gateways and mist where our firewalls used to be, and persistent cybercriminals who want to hang out in our networks for months, years, or indefinitely if we let them. They will use the easiest method possible to gain access but will stop at nothing to get in. We also learned that the attack surface is infinite.

Why did I review this scope of problems? Because I believe the challenge is to design a monitoring approach that recognizes and adapts to the increasing number of attack vectors, and that critical to this is always to be aware of what you are protecting and avoid the temptation of becoming distracted by the constantly changing landscape. You'll want a combination of legacy and next-generation cybersecurity monitoring techniques. Legacy techniques look for evidence of altered files or assets: malfunctioning applications, corrupted files, complaints to the Help Desk, access log entries that show inappropriate access.

Chapter 12 Key Point and Action Item 1

It is essential that you have sensors on every critical part of your network. When you inherit a monitoring program, it's safe to assume that time pressures, budget pressures, or less-than-ideal change management have left part of your network unwatched. These failures create dark zones that could leave your infrastructure exposed.

You should conduct a thorough review of your assets and the activity and log data you are collecting to make sure all critical flows can be monitored.

Artifacts left behind, for example, an altered file, device, or configuration setting, are indications that something has occurred. Sometimes you notice these "Indicators of Compromise" (IOCs) before the exfiltration or vandalism happens. More often, you don't catch them until you are performing forensics on compromised systems after you've become aware of a breach. In some cases, it is initially difficult to distinguish error from malfeasance, which impacts speed to detection.

But even though you may not notice the cyber-attack until it is further along the kill chain than you'd like, it's still important to look for these IOCs as your resident cybercriminals may not consider you a "one and done" target. Your monitoring program should start with routine sweeps of file systems for malware, reviews of access log files, responses to Help Desk tickets, and a root cause analysis for application errors and network slowdowns (as ITIL best practice, of course, would require).

There are other logs and events you should track and investigate as well, including failed authentication attempts, data transfer logs, and error logs. The limiting factors are how much data you can process and store, and how many events you can handle.

There are techniques (using tools) for increasing the amount of data you can handle. These range from simple scripts, such as running specialized Perl scripts against log files looking for error conditions, to purpose-built SIEM (Security Information and Event Management) applications that analyze and correlate multiple, disparate log files looking for pre-defined patterns that indicate a high probability of unauthorized activity worthy of investigation.

It is true that these tools take a fair amount of skill to use correctly and require a fair amount of "hands on keyboard" to maintain the rules and target the right data sources. But, you can limit the blast radius, and you can halt the exfiltration before losing all the data. However, this is usually not enough.

What Should You Be Looking For?

What other types of monitoring should you do? Depending on the industry and the size of the target painted on the data you are protecting:

- Monitor your network and endpoint devices for malware. The vast majority of attacks originate from opportunistic malware. SPAM and Phishing are attacks that cybercriminals use indiscriminately, like casting a fishing net. These attacks are designed to round up any device that becomes infected for later exploitation.

- Monitor your network for vulnerabilities. In addition to malware, using known exploits for unpatched vulnerabilities is extremely common. Keep in mind that the whole world knows about every detected vulnerability on the technology you deploy. The more valuable the vulnerability (in other words, the larger the hole it punches through your defenses), the faster the cybercriminals will try to exploit it. Expect immediate scanning for vulnerable systems. Remember that any other scan done by cybercriminals against your network (which you may or may not have noticed) will be mined and sold to accelerate finding an easy way past your defenses. Monitor your network for unauthorized scanning and realize this probing will be patient and stealthy.

- Monitor the dark web for activity about your organization. The dark web may be out of your direct reach. You might not be able to afford to hire staff that can lurk on the dark web, waiting for your data to appear for sale, or waiting for your organization to be talked about, which may be an early precursor to attack. If this is not something you can staff directly, consider threat intelligence services that include monitoring of a range of data points, including the dark web.

- Conduct penetration testing (pen testing) on your network. Vulnerabilities are significant, but successfully penetrating your network through unpatched vulnerabilities usually requires successfully exploiting several low-level to moderate-level vulnerabilities (because you perhaps patched all the highs?). While the cybercriminals are willing to put in the amount of effort warranted by the size of the prize, you can monitor what they could exploit by pen testing yourself. While pen testing with specific parameters is necessary for certain types of compliance (most notably PCI-DSS), using an automated pen testing tool that allows you to simulate exploits proven in the wild can help you close gaps before the breach occurs.

At a high level, you'll need to watch the following:

- The accounts (human and system) provisioned in your environment, including privileged access (root, admin) to your systems (account creation, change in access rights)
- The assets these accounts access and attempt to access
- The data flow across your network (to internal and external destinations)
- The vulnerabilities left unpatched in your environment
- Viruses detected and remediated on your network and the endpoint devices connected to your network
- The dark web market for your firm's information
- The unapproved traffic on your network
- The configuration drift for both physical and virtual assets from approved secure baselines (including servers, endpoints, as well as the network infrastructure such as

routers and switches and network protection such as firewalls)

- The third-party applications (approved and unapproved) deployed on or accessed from your network
- The devices (approved and unapproved) connected (physically or wirelessly) to your network and clear text or encrypted traffic they generate
- The applications (approved and unapproved) generating traffic on your network
- The third-party accounts that have access to your network, especially service accounts
- The events generated by system accounts

Chapter 12 Key Point and Action Item 2

Due to the large volume of data collected, it is often impossible to look at all of it, and it's rare to have the spare time needed to conduct random threat hunting. While being able to reconstruct what happened after a breach can help you tighten your defenses, looking at real-time indicators of compromise is critical to reducing the mean time to detect nefarious activity on your network.

You should continually assess your most critical business processes and make sure that you have event monitoring in place to detect indicators of compromise for potential breaches with the greatest potential to do your organization harm.

So far, we've talked about firewalls and SIEMs. Any conversation about rules-based security tools should also include Intrusion Detection Systems (IDS), their big brothers, Intrusion Prevention Systems (IPS), and for outgoing traffic, Data Loss Prevention (DLP) systems. IDS, IPS, and DLP systems are like firewalls and SIEMS in that they are all rules-based systems.

Firewalls allow or block traffic. IDS detect traffic patterns that violate rules and log these events. IPS detect traffic patterns that violate rules and rejects that traffic. DLP systems detect and alert on (and sometimes block) data leaving the network. SIEMs analyze logs and alert on log entries that violate rules for appropriate events.

These devices rely on rules that are set up using conditional pattern matching based on known signatures representing previously detected patterns. These patterns can be detected either by the organization itself or other customers or subscribers to the manufacturers of the devices, providers of the services, or consortiums that collect pattern samples on behalf of many member companies.

The supporting ecosystem consists of databases with hundreds of millions of signatures of viruses, patch and vulnerability databases, blacklists and whitelists. There is a lot of effort expended to catalog as many bad things as we can recognize and program our defenses to close that proverbial barn door, but it is often too late.

As I mentioned before, the barn doors often represent the most economical way to penetrate a network, and therefore, we must defend them. But with the rate at which technology is proliferating and the number of vulnerabilities discovered, an ecosystem built only around gathering and applying some logic that stops something known to be bad from happening again is bound to be overwhelmed.

To try to keep up, we've automated much of the reporting, and we're now automating much of the response. We therefore now have machines diagnosing machine problems, communicating antidotes to each other, applying those remedies and hoping we can do it fast enough to keep the cybercriminals out. All the while, older systems are becoming unpatchable, and the ecosystem for recognizing known problems cannot keep up with the hundreds of thousands of new attacks developed every day.

Don't Bring a Knife to a Gunfight

We've talked about looking for the signs, the IOCs, that cybercriminals might have been in your network, indications that they might be targeting your network, and evidence that there are openings in your defenses they are able or known to exploit. But these approaches share something in common. In each case, you are defending a large number of assets and monitoring a large number of signals with humans and rules-based tools.

Does it strike you that the cybercriminals are outgunning you? They are. Among the many clichés we've abused in this book, here is one more: You must be right 100% of the time, but the cybercriminals only need to be right once to penetrate your network.

We have established that you very likely have already been breached. We've also made it clear you have more data available to you than is humanly possible to analyze. So, give the humans some help, some artificial help, as in, artificial intelligence. By the way, the cybercriminals have. AI tools are already being used to probe for weaknesses, and AI-driven twitter bots are well known as constant sources of phishing campaigns.

As much hype as AI has received, and it's a lot, one of the areas where AI is already proving useful is cybersecurity. AI tools are helping to detect malware and unauthorized (inappropriate) activity using several different approaches. One approach is to use a branch of AI called machine learning that allows machines to learn to recognize good versus bad patterns of behavior. You'll often hear this referred to as behavior analysis. The machines learn how to distinguish good behaviors from bad by cataloging good behaviors (establishing a baseline) and discerning behaviors that diverge from goodness by a sufficient delta.

Another approach uses clustering algorithms to find aberrant files that have been masked to appear to be normal files. By examining attributes of the various binaries, the machine can group files that seem to be similar. In both cases, what makes the AI systems truly useful is their ability to learn the baselines and determine the attributes most useful for clustering on their own.

We call this branch of machine learning "structured learning." Engineers direct the learning by feeding data to the machines and teaching the AI algorithms how to make decisions about the best paths to pursue. While engineers direct the learning is initially, the machines eventually become sufficiently autonomous, which improves the speed at which the machines can learn and react.

These tools are still biased toward the past, though. Another approach is called predictive analytics. In this case, the mathematical models used by the AI systems are focused on predicting the possible outcomes that certain behavior patterns are likely to achieve. In this scenario, the analytics might predict a probability that a certain pattern of actions might achieve an outcome that is negative versus an outcome that is neutral or positive and raise an alert about this potential.

Predictive analytics require more data and more compute power, and the science is less mature than behavior analytics and clustering, however, these and other technologies also based on AI are coming to market for cybersecurity.

Given the sheer volume of attacks and the number of endpoints, systems, and approved communications channels you are protecting, it's going to be essential to incorporate products that use AI into your tools portfolio and train your staff to include AI in their experiments and ad hoc tools. My point is not that you should abandon your existing monitoring processes in favor of only those that feature AI. But I do believe you should monitor the cybersecurity tools space and, where practical, encourage and deploy AI to both enhance the protection of your environment and learn more about how to use these tools to help protect your organization in the future.

In the following essays by Matt and Gary, you're going to get many practical suggestions for steps you should take for monitoring your systems. All of them are worth considering for your network, and what you ultimately choose to deploy should be tailored to your unique circumstances.

Security Program Monitoring – Stamper

> "The touchstone of the FTC's approach to data security is reasonableness: a company's data security measures must be reasonable in light of the sensitivity and volume of consumer information it holds."
>
> (Federal Trade Commission)

Just how good is my security program? Every CISO needs to ask this question continuously. So too should their colleagues in executive management as well as the board of directors. How you frame this question is equally important. In basic terms, is your security program reducing risk to a business-acceptable level? Cyber risk is a component of enterprise risk management (ERM), albeit a type of risk that is often more nuanced and complex to qualify and quantify than other, more traditional, risk management disciplines such as financial and operational risk. Monitoring your security program is key to determining if your organization's risk profile and appetite are consistent with your organization's overall strategic goals and objectives.

Broaden Your Approach to Monitoring

For many of us, when we think of monitoring, we immediately think of our networks and the packets that traverse them. It's my view that this monitoring, while crucial to our security program, is only a small part of the overall effort. CISOs must take a more comprehensive and expansive view of monitoring to ensure that they adequately align their security program with the objectives of their organization.

How you monitor your security program can be broadly categorized into two distinct forms: Technical Monitoring and Security Program Governance Monitoring.

- **Technical Monitoring:** In its purest form, this type of monitoring oversees what is allowed into the organization and what should be allowed to leave. Areas of focus include basic security hygiene related to network boundaries, network segmentation, user behavior, and which protocols and services to either allow or deny. Effectively, this is all about policing packets. Allow good packets in and deny bad packets because their payloads put the organization at risk. Your job is to monitor for and prevent bad traffic.

Over time, this traffic (packet) monitoring has expanded to incorporate additional business context. For instance, data loss prevention (DLP) and other tools are designed to preclude the exfiltration of particular data objects. These include payment card data, social security numbers, personally-identifiable information (PII), protected health information (PHI), intellectual property (IP), and the like unless these traffic flows are duly authorized.

More recently, and a source of some impressive detective capabilities, we have enhanced the monitoring of the security of our systems with tools that allow us to look for anomalies within the network as well as with the behavior of users. Technical monitoring discovers rogue devices, unauthorized activity, and other indicators of compromise. Ultimately this more sophisticated monitoring improves the detection and timely response capabilities of the organization.

Security monitoring has also incorporated tools from other disciplines such as traditional intelligence and counter espionage. Much of our threat intelligence effort today is akin to that of a private investigator looking at the actions of a suspect. Threat intelligence frequently looks at the profile of the organization and its principal executives in the "dark web," helping the CISO to assess the discussions about the organization across *alternative* channels. Proactive threat intelligence – hunting for scenarios that could place the organization at risk – is an essential element of a technical monitoring program for organizations that are in high-profile industries or critical sectors of the economy.

In the aggregate, technical monitoring provides essential value to a security program. It highlights areas where misconfigurations are placing networks, applications, systems, and, most importantly, our information and data, at risk. It also highlights the threat actors who look to cause harm to the organization and its operations and people. Strong competencies with technical monitoring – both personally and organizationally – are a must for a CISO. But these skills alone may not be sufficient to protect your organization.

- **Security Program Governance Monitoring**: Admittedly, this is the less-visible side of monitoring but every bit as necessary. Program monitoring is, in many ways, the foundation of your overall security program and calls on many of the business skills associated with risk management and security program administration. CISOs who excel at this type of monitoring will have stronger, more effective security programs than those that ignore these critical competencies. The C-suite views these CISOs as trusted advisors and colleagues. The pay for these individuals is higher than that of purely technical CISOs – who are frequently a layer or two below in the org chart – because of their engagement with organizational strategy and the higher-level audience with whom they work. I cannot overstate the return on investment for developing competencies with this type of program monitoring.

Security Program Governance Monitoring

Let's take a more in-depth look at security program governance monitoring. Every organization will differ on what material in this regard means, but the CISO should begin with a basic set of questions to inform this effort. "What is it that I don't know that I should know about my organization that could impact our organization's ability to achieve its objectives?" The CISO should also ask "What is it that I don't know that I should know that will put my organization at risk?"

The premise is that there is essential, not necessarily technical, risk context that can influence the success of the security program. As a CISO, you want to avoid risk blind spots...those areas that can cause harm to your organization but that you are unaware of until it's too late. The goal of security program governance monitoring is to go from a reactive security posture to a proactive, informed, and engaged security posture.

Let's think about some of the critical elements of your security program for governance monitoring.

- **Legal Obligations**: CISOs have an important role liaising with legal counsel. Specifically, the CISO offers the organization's counsel a technical resource and sounding board to ensure that the organization's security practices are consistent with contractual and regulatory obligations. Indeed, the proactive CISO will review these obligations in advance of the organization entering into any material agreement.

A CISO may want to ask if the organization's current contracts obligate certain security practices, staffing levels, or infrastructure requirements that simply are not in place or currently available. This review will highlight areas within the security program that may require additional resources. Requesting these resources should not be conveyed in technical terms. For instance, "We need to expand our SAN to store more security logs. Can I please have $75,000?" is not likely to be effective.

A better way to approach this is to put it in business terms. For example, "Our contract with XYZ Company requires that we store security logs during the life of the contract. Fulfilling this obligation will require an increase in our current infrastructure that is likely to cost $75,000. We estimate $2.1 million in increased business from the XYZ contract."

Knowing what the organization is committing to concerning privacy and security controls and associated practices can reduce the organization's legal exposure and risk as gaps can be remediated and addressed in a business context. Simply stated, CISOs will want to meet with their organization's counsel to review these and similar scenarios.

- **Regulatory Obligations**: Similar to being consulted on contractual obligations related to material contracts, the CISO plays an integral role in ensuring that security (and privacy) practices are consistent with state, federal, and international laws such as the European Union's General Data Protection Regulation (GDPR). Specifically, the CISO should be aware of and validate whether his or her security program is meeting the intent of the law.

As a case in point, CISOs in healthcare organizations should review their organization's business associate agreements (BAAs). Do current practices meet the obligations defined and required within the BAAs? Areas that are frequently overlooked include – as in the example above – mandatory requirements to retain security logs for a specified period of time. Similarly, we often ignore the need to assess the security and privacy controls of vendors. Assessing this risk is a legal obligation of HIPAA-HITECH compliance (see CFR 164.314 for further detail).

Regulatory compliance is frequently an ambiguous topic for many organizations. Department heads often assume that another department is responsible for compliance activities. Declare war on this ambiguity. Work with your internal audit, procurement, legal, and other colleagues to validate requirements and determine if your security program is adequately addressing these obligations (including third-party vendor assessments). To the extent that there are gaps in the program, that presents a risk to the organization. Surface this risk and what's required to address it with your colleagues. Express this risk in business terms and impact to the organization and allow your colleagues to weigh in on the solution.

Ultimately, compliance is the responsibility of executive management – notably the CEO and CFO. Your job is to ensure that they are aware of these obligations and understand the risks and, more importantly, the impacts of non-compliance. You need to offer a solution that is expressed in business terms and not security-related fear, uncertainty, and doubt (FUD). How the organization chooses to treat this risk is a business and not a security decision. Many organizations will accept this risk and continue with the status quo. That is ultimately the CEO's or other executives' prerogative.

- **Program Budget:** Let's face it, budgets and the budget process are the organizational equivalents of going to the dentist. Nevertheless, budgets and overall financial responsibility for security programs are a core element of the CISO role. The board of directors does not like surprises. They are not alone. CFOs take this trait to an extreme. Non-budgeted requests, especially those that involve capital expenditures, are a surefire way to get off on the wrong foot with the CFO. CISOs need to be good financial stewards of their security programs.

  To facilitate this, it's important that the CISO understands the financial costs of delivering proper security for the organization. As part of this effort, know the status of your security infrastructure. Do you have systems that are close to being declared end-of-life? Do you have maintenance and subscription fees (notably for threat intelligence services) that are coming due? Will there be training for your team that is required to maintain compliance with specific regulations or contractual obligations? Do you have new systems coming on-line that will require security services? Do you need more storage for logs? Being on top of your organization's infrastructure, strategy, new applications, staffing levels, and training competencies is a core element of the CISO role given their financial impacts.

Develop a budget that has some sensitivity analysis incorporated. I would recommend two scenarios: a reasonable budget (addressing minimum requirements to keep the security lights on), and an aspirational budget. The reasonable budget should cover the core elements of your program including estimated costs for training, maintenance of subscriptions, staff salaries and their benefits, as well as some anticipated growth for security services that are consumption based (e.g., seat-based licenses, SIEM and logging infrastructure, etc.).

The aspirational budget is effectively a wish list that could include additions to your security team and newer tools that support analytics and detective or forensic capabilities within your security architecture. The aspirational budget requires alignment between the organization's strategy and your security program. You don't want the CEO or CFO to ask you what you need to address an issue and have to say, "Let me get back to you." Be prepared.

Your budgeting process should not take place in a vacuum. Coordinate and work closely with the CFO (or his or her delegate) to ensure that you are conveying your budget materials in a format that they understand and can incorporate into the organization's overall budgeting process. Under ideal circumstances, plan quarterly meetings to review the financial performance of your department and program with the CFO.

This review offers an opportunity to convey to the CFO the vital work you and your team are doing, address any unforeseen issues that may arise, and equally important, learn of any new initiatives or challenges that could impact your security program. A healthy working relationship with your financial colleagues is a must.

- **Board Communication**: Today's CISO must know that part of their security monitoring program will include evaluations by the key stakeholders of the organization, such as the board of directors, of their performance and the performance of their program. Boards are becoming increasingly aware of the risks associated with poor security practices and the resulting damage that can be caused to an organization. Boards are also, in many cases, ill-equipped to understand the more nuanced elements of security programs. As a CISO, you should anticipate that the board of directors or, minimally, senior management are going to want to understand the risk profile of the organization.

In many cases, the board's expectations may not be realistic. They may have a perception that because they have invested in you and your security program, the organization is "secure." It's incumbent upon you to educate the board that there is no such thing as absolute security and that the likelihood of some security-related event will never be zero. Indeed, security incidents should be anticipated and addressed with planning.

Help your board understand the value of your security program based on how your program aligns to the risk appetite of the organization, how it supports and facilitates organizational resiliency, and how the program is designed to minimize the legal and contractual risk that would result from inadequate, incomplete, or untested security practices. CISOs who can translate security risk into actionable insight – conveyed in business terms – to the board of directors become trusted advisors for their board. CISOs should anticipate and plan to communicate periodic status updates to their executive team and the board as part of their core responsibilities.

- **Procurement and Line of Business Initiatives**: Just like looking for nefarious actors and suspicious activity within your network, the proactive CISO will seek out details related to the procurement of third-party services and initiatives from colleagues across different lines of business within the organization. Schedule meetings with your procurement or vendor management teams to evaluate which services the organization uses that you or IT do not control. Build a collaborative relationship with these colleagues by conveying how you and your security team are there to help them evaluate risk related to third-party services or other initiatives.

To avoid being blindsided, you want to anticipate activities that present a risk to the organization. You can ask your colleagues which vendors they are using, what types of information they share with these vendors, whether the vendors connect to your internal networks, what services the vendors support, and other detail that will help you evaluate the risks associated with this provider or initiative. Be known as someone your procurement team and other colleagues can rely on to help assess the risks of the initiative or the vendor. Don't rain on their parade, either. Look for ways to help these prospective vendors improve their security posture while protecting your organization's data and infrastructure. Think of this as a highly collaborative effort – both inside and outside the organization.

If you have a reputation of always saying no to new initiatives or precluding valuable services from being procured, this effort will fail. Your objective is to help qualify and quantify the risk associated with these activities, develop a governance model to address this risk, and facilitate the strategic goals of the organization generally and your colleagues' goals specifically.

- **Training and Professional Team Development**: As CISOs we also need to protect our own. Your team deserves your commitment and support. Know the professional aspirations and career goals of your people. Just like not monitoring your network and the behavior of users across your application portfolio presents a risk, failing to be engaged with your people presents a significant risk. If you are distant, quick to judge, authoritarian, or otherwise a pain in the ass to work with, your people will leave.

There's too much opportunity to find bosses who are engaged, a job with enhanced or more exciting responsibilities, and, of course, a salary increase, if someone on your team decides to look outside of the organization for their next career move. You cannot execute your security program without your team. Invest the time to help your team grow professionally and you will reap the rewards.

To ensure that your team is doing well, I recommend having regular one-on-one meetings with your staff. Your job is to listen and learn. Which tools are working well, which systems have challenges? Know their preferences and understand what they need to be successful. Does the team need specific training on specific tools or applications that you use as part of your security architecture?

If so, make sure they get the training they need. Too many organizations fail to train their staff for fear that they will leave the organization for a better opportunity once trained. They will go regardless, and probably under the worst of circumstances, if you do not demonstrate that you are listening to them and respecting their needs. CISOs who fail to train their people are shortsighted and put their organizations at risk.

Ultimately, the CISO role is about shedding light on the myriad cyber risks confronting an organization and helping colleagues – notably those in the C-suite as well as the board of directors – place this risk in an appropriate business context, noting the potential impacts to the organization's strategy and mission. Business-focused CISOs excel at translating the more technical elements of cyber risk into business and operational risk characteristics that are easily understood and addressed.

They also do not shy away from the less technical aspects of their role: monitoring risks related to their organization's contracts, regulatory exposure, and vendors, as well as the financial well-being of their security program. These CISOs also recognize that ultimately the success of their programs depends heavily upon their direct teams. Ensuring team engagement, career advancement for talent within their departments, and the overall morale of their team is one of the most important "monitoring" functions a CISO will have.

Monitoring the Enterprise and Your Cybersecurity Program – Hayslip

"Reasonable care is important because cybersecurity is a continuous lifecycle and breaches are part of that lifecycle."

It's 2:00 AM and the smartphone on a nightstand is chirping a lonely message for Alice Bentlee (fictitious). Alice is the Vice President, Cybersecurity and Risk Operations Director for a local bio-technical research facility and right now she is trying to brush the sleep from her eyes as she reaches for her phone. In the next fifteen minutes, she will become wide awake as she learns the news. The organization, which is her employer, has had a data breach and has activated the incident response plan. In the days to come as she triages the breach, she will use forensics to understand how it happened and what data was accessed.

The company will leverage its cyber insurance policy to help cover its costs as it initiates an internal investigation into Alice's cybersecurity program, and as the CISO she will need to answer questions to prove her program was meeting the definition of "reasonable care." Did she, as the senior security executive for the company, implement a cybersecurity program to the best of her ability that met industry best practices and as an organization met the standards of care for protecting the critical intellectual property data her company had stored within its enterprise networks?

As a CISO, it is essential to understand the idea of "reasonable care" and why it is a minimum strategic standard for the business. This concept is based on several core principles:

1. The organization, or the CISO acting on its behalf, shall be considered to have complied with reasonable security practices and procedures if an industry standard framework was used to implement the procedures (i.e., NIST, ISO, COBIT, and CIS), and there is a current documented information security program. This program should have mature information security policies that contain managerial, technical, operational, and physical security control measures that are at a maturity level commensurate with the level of sensitive information being protected by the company.

CISO Desk Reference Guide, Volume 2
96

2. In the event of legal action or a request from regulators stemming from a data breach, the organization, or the CISO acting on its behalf, may be required to demonstrate that security control measures were implemented, and they are documented in the organization's information security policies.

3. The security procedures are certified or audited on a regular basis by an independent auditor. The audit of reasonable security practices and procedures must be current and therefore conducted within the last year.

I am sure by now you are wondering why this is so important. The reason is that, as we've previously discussed, cybersecurity is a continuous lifecycle and breaches are part of that lifecycle. To reduce the risk to our organizations, as CISOs we create and implement enterprise cybersecurity programs and deploy policies, procedures, security controls, and standards to reduce risk and protect our assets. However, even with a mature cybersecurity program, we will at times remediate security breaches and then be required to prove that we are meeting reasonable security standards.

Continuous Scanning, Monitoring, and Remediation

We're now ready for our next discussion topics. One of the primary processes that your cybersecurity program will be responsible for is "continuous monitoring." In many network/organizational environments, there may be extreme technology change as organizations try innovative solutions to compete in their specific business markets. This dynamic change environment makes providing enterprise risk management and cybersecurity as a service extremely challenging.

To bring balance to my security teams and be effective as a security leader, when operating in chaotic business environments where there is no stable risk baseline, I implement the concept of continuous scanning, monitoring, and remediation to provide an effective security practice for my business and our stakeholders. Understanding the answers to the questions for this chapter will enable you as a CISO to state that you are meeting the requirements of "reasonable care."

Continuous monitoring provides a critical service to security operations teams through detection, response, and remediation. When such a program is aligned with the organization's enterprise security program and implemented with appropriate security controls, it enables security organizations to detect security incidents, remediate security gaps, and analyze trends to reduce the company's risk exposure. I believe it is essential to understand that continuous monitoring is a component of a lifecycle, a cybersecurity lifecycle.

I have written about this lifecycle and its five stages: inventory, assessment, scanning, remediation, and monitoring (Hayslip, Pulse, Articles by Gary Hayslip 2015). This graphic is a depiction of the final stage, continuous monitoring, and will be our guide in the discussions that follow.

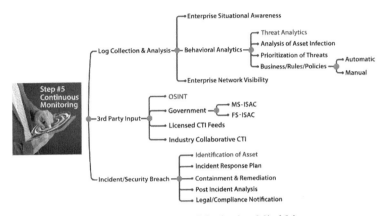

Figure 12.1 Continuous Monitoring Mind Map

The first question that we will review will provide some insight into the components that make up continuous monitoring and why I believe it is an essential business process. Numerous strategic frameworks address continuous monitoring. I have implemented the National Institute of Science and Technology (NIST) guidelines, NIST SP800-137 (NIST 2011) at multiple organizations over the last several years. I consider it to be a best practice for a CISO standing up a security program.

I believe it is a critical business process for organizations to understand and maintain their situational awareness and oversee their enterprise risk management portfolio. While I used the NIST guidelines for continuous monitoring, the framework you select should be decided through input from your stakeholders, including legal staff and executive management, and depends on your technical requirements.

With that said, let's review our first question: *"As a CISO, what frameworks, security controls, or processes would you recommend to continuously monitor your organization to prevent or mitigate a data breach?"*

To design and implement an effective continuous monitoring program, a CISO will need to take into account answers to the following questions:

- *Purpose of the monitoring system* – From the viewpoint of the organization, what are the overall business reasons to develop a monitoring system? Is it a compliance/regulation requirement? Are there technical requirements? As a CISO you must be able to answer the question of why resources need to be expended to develop this program.

- *Requirements* – Now that you understand why you need to implement it, what are the technical, security, legal, business, and compliance requirements for the program's creation, management, report structure, and data views?

- *What needs to be monitored* – This question is critical. It is imperative for the CISO to work with stakeholders and trusted partners to identify what systems, applications, and data to monitor.

- *How will it be implemented* – From a technology perspective, will this monitoring be on-premises, will it be in the cloud, or would it be better to use a hybrid approach? If deploying sensors or agents, determine if the deployment is a one-to-many configuration or a distributed site-to-site configuration. Once you have identified the data to pull, you can create the architecture to move the data to a location for analysis and storage.

- *Data, data, and more data* – You have identified what data you will monitor, and now you need to ask yourself, where will the data be stored? Do I have a data retention policy? Do I have a data governance program that specifies who is allowed to access it and why?

- *Metrics and reports* – Collecting information from the monitoring program should have a purpose. Do you have any metrics? Do you have specific reports based on the analyzed data? What is the story, and to which audience are you providing this data?

- *911* – You understand your requirements, you have built a continuous monitoring program for the organization, you are collecting information, and now the question is who will use it to protect the organization?

As you can see from these questions, there is an extensive amount of information you need to collect before you begin architecting a monitoring program. I typically start with conducting an inventory of my security suite to identify all of my security assets such as firewalls, IPS sensors, honey pots/nets, endpoint platforms, and vulnerability scanners. I then proceed to document what logs I can collect from these platforms and meet with my peers in our data centers, desktop support, and network services teams to verify what assets they have and what logs I can collect from them. Once I have identified these assets and log types, I research and deploy a security information and event management (SIEM) platform that enables me to build dashboards to analyze the collected information. This allows me to make decisions about reducing risk and focus on how to best use my limited resources.

You will need to review several issues if you plan to use a SIEM platform as one of the core elements of your continuous monitoring program. The SIEM platform will provide your monitoring program with extensive capabilities for reviewing and analyzing collected data for actionable threat mitigation. However, you will need to verify some information before you start analyzing the collected data. Some of the issues I would recommend you check are:

- *Deployment of Security Suite Assets* – Review where you have your security assets deployed in your enterprise network. Assets such as intrusion prevention systems (IPS) or unified threat management (UTM) appliances become primary sources for data logs and it is critical to position them at locations in the network with the best visibility into data flows to ensure you are collecting optimum data. Whether it's at the network edge, chokepoints between sites, or within enclaves that manage sensitive data – review your network maps and the position of your security suite's assets.

- *Log Filtering* – Next, I would recommend that, depending on the data type you collect (for instance, if the data is from security components like firewalls or IPS systems), you incorporate filters or pre-defined rulesets to remove basic informational data so your analysts don't get overwhelmed. There are configurations for many of your security components that will allow you to filter out informational data and only send alerts for data that meet specific criteria for review by one of your security personnel. The use of these filters and automation for specific analysis will help provide relevant data and meaningful metrics for review. As a result, security staff will be able to spend less time analyzing the data and more time remediating any issues they find.

- _Log Management_ – You are collecting logs and sending them to a central repository for your SIEM to review, however, what events are you collecting? Some events that I have collected in the past (and by no means is this a complete list) are:
  - Asset boot/shutdown
  - System process initiation/termination
  - Invalid Login attempts
  - File Access/File Close
  - Invalid File Access attempts
  - Network activity
    - Ports/Protocols
    - Flagged application activity (Tor, Web Proxy, File Sharing)
  - Resource Utilization information

- _Log Retention/Access_ – It is critical that you understand your log retention requirements. If you must keep logs for several years due to federal regulations or industry compliance, you will need to factor storage and encryption of the data at rest as part of your program for managing this data. Another critical question you will need to address is who needs access to these logs, why do they need access, and what rights do they need to this data? You will need to incorporate an access control mechanism for this information, so you can demonstrate you're a good steward of the data entrusted to your program. I have found that discussing this issue with my stakeholders will help identify who needs access and the business requirements for the information, so collaborate when setting your access control mechanisms.

Chapter 12 Key Point and Action Item 4

All breaches are not created equal. While we'd like to ensure perfect protection for all business assets, the reality is we need to make hard choices every day about where to put our time and attention.

You should evaluate your business processes along with your scanning and monitoring to verify that you are focusing your attention on the assets that are vital to your most important business processes.

As you incorporate your selected framework, you should ultimately get to a state where you have a continuous monitoring program with dashboards to review and analyze your collected, aggregated information for trend analysis. To get to this point may require you to research, source, and install a vulnerability management platform, as well as an SIEM management platform, and possibly a storage platform for all of the collected system log files. I have often found that I needed to install a vulnerability scanning solution to monitor my enterprise for risk and quickly mitigate identified threats. This allowed me to continually scan for vulnerabilities and misconfigurations and helped me identify asset mismanagement.

Understand that when using a powerful scanning solution like this, you will need to work with stakeholders to again identify what to scan, what logs to collect and store, and what reports to generate. I highly recommend that you ensure the vulnerability management platform integrates with your SIEM and your SIEM collects the data for review and assignment to team members for investigation and remediation. Having both of these platforms gives you the ability to continually assess your security controls and network assets and collect information from your current data flows to analyze for actionable risk mitigation.

The discussion above describes a program of continuous assessment and review of data from enterprise assets and network data flows. Through continuous monitoring, you will have a strategic picture of the business enterprise and how it is using its technology. You will still need to incorporate a framework/methodology to assess the risks for the applications that are developed, updated, managed, and deployed on your organization's networks. Whether these applications are cloud-based or deployed on your premises, there are industry best practices for how to manage application development.

That brings us to our next discussion, "*What framework and/or processes should a CISO use to remediate vulnerabilities and search for malware in their organization's application portfolio?*"

You Must Secure the Applications

Application security is defined as measures taken throughout the software development lifecycle to prevent gaps in the security policy by an application or the underlying system through flaws in the application's design, development, deployment, upgrade, or maintenance (Wikipedia 2016). Insecure software code puts your organization at risk; it undermines all of the security controls and policies you have put in place for your company. I have selected this visual from the Open Web Application Security Project (OWASP) community (Open Web Application Security Project (OWASP) 2016) to demonstrate the importance of application testing and how insecure code can significantly impact your organization.

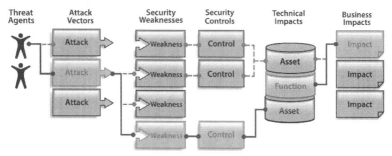

Figure 12.2 Paths Through Your Application to Harm your Organization

Use a vulnerability scanner to monitor your security controls continuously and remediate weaknesses such as misconfigured assets or poorly implemented application updates. Weaknesses in software code are doorways for exploitation if the security controls of an organization are not mature enough to prevent the attack from an outside agent. As we have seen in today's environment, the capacity of organized criminal elements to exploit vulnerabilities created by the rate of technology change vastly outpaces our ability close these loopholes.

To address this fundamental risk, you must start by ensuring management awareness of the issue and getting formal approval to establish an application security testing program. Once you have management's approval, get up close and personal with the applications inside your organization. I have worked with teams of developers and stakeholders from various units within my organization to identify the applications in our portfolio. Once we had an inventory of our applications, we sought to answer questions such as:

1. Is this application custom built or off the shelf?
2. Is this application written in a language that is no longer part of our technical roadmap, i.e., is it an older legacy application that we lack resources to support?
3. Do we have current licensing for these applications?
4. Do we have maintenance contracts for these applications?
5. Are these applications on-premises or are they in the cloud? If in the cloud, are you familiar with Cloud Security Alliance (Cloud Security Alliance 2017) and their controls matrix for managing cloud environments?

From the answers to these questions, you can start to prioritize your list of applications based on their risk exposure to the business. I would suggest that you create a risk model (OWASP 2017) to rate these applications and prioritize them in a list with the riskiest at the top and the less risky at the bottom. Obviously, for those applications with higher risk scores you will want to allocate resources, when available, to either replace them or update them and remediate their issues.

Once you have established your risk model for how you will evaluate the applications in your current portfolio, it's time to get down to focusing on creating policies and standards with the software development team. These policies should provide a baseline for the developers, so that they understand the security controls. A good reference I would recommend is OWASP's Enterprise Security API page (Open Web Application Security Project (OWASP) 2016). This page offers security control toolkits for your developers to make it easier to incorporate "security by design."

At this stage in the process, you have an inventory of your applications, you have created risk models, and you have prioritized your applications based on their risk scores. You have helped develop policies and standards for the software development teams for the security controls they will use as a baseline, and finally, you almost have a full application security program. What I would do next is identify an application security framework that you want your developers to use. This framework will aid in evaluating the team's efforts and assist them in establishing a formal continuous risk baseline for their ongoing software development efforts.

Two security application frameworks I recommend evaluating are the OWASP framework (Open Web Application Security Project (OWASP) 2016) and the BSIMM framework (Building Security In Maturity Model (BSIMM) 2017). Both frameworks are open standards. The OWASP framework has numerous components that your development teams can leverage, and the OWASP Top 10 Project (Open Web Application Security Project (OWASP) 2016) is an excellent cyber hygiene standard for your teams to use for assessment. The BSIMM framework has extensive information collected over 113 developer activities categorized into 12 practices that equate to four overall domains. The BSIMM framework information comes from a multitude of corporate developer teams and provides context on implementing security controls, whereas the OWASP framework is an open community of content provided by a very dedicated community of developers across the planet. I would recommend you start with OWASP to establish your program and then use BSIMM to grade the maturity of your efforts.

The final step in establishing an application security program and answering the question under discussion is to incorporate the program into the formal change management process of the Information Technology department. As the CISO, you will want the development teams to follow the established change management and technology review processes for the organization. You will want the software development teams to have a process for code review, security testing of code in development before it goes to production, and periodic testing of code to verify there are no misconfiguration issues. Code testing, configuration testing, and user acceptance testing will be part of the policies and standards created for the application security program, and you should also require the collection of metrics for these activities.

Analysis of these metrics will help prioritize funding decisions based on the analysis of data captured and the resultant risk scores. The metrics you track will help provide visibility into the adherence to security practices and controls, new vulnerabilities created, and development defect rates. I have also seen development teams supplement the use of security controls and frameworks by using vulnerability scanning tools similar to those employed by the cybersecurity team. These application security toolsets would be used to review code as it is tested and moved through its various stages of development. The code would also be scanned periodically, even after the program passed service delivery inspection and was in full production.

Chapter 12 Key Point and Action Item 5

As the hard, defensible network perimeter has become soft and permeable, your applications are now accessible from virtually every corner of the world by your workforce and your customers using any device they can access, carry or wear.

You should threat model your applications and add monitoring to detect the attempted exploitation of your applications' vulnerabilities.

The CISO must effectively manage the risk of the organization's application portfolio by championing the establishment of a mature application security program that is funded and supported by executive management. If you have operational development teams that are following these types of mature processes, you should also have a team of professionals to partner with your security program in continuously monitoring and mitigating evolving risks within your corporate networks, inside the enterprise application portfolio, and in the data flows throughout the organization.

It is this last component of data flows that leads us to our next discussion. From the beginning of this chapter, we explored how continuous monitoring provided strategic value to the organization by providing visibility into whether the company's networks had been compromised. We then discussed how we should look at security within the application layer of the enterprise and how using frameworks and establishing an application security program could inject cybersecurity into the development lifecycle of applications created and maintained by the company.

Now we need to move our view of security and risk to the data layer, the layer of ones and zeros. Down here at the bottom, what policies and processes can be followed to incorporate risk management and remediation into the management of the company's primary means to conduct business, the governance of its data? This leads us to the third and final topic for discussion: *"Your organization experiences numerous unauthorized attempts to breach its enterprise networks. What metrics are important to your enterprise cybersecurity program to see these attempts?"*

Let's return to the beginning of our story, with CISO Alice Bentlee who was woken up very early in the morning by her company's MSSP security team. As she listened to the reports and evaluated what was known about the ongoing data breach, she reviewed the status of the activated incident response plan. As she collected data from the various stakeholders on her corporation's incident response team she was already thinking of the executive status report she would need to give her management team. The report would consist of what's currently known, the impact to operations, and recommendations for the activation of the current cyber insurance policy to field a forensic team for full breach analysis and data remediation.

This incident depicts an all-too-common day in the life of a CISO. How it relates to the subject under discussion is that Alice's understanding of the impact of this breach and the forensic team's understanding of the context for how it occurred will depend completely on data and collected logs. The data collected over time and used for analysis, security metrics, and executive reports by Alice and her security teams will prove crucial in identifying when the network was compromised and what data was accessed.

The Metrics Data You Should Collect

Metrics are data collected to tell a story. The data is being collected for a reason. That reason could be funding, to prove the viability of an asset, or it could be part of a governance requirement to enforce compliance. I look at this collection of data and the metrics derived from it as a decision aid – it supports making strategic decisions with the best information available. Now understand, the metrics you create from this data should be quantitative – they measure something, they are formula driven, there is a time component, they are controllable, and they are repeatable.

To do this effectively, you will first need to understand why you need security metrics. As I have stated before, we don't collect metrics without a reason, and the reason is tied to the business. You need to understand what the organization's business purpose is for cybersecurity. Why is it needed? What do they want you to achieve? Of what use or value is it to the company? What data is important to the company? What could be the business repercussions to operations if we have a data breach?

Understanding these questions will provide you with invaluable intelligence on the business drivers for your cybersecurity program. They will also help you decide which security metrics you should collect because *security metrics help tell the story of how your cybersecurity program mitigates business risks that impact operations in a way that management finds unacceptable*.

So, to get started, let's think of some questions your executive management team may ask you that your metrics should help you answer:

1. How secure are we?
2. How secure are we relative to company X or company Y?
3. Which are our strongest or weakest security issues?
4. What are our most significant security threats or risks? What are you doing about them?
5. Are we spending the right amount on cybersecurity? Is there a baseline against which we could measure ourselves?
6. Are our security suite and assets deployed optimally?
7. Are we meeting the standard of reasonable care? Are we using best practices to address all reasonable, identifiable risks?
8. Are we resilient? Can we handle a compromise without losing the ability to operate?
9. Are we going to be able to meet our compliance requirements?
10. How do we rank versus other peers/competitors/partners in our business vertical?

As you can imagine, any of these questions answered the wrong way could significantly impact your cybersecurity program and result in a "resume-generating event." To capably answer these questions as well as the question currently under discussion, we need to collect data and implement a security metrics/measurement methodology to turn that data into quantifiable information.

Collecting metrics will help improve your cybersecurity program's productivity, and the information can be used to verify that you have aligned your security program with business operations. These metrics can also be used to improve risk management by showing over time that installed security controls are effective and reducing the rate of compromised desktops or number of intrusions into a system. An example of this is:

- I know my organization's strategic business is aligned with e-commerce and that our web portal help desk is critical to customer satisfaction and the return rate of paying customers.
- So, some of my metrics will focus on the time it takes to return a compromised help desk asset to full capability and also why help desk assets get compromised. I know that one hour of lost productivity for a help desk employee costs my company approximately $142,000 in lost customer revenue.
- I may have several metrics related to this critical asset – my company's help desk teams.
  - o The number of assets compromised per week.
  - o The number of assets compromised per shift.
  - o The percentage of help desk assets fully patched per week (report period).
  - o The percentage of help desk assets anti-virus/anti-malware signatures updated.

These are just basic examples. What I want to illustrate here is that the metrics you collect should be for specific reasons related to supporting your company. Those given above are simple metrics that could help security analysts on a security team understand if compromised help desk assets were missing patches or had outdated anti-virus, and also if specific shifts were more susceptible to infections and downtime.

A good reference for building metrics is the CIS critical controls website (Center for Internet Security, 2016), which lists metrics for the CIS Top 20 security controls. An excellent article that I recommend for explaining the importance of collecting data to measure security concerning governance is by Andrej Volchkov. This article is available on the ISACA website (Volchkov, 2013). The table provided below is from this article and I believe is a good representation of metrics used to support a security program.

Examples of Operation Efficiency Metrics				
Deliveries of a Team	Metric	Efficiency Trend	Cost	Cost Trend
Awareness Efforts	Cost of awareness program vs. number of security incidents due to poor awareness (ratio)	↓	$	↓
Compliance Strengthening	Average delays in improvements according to audit findings	↑	$	→
	Number of systems in compliance vs. number of systems to be made compliant (ratio)			
Incidents processed	Number of security incidents vs. number of employees (ratio)	→	$	→
Unavailability rate of security components	Number of hours of unavailability vs. components (ratio)	→	$	→
Efforts to ensure that IT projects are compliant	Number of employees devoted to security projects vs. total cost of complex projects (with high security impact) (ratio)	↑	$	→
	Number of accounts still open after end users leave			
Effectiveness of identity management	Number of changes in privileges	↑	$	↑
	Total number of different systems and applications under management			
	Average delay in processing requests			
	Error rate			
Efforts in processing alerts and other security events	Number of specific investigations	↑	$	→
	Number of working days spent on analyses vs. number of employees (ratio)			
Effectiveness of controls	Checks carried out vs. number of employees (possibly by nature of checks or severity of checks) (ratio)	↓	$	→
	Number of breaches vs. checks carried out vs. checks carried out (possible by nature or severity of controls) (ratio)			

Figure 12.3 Operation Efficiency Metrics

The table above demonstrates the work processes the security team must initiate to collect data for the specific metrics. The collected metric data will enable you to monitor trend analysis to show your security program is improving, hence providing value to the organization.

Be aware that there are numerous tools, assets, and processes within an organization's cybersecurity program that can be used to provide the raw data to create mature security metrics. Some examples include:

1. Anti-malware / Anti-Virus endpoint systems
2. Firewalls / IDS / IPS suites
3. Managed Security Services
4. Asset Management / Patch Management solutions
5. Vulnerability Management platforms
6. Unified Threat Management platforms
7. Operating Systems / Databases
8. Website / Web Portal Statistics
9. Governance, Risk and Compliance platforms
10. SIEM

You may also have service delivery platforms that can provide statistics on workflows such as the number of support tickets for an incident or the number of specific incident type tickets associated with a new workflow in production. What I want you to understand is that you will have more than just tools and sensors, you will take data from related work processes that are crucial for your teams and impact your company's business operations. Establishing a security program that collects data and provides measurable information that can be used for trend analysis and provide insight into the maturity of the current security controls, is a valuable asset to the business.

With this type of information, the CISO can make strategic decisions on the priority of issues for remediation and can provide insight into how the cybersecurity program is meeting the objectives of its executive charter. It is crucial for you to socialize your security metrics program throughout the company. You must act as an evangelist when the opportunity presents itself. You need to be quick in sharing your data and information with stakeholders when appropriate to assist them in making decisions. The more you circulate your cybersecurity metrics reports to your stakeholders, the more they will have visibility into the strategic value you provide to the organization.

You should now have a cybersecurity program in place using industry best practices for "continuous monitoring." You also should be supporting the organization's application security program, and your team should be assisting the development teams as they follow OWASP or other frameworks and establish a "security by design" mentality for software development and maintenance in your organization.

You have established a data governance program that uses data to tell a story. This governance program is designed to track and manage the lifecycle of the most important asset in your company – data. You will then use the collected data to measure maturity. The maturity data you collected is incorporated into actionable metrics to drive executive decision making and long-term strategic planning for the business. Using the recommendations from this chapter, you will have completed several major tasks that are integral to your security program:

- Monitoring the organization for vulnerabilities and using scanning reports to inform remediation
- Verifying that the company's application portfolio is following best practices
- Protecting the company's data and using it to measure your security program for continuous improvement

Summary

For Chapter 12, we began our discussion by asking these three questions:

- As a CISO, what frameworks, security controls, or processes would you recommend to continuously monitor your organization to prevent or mitigate a data breach?
- What framework and/or processes should a CISO use to remediate vulnerabilities and search for malware in their organization's application portfolio?
- Your organization experiences numerous unauthorized attempts to breach its enterprise networks. What metrics are important to your enterprise cybersecurity program to enable it to see these attempts?

Given the overwhelming volume of data and the exponentially expanding number of devices and breadth of your network, we can't emphasize enough how important it is to think strategically about what you need to monitor and how you'll build an infrastructure to do so.

In closing, we would like to leave you with these five key points and next steps:

1. It is essential that you have sensors on every critical part of your network. When you inherit a monitoring program, it's safe to assume that time pressures, budget pressures, or less-than-ideal change management have left part of your network unwatched. These failures create dark zones that could leave your infrastructure exposed. **You should conduct a thorough review of your assets and the activity and log data you are collecting to make sure all critical flows can be monitored.**

2. Due to the large volume of data collected, it is often impossible to look at all of it, and it's rare to have the spare time needed to conduct random threat hunting. While being able to reconstruct what happened after a breach can help you tighten your defenses, looking at real-time indicators of compromise is critical to reducing the mean time to detect nefarious activity on your network. **You should continually assess your most**

critical business processes and make sure that you have event monitoring in place to detect indicators of compromise for potential breaches with the greatest potential to do your organization harm.

3. It is easy to become so focused on day-to-day operations that we fail to make time to look at the bigger picture with as much rigor as we do to metrics such as mean time to detection and processes like incident response. But having a good understanding of the entity-level health of your security program can ensure that you avoid the process breakdowns that often lead to control failures. **You should review your security program governance processes and the checkpoints that you have in place to validate that these processes are operating both at the necessary level to ensure regulatory compliance and adherence to contract obligations, and to ensure the timely flow of information to operations teams.**

4. All breaches are not created equal. While we'd like to ensure perfect protection for all business assets, the reality is we need to make hard choices every day about where to put our time and attention. **You should evaluate your business processes along with your scanning and monitoring to verify that you are focusing your attention on the assets that are vital to your most important business processes.**

5. As the hard, defensible network perimeter has become soft and permeable, your applications are now accessible from virtually every corner of the world by your workforce and your customers using any device they can access, carry or wear. **You should threat model your applications and add monitoring to detect the attempted exploitation of your applications' vulnerabilities.**

As Gary mentioned above, weaknesses in software code are doorways for exploitation if the security controls of an organization are not mature enough to prevent the attack from an outside agent. As we have seen in today's environment, the capacity of organized criminal elements to exploit vulnerabilities created by the rate of technology change vastly outpaces our ability close these loopholes. Rigorous monitoring is essential to staying in the fight.

Chapter 13 – Threat Intelligence

Introduction

In the first three chapters of Volume 2 we have been focused internally. In Chapter 13, we turn our focus to outside your organization. Threat intelligence, like situational awareness, is the discipline of becoming conscious of the environment in which you are operating with the intent of decreasing the potential impact of harms that are presented to you or your community. You'll need to use a combination of data about the relevant threat actors and the vulnerabilities of your high-value assets along with your judgment about the combinations that pose the greatest risk to your organization.

Bill starts the discussion where we have traditionally associated protection from risk, with the law enforcement community. Every organization operates in the context of local, state and federal jurisdictions, some grounded in the physical world and many increasingly incorporating the digital realm. From there, Bill expands the scope to include the entire human network that all three authors have repeatedly highlighted.

Matt asks us to look inward again to establish the context in which threat intelligence is most effective. He guides us on an exploration of six keys to threat intelligence that teach us how to use that context to make better decisions about which threats are most real to us and build a program around that knowledge.

Gary gives a thorough analysis of the sources for threat intelligence and leaves us with an understanding of how these sources are structured, characterized, and effectively utilized. He concludes with an extensive review of Open Source Threat Intelligence and how you should incorporate that into your threat intelligence program.

Some of the questions the authors used to frame their thoughts for this chapter include:

- What is threat intelligence, and what types of external threat intelligence sources should the CISO use to augment their cybersecurity suite?
- What are the business scenarios for incorporating threat intelligence services into an enterprise cybersecurity program?
- Which Open Source Threat Intelligence (OSINT) resources should a CISO consider for enhancing their threat vulnerability management program?

"Good threat intelligence should be actionable. When we learn of threats, we should have a process by which we determine if it applies to our organization. Do we have similar assets? Are we susceptible to that attack?"

What Is Threat Intelligence?

Before answering the questions that we have posed for threat intelligence, I'd like to define what threat intelligence is, or what it means to me. Some threat intelligence products and services might include phrases like "organized, analyzed and refined information" and reference "potential and current attacks" somehow targeted, generally or specifically, "at your organization or industry." That's certainly one aspect of a good threat intelligence program. That kind of information is consumed at a knowledge level, in other words, informing the people on your team about the current threats that they should focus on, how to recognize them, how to prepare for them, and how to defend against them.

Threat intelligence information can also refer to specific vulnerabilities and the techniques that might be used to exploit those weaknesses in a way that your people and your defensive systems can immediately use to prevent or mitigate specific threats. Threat intelligence can also refer to specifics about the adversaries (who is posing a threat) and the victims (who is the target). Good threat intelligence should be actionable; you need to know what the adversaries want to do, to what, and you need to know if that applies to your organization.

We have to assume that you know what assets you have that are susceptible to any threat. Much of what I've listed above is available through commercial and cooperative services. Depending on the scope and capabilities of your organization, you might consume one or more commercially available sources of threat intelligence.

There is a tendency to believe that once something like threat intelligence is packaged commercially, that "buying" your threat intelligence is the most comprehensive and practical approach. Let the experts collect the data from their millions of sensors and their honeypots, and let their analysts review that intelligence and monitor the dark web for you and tell you where you should focus your attention. It's true that very few companies have the means to run a comprehensive threat intelligence program on their own, and even those that do still consume commercial feeds to support their efforts. But there is another aspect to threat intelligence that does involve work that you do on behalf of your organization. You now have an excellent opportunity to work with your human network, especially your external network of peers, subject matter experts, law enforcement, vendors, and partners.

With this context for threat intelligence, I want to ask an additional set of tactical questions:

1. What is our current working relationship with law enforcement?
2. What are our sources of international cyber threat intelligence?
3. What organizations are we sharing our cyber threat knowledge with, and what are we learning from them?
4. What is our working (information sharing) relationship with the most high-profile firms who have had breaches? Do we have information coming to us from them? What have we learned?
5. Do we track social media sites and blogs referencing us for clues about our vulnerabilities?
6. When we hear of a breach in another organization, what do we do? When does that process start, and what is the routine reporting in the organization? What are the criteria that determine who to notify and when to notify the board of directors?
7. As we look at the data for intrusions, penetrations, or attempts to gain unauthorized access, what has been the primary category of threat actors who seem to have made these efforts? How has that information influenced our defensive efforts?

Threat Intelligence Is More Than a Service

Let's look at what these questions are getting at and how we, as CISOs, might go about responding. Starting with number 1, our relationship with law enforcement. We've all heard that law enforcement wants to have a relationship with us. They would like organizations to tell them when suspicious events occur and identify potential bad actors for them. Then, they will share information with industry about threats they become aware of through various means. Each party would be able to use this information without additional jeopardy.

Just a few years ago, this statement met with a fair amount of skepticism. However, through organizations such as InfraGard, which is an FBI public-private partnership program, and concerted efforts by law enforcement and various supportive industry groups, cooperation and trust has been building. While it still varies by region and community, there has been significant progress.

If your organization has a relationship with local law enforcement through its physical security organization, partnering with that group and leveraging that connection is a great place to start. Usually, this involves at least local law enforcement, such as city police departments, county sheriff's departments, and state troopers across the United States. If your organization does not currently maintain any federal relationships, you should consider connecting with the FBI (through regional associations such as InfraGard) and the Department of Homeland Security (DHS).

The DHS was created in the aftermath of the events of September 11, 2001, to manage and coordinate the activities between several existing agencies. The combined organization addresses land and marine borders and immigration, with the U.S. Customs and Border Protection (CBP), the U.S. Immigration and Customs Enforcement (ICE), and the U.S. Coast Guard (USCG). It also addresses accidents and several types of threats, with the Federal Emergency Management Agency (FEMA), the Transportation Security Administration (TSA), the U.S. Secret Service (USSS), and the Office of Intelligence and Analysis (OIA).

In addition to the FBI's InfraGard program, there are many cooperatives and public-private partnerships. Among them are the ISACs (Information Sharing and Analysis Centers), which exist for all of the elements of the U.S. critical infrastructure. The graphic below (courtesy of the National Fusion Center Association - NFCA) depicts the 16 components of the U.S. critical infrastructure. The U. S. DHS declared a 17th component, the U. S. Electoral System, a part of the nation's critical infrastructure in January 2017.

Figure 13.1 The 16 Original Industries in the U.S. Critical Infrastructure

In addition to the NFCA, the ISACs, and your local law enforcement, there are the 76 regional "Law Enforcement Coordination Centers" (LECC)[11]. Reach out and connect with these groups and then leverage these groups to find local industry associations if you are new to the region or just don't know who to ask.

Regarding question 2, not every organization will need sources of international threat intelligence, but if your team has a global footprint, there are significant considerations. First, some cyber-criminal gangs are very regional, and intelligence is limited outside their region. Second, if you do not have a substantial presence in international markets, your international field offices might be especially vulnerable to local cyber-criminal activity if you aren't able to keep the cyber education level high among your global workforce. To address this, ensure that any vendors you use for threat intelligence have sufficient coverage in the markets where you are present.

---

[11] See table below for contact information for the National Fusion Centers

In addition to the cross over between threats that operate in the physical and digital worlds, the law enforcement community has enormous experience in gathering threat intelligence.

You should uncover all of the touchpoints between your organization and both the law enforcement and regulatory communities. Ensure that you have defined an appropriate two-way information flow in each case and develop a process to regularly utilize that information flow.

Good Follow-up Is Essential

Let's take questions 3 and 4 together: What organizations are we sharing our cyber threat knowledge with, and what are we learning from them? What is our working (information sharing) relationship with the most high-profile firms who have had breaches? Do we have information coming to us from them? What have we learned?

Notice that in both cases we're asking the same follow-up question: what are we learning? Good threat intelligence should be actionable. When we learn of threats, we should have a process by which we determine if it applies to our organization. We assess the nature of the threat, focusing on the type of asset under attack. Do we have similar assets? What is the method of attack? Are we susceptible to that attack? What breaches have occurred, and could the same attack scenario work against us?

Sometimes that is a simple question to answer – we might not have those same kinds of assets, and sometimes that is a very complicated question to answer – we might need to perform a vulnerability scan or stage a penetration test to find out. Once we know that an attack could work, and we determine that the assets at risk are worth taking extra measures to protect, we need to validate that a breach has not occurred, and then patch, upgrade, disable, back up, and take whatever other actions we deem appropriate to protect against that attack scenario.

The next two questions, 5 and 6, both pertain to the media. For number 5, the issue is how social media responds, and for number 6, we're looking at the national news media. Social media is focused outward, but with our organization as the subject. The national news media is focused outward too, but on how the news media is treating various high-profile breaches, along with how the public (citizens, industry, and government) is reacting. What we hope to learn from these sources and how we might respond to what we learn is very different.

Our approach to social media as a threat intelligence source should not be confused with our organization's policy on the use of social media by our marketing department or our workforce. Using social media as a threat intelligence source means monitoring and reacting appropriately to mentions about our organization. Are we being disparaged by customers or activists? Are specific actions being advocated? Are our commercial practices being denigrated or are our lobbying efforts, our third-party relationships, our community relations, or our organizational governance policies generating controversy? Are we being associated (even inaccurately) with other organizations, or actions taken by or against those groups or activities in response?

Monitoring the national news media is another valuable source of threat intelligence, but with an interesting caveat. Effective threat intelligence programs should make you aware of threats that are specific to your industry before you read about them in the national news. It is essential to understand that public opinion can create a sense of crisis very quickly, and that sense of crisis can either amplify the threat to your organization or generate concern within your organization, from management, the workforce, or the board of directors. This fear can, in turn, create an urgency to act. Knowing that threats specific to your industry are active before the national news broadcast can give you a critical head start to understand the danger, devise an action plan, and prepare to execute that plan without an aura of crisis.

In addition to lowering the stress level for you, your department, and your organization, being prepared before the crisis becomes well-known will allow you and your team to project confidence that will help put management at ease. Nonetheless, by monitoring key publications for information about your organization, your practices, customers, partners, shared agendas and associations, you can add another vital source of intelligence that can help prepare you for adverse action or reaction.

The last question, number 7, challenges us to do more with the output of our scanning and testing programs than just patching the vulnerabilities we discover. There are various kinds of indicators of compromise, such as the presence of a piece of malware known for specific types of attacks, inappropriate authentication attempts against assets, and evidence of targeted unauthorized scans against our network. When we detect these indicators, we should develop a working theory of the methods used to attack our assets, and by whom, so that we can improve our countermeasures against the immediate threat and future threats as well. We should also share as much of this information as we safely can with our partners in law enforcement, our vendors, our colleagues, and our peers.

The Human Network

This last point brings us back to the human network, which we identified as your network of peers, subject matter experts, law enforcement, vendors, and partners. I advocate meeting regularly with these colleagues and building trust relationships with the people with whom you can effectively partner.

Many regions have locally organized groups, including local chapters of national organizations such as InfraGard, ISACs, and LECCs, and roundtable groups, professional associations, and others who are motivated by the same objective as you: to build and nourish a human network to share intelligence, best practices, and advice. If you can't readily identify the groups in your area, start with law enforcement, vendors, and third-party partners and ask them who they meet with and who is or might be open to cooperating.

If a group doesn't exist in your area, one tactic might be to partner with established vendors in your region and found a group yourself. If you choose that route, remember that your objective is the open and honest sharing of information, and to that end, you might want to set some ground rules, such as invoking the Chatham House Rule[12], or something similar.

In a nutshell, the Chatham House Rule allow you to share what you've learned, but not attribute specific comments to a person or an organization or share enough details that this becomes obvious. You may opt for a formal charter or an informal association, but the key is to build a circle of trust that allows you to cooperate with your human network.

---

[12] The **Chatham House Rule** is a system for holding debates and discussion panels on controversial issues, named after the headquarters of the UK Royal Institute of International Affairs, based in Chatham House, London, where the rule originated in June 1927.

At a meeting held under the Chatham House Rule, anyone who comes to the meeting is free to use information from the discussion but is not allowed to reveal who made any comment. It is designed to increase openness of discussion. See: https://en.wikipedia.org/wiki/Chatham_House_Rule

The informal human network that you have been building serves as an invaluable source of threat intelligence, from pooled and shared feeds to side-channel discussion to a short list of who to call and who might warn you of impending threat.

You should review how the people in your human network prefer to interact and look for opportunities to join or organize your colleagues. Take advantage of existing communities or form your own if needed.

The tables below give a little guidance for the public-private partnerships. The point here is not that government-sponsored threat intelligence is the only option, but you can rightfully infer that the public-private partnership model plays an essential role in threat intelligence.

Organization	How to Contact
DHS-designated Fusion Centers and contact information	Under the auspices of the Office of Intelligence and Analysis **https://www.dhs.gov/fusion-center-locations-and-contact-information**
InfraGard	InfraGard is a partnership between the FBI and the private sector. It is an association of persons who represent businesses, academic institutions, state and local law enforcement agencies, and other participants dedicated to sharing information and intelligence to prevent hostile acts against the United States. **Visit: https://www.infragard.org**
ISACs	ISACs are member-driven organizations, delivering all-hazards threat and mitigation information to asset owners and operators. **http://www.isaccouncil.org/**
National Fusion Center Association - NFCA	**The Mission:** To represent the interests of state and major urban area fusion centers, as well as associated interests of states, tribal nations, and units of local government, to promote the development and sustainment of fusion centers to enhance public safety; encourage effective, efficient, ethical, lawful, and professional intelligence and information sharing; and prevent and reduce the harmful effects of crime and terrorism on victims, individuals, and communities. **https://nfcausa.org/**
Law Enforcement Intelligence Units (LEIUs)	**http://leiu.org/**

Figure 13.2 Selected Public-Private Partnerships

Cyber Incident Reporting

Organization and Key Points of Contact	What to Report?
U.S. Department of Homeland Security (DHS)	
National Protection and Programs Directorate (NPPD)	
National Cybersecurity and Communications Integration Center (NCCIC) (http://www.dhs.gov/about-national-cybersecuritycommunications-integration-center) NCCIC@hq.dhs.gov or (888) 282-0870	Suspected or confirmed cyber incidents that may impact critical infrastructure and require technical response and mitigation assistance
United States Secret Service	
Secret Service Field Offices (http://www.secretservice.gov/field_offices.shtml) Electronic Crimes Task Forces (ECTFs) (http://www.secretservice.gov/ectf.shtml)	Cybercrime, including computer intrusions or attacks, transmission of malicious code, password trafficking, or theft of payment card or other financial payment information
Immigration and Customs Enforcement Homeland Security Investigations (ICE HSI)	
ICE HSI Field Offices (http://www.ice.gov/contact/inv/) ICE HSI Cyber Crimes Center (http://www.ice.gov/cyber-crimes/)	Cyber-based domestic or international cross-border crime, including child exploitation, money laundering, smuggling, and violations of intellectual property rights
U.S. Department of Justice (DOJ)	
Federal Bureau of Investigation (FBI)	
FBI Field Offices (http://www.fbi.gov/contact-us/field) Cyber Task Forces (http://www.fbi.gov/about-us/investigate/ cyber/cyber-task-forces-building-alliances-to-improve-thenations-cybersecurity-1) Law Enforcement Online Portal (https://www.cjis.gov/CJISEAI/EAIController) or (888) 334-4536	Cybercrime, including computer intrusions or attacks, fraud, intellectual property theft, identity theft, theft of trade secrets, criminal hacking, terrorist activity, espionage, sabotage, or other foreign intelligence activity

Figure 13.3 Incident Reporting - Reproduced from: DHS Publications

Contextualized Threat Intelligence – Stamper

Threat intelligence without context is just a laundry list of threats that create fear, uncertainty, and doubt in some scenarios and the "boy who cried wolf" syndrome in others. To build a good threat intelligence program, you need to understand what you are protecting. Specifically, know your industry, your employees and key stakeholders, your organization's processes, the applications that support these processes, and the underlying infrastructure (operating systems, hardware, and networks).

Let's take a look at how you can develop a threat intelligence program for your organization that does not necessarily require expensive threat intelligence services. Once you establish this structure, your organization can make an informed decision regarding what, if any, threat intelligence program is appropriate for your environment.

Six Keys to Threat Intelligence

The steps below can be completed in relatively short order but will require that you collaborate with other members of the organization, including your counterparts in legal, human resources, and operations.

1. **Know your industry:** Certain industries have intrinsically higher risk than others. The defense industry's threat landscape differs dramatically from that of the agricultural sector. Analyze the dynamics of your industry. Do you face stiff international competition? Is the industry consolidating? Do you collect and retain sensitive information as part of your industry's business model? If you answered "yes" to any of these questions, you may be facing a more dynamic and inherently high-risk threat landscape.

To facilitate your analysis of your industry, look for trade publications and industry-specific websites. Have there been cyber-attacks on companies in your industry? What is the role of technology in your sector? Effectively, how extensive is your industry's technological exposure? One simple way to capture this detail is to create a mind map of your industry such as the one shown below. Use the mind map as a brainstorming exercise to capture potential sources of risk for your organization.

Figure 13.4 Industry Mind Map

2. **Know the profile of your business:** While there are common threads across industries and sectors, internal dynamics within your organization are equally important and provide a crucial contextual foundation for your threat intelligence program. Begin with a clear understanding of your organization's board of directors and executive management. Do they have unusually high profiles in your industry? Essentially, are they targets?

   Equally important, spend some time to understand how your organization derives its income. In which markets does it participate? What is a typical client profile? For government agencies and non-profit organizations, you will want to understand the core functions of the organization and the constituencies that they serve.

3. **Know the critical business processes or functions of your organization:** Most organizations have similar core functions including human resources, accounting, sales and marketing, and operations, among others. Know the basic organizational structure of the business. Inventory these processes and functions. Understand the basic process flow and key participants in each process. As I've discussed in Volume 1 of the CISO Desk Reference Guide, data flow diagrams are a CISO's friend.

Use your judgment to diagram and document the more critical functions within the organization. An easy way to determine which functions and processes are more material than others, beyond their financial impact, is to validate if the process would impact the confidentiality, integrity, or privacy of the organization's information, should availability be interrupted. With operational technology more frequently connected to traditional networks, materiality can also be gauged by whether an issue with the process would impact the safety of employees or clients and whether there's the potential to create physical damage to the organization's assets.

4. **Know which applications support specific processes:** Few organizations today have genuinely manual processes that don't have some reliance on technology. Similar to the processes discussed above, document and inventory those applications that directly support essential organizational functions and processes. Here is where our work becomes a bit more detailed. Your inventory of applications should include relevant details including the application's manufacturer, its version, and other pertinent information that will provide context related to the application. Don't overlook SaaS and hosted applications. I'll touch upon these below.

   If you have software developed in-house, capture detail related to its development including, who was on the development team. Find out whether they are still part of the organization. If they've left, who has assumed responsibility for the application's ongoing care? Where is the source code maintained (e.g., on-premises or in a hosted repository)? Who has access to this source code? Your goal is to have an accurate and complete understanding of your organization's application portfolio and to start capturing detail related to application-specific dependencies.

5. **Know your infrastructure:** Here is where more sophisticated tools can be useful, including configuration management databases (CMDBs) with their detail on specific configuration items within your environment. At a minimum, make sure that for every material application you have identified, you also have a good understanding of the operating system it runs on, which server or virtual machine the OS is running on, and its storage, network, and backup dependencies. Know the hardware manufacturers, the versions of the firmware, and the status of all OS and firmware updates. This level of detail

can make the difference between a well-managed response to a known issue versus a panicked "what's our exposure to 'x' or 'y' issue?" This process is one where close collaboration with the CIO is in order.

6. **Know your vendors and suppliers:** One thing the well-publicized Target breach taught us is that our vendors can have a material impact on our security operations. Make sure that you can adequately map vendors and suppliers to specific business processes and functions. Returning to the SaaS example mentioned earlier, know the details related to your SaaS providers. Do they deliver services from their own data centers or do they leverage managed services and public cloud providers such as AWS or Azure to deliver their application?

   While a separate topic from this discussion on threat intelligence, ensure that you have conducted appropriate due diligence on material vendors (e.g., those that could impact the confidentiality, integrity, and availability of your organization's information and systems). Are suppliers and vendors financially stable? Does your contract with the vendor include a right-to-audit clause, breach notification, and minimum-security practices?

   These are some of the essential components you'll want to assess. Create an inventory of your vendors (your accounting team can assist with this effort). Collaborate with your procurement team to make sure you include basic security expectations in vendor and service provider contracts.

The items above are all about context. They help us address some fundamental issues, including the overall profile of your industry, the profile of your key executives and board members, and the types of business processes and functions that ultimately run the organization. Much of this information – notably the process and application detail – can be found in your organization's business impact analysis. The detail captured above will facilitate contextualized threat intelligence.

Application and infrastructure detail can be challenging to obtain, especially for larger, geographically dispersed organizations. Nevertheless, it is critical. It will help highlight dependencies on specific manufacturers, exposure to particular vulnerabilities, and other items that can become actionable. As noted above, with the exception of infrastructure dependencies, most of the detail should be relatively straightforward to obtain and should not require any complicated or costly tools to address.

With this information ready, the question now becomes *"How can I create a contextualized threat intelligence program for my organization?"* We'll look at this systematically, taking a top-down approach.

How to Build a Program

Beginning with your industry or sector, determine if there are information sharing and analysis centers (ISACs) that are specific to your industry. There may also be chambers of commerce, industry associations, and other entities that can serve as a focal point for collaboration. Depending upon your industry, the Federal Bureau of Investigation's (FBI's) InfraGard program may have sector-specific details to share with vetted members of the program. Beyond these, determine a list of industry sites and have members of your team assess these sites for issues that could impact your organization.

Moving to the board and executive management, have vetted members of your team monitor their specific details on sites that trade in executive profiles. Your threat intelligence program also offers an excellent opportunity to speak with these individuals about good social-media hygiene. They should know that photos contain geolocation data, that not all followers on Twitter are benign, and that their profiles on LinkedIn and Facebook are used to facilitate social engineering. Use of social media can be a sensitive topic, so you may want to review approaches for this "executive monitoring" with more cyber-friendly members of the executive team before addressing the broader team.

At the process and function level, coordinate with internal audit or other stakeholders to understand how they categorize anomalous behavior and hard-to-explain transactions. What does normal look like in a given process? Are there dependencies on specific employees or suppliers? Try to get as much insight as possible into how these processes are currently being monitored (or audited) by departments outside of IT.

Moving to your inventory of applications, validate whether the manufacturers are obligated to inform clients of known threats and specific compromises used against the application. Most of the larger software manufacturers have alerting systems that you can incorporate into your program. To the extent that they don't provide that service, start requesting it.

I anticipate significant challenges with software manufacturers' disclaimers of warranty provisions moving forward. When we contemplate physical safety as a substantial risk component to the software we operate in our organizations and the real likelihood that material harm, injury, and even death can occur because of poor code and security practices, the veil of disclaimed warranties and limitations of liability will likely begin to lift. While not to the extreme of vehicle recalls in the automotive industry, we should anticipate software manufacturers being held to a higher standard as cases surface where real harm has resulted from poor coding and security practices.

The manufacturers of your core IT infrastructure are also crucial to your overall threat intelligence program. Most network, server, storage, and backup manufacturers have notification services to alert customers of issues related to firmware and software updates. Use your CMDB to validate the type of infrastructure in your environment. Also, ensure that your team receives alerts from these manufacturers. Many of the big networking and firewall manufacturers have some limited threat intelligence that they share with their customers, though most have a more comprehensive fee-based service that ties into their platforms.

Vendors and other suppliers for your organization are also good sources of threat intelligence. Ask them to share their threat intelligence feeds. Not every vendor will do this, but some will. For those that don't, consider this as a negotiating point when your service agreement or contract is coming up for renewal.

There are other feeds of public-source threat intelligence. In the U.S., US-CERT provides a free threat intelligence feed. The options described above are specifically designed to be low-cost and contextualized to your organization and the industry in which it operates. There are other approaches to building a threat intelligence program that can be costly, including feeds from your service infrastructure manufacturers (endpoint detection and response platforms, firewall and IPS manufacturers, etc.).

Equally important, some services will mine "dark web" environments to look for evidence of trading details of your organization (e.g., emails of key executives, personally-identifiable information, intellectual property). There is some value in having these services outsourced. Specifically, threat intelligence providers are skilled in these practices, and the arm's length nature of these investigations can also obfuscate attribution during a search.

Tie your threat intelligence program to your organization's overall risk environment and risk tolerance. Organizations in defense, retail, and those with a significant amount of intellectual property will want to incorporate this function into their security programs and likely devote essential resources to this capability. For those organizations facing a less-threatening external environment, threat intelligence on the cheap – leveraging some of the resources described above – could be sufficient.

A final point about infrastructure and contextualized threat intelligence. I've tried to highlight how important context is to this discipline. It informs how the organization evaluates and assesses external factors. There are also pervasive influences that impact your threat intelligence program regardless of industry.

As a case in point, if there's a zero-day vulnerability that impacts a given network switch, operating system, application, or router that hackers can exploit, all companies that employ that technology, regardless of industry, could be impacted. Zero-day vulnerabilities are one of the reasons why the Center of Internet Security's Critical Security Controls[13] top two controls are so important. An accurate inventory of assets and systems is necessary to know how much of a threat a given exploit could be for your environment.

---

[13] Here is the link to the Center of Internet Security's list of the 20 most basic security controls: https://www.cisecurity.org/controls/

We cannot control external threats. We can, however, control how we analyze and respond to them. Contextualized threat intelligence – informed by your industry, the profiles of your board and executive management teams, and your core processes, applications, IT infrastructure, and vendors – can play an essential role in deciding how our organizations respond to these external forces.

Threat Intelligence: The Strategic Resource Providing Clarity to Organizations' Cybersecurity Programs – Hayslip

"No one data feed will meet all of the requirements of an organization, so you should look at a mix of sources from commercial, open source, vendor/industry specific and internally created feeds."

In today's dynamic cybersecurity landscape, executive leadership teams continuously assess the value of their organizations' security investments while cyber attackers innovate and leverage new technologies and capabilities. In today's world, CISOs and their security teams often find themselves triaging a breach after the attack, analyzing digital artifacts as they try to piece together the steps for a breach event that happened in the past.

Hopefully, the information they glean from the files, logs, and data provides enough information to remediate any defined security gaps and provides intelligence on possible future events. Unfortunately for CISOs, this is a losing equation. The adversaries we face are far nimbler and adept at making changes that thwart our attempts to stop them. It is this untenable situation that drives organizations and CISOs to use threat intelligence services to provide context about the adversaries they face, along with the techniques, tools, and processes they employ against them.

Threat intelligence is the process of using the information that is available to understand the threats to an organization based on such identifiers as their technology portfolio, their industry, or the types of data they create, use, process, and store. Many companies use multiple threat intelligence data feeds to provide a range of information on the adversaries they face.

However, for these threat intelligence feeds to be useful, they need to be more than just information about current threats. Threat intelligence should provide some relatable context to the company's strategic business processes. For threat intelligence to be of value, it must apply to the organization and provide enough context for the CISO and security teams to determine if the threat data is relevant to business operations. Furthermore, it needs to be actionable intelligence, data that the CISO and the information security team can use to respond and mitigate threats to the business. It is with this context that we begin to consider the questions for this chapter, about threat intelligence, including what it is, some uses cases for it, and how it should be used to prioritize vulnerability remediation.

In a recently released cyber threat report (Webroot Inc., 2017), the cybersecurity firm Webroot noted that in 2016 approximately 94% of the malware executables they observed were being seen for the first time. They cited a rise in polymorphism, a technique that attackers use to make changes to malware packages to make them appear different than other malware in order to fool anti-virus tools. The report also noted that the growth of traditional malware creation has declined as more attackers are switching to automated, polymorphic file creation techniques to generate unique executables that are harder to detect and provide the attackers with more chances to access corporate networks. Also noteworthy was that ransomware had matured into a "ransomware-as-a-service" solution offered to cybercriminals who lack the knowledge and resources to create malware on their own.

In addition, phishing attacks against organizations are on the rise and 84% of phishing websites used in attacks now last less than 24 hours, making updates to URL black and white lists impractical. These examples, and the estimated impact to the organizations that must deal with the consequences of these types of attacks in the billions of dollars (Fitzpatrick & Griffin, 2016), is why I believe CISOs should use threat intelligence as a critical resource. With this backdrop, let's discuss our first question: "*What is threat intelligence, and what types of external threat intelligence sources should the CISO use to augment their cybersecurity suite?*"

Gartner defines threat intelligence as "*evidence-based knowledge, including context, mechanisms, indicators, implications and action-oriented advice about an existing or emerging menace or hazard to assets.*" When there are deficiencies and vulnerabilities within the security controls you've deployed, it is possible to use these menaces and hazards against your organization and its assets. Every network has deficiencies and vulnerabilities. Whether it's legacy apps left over from a previous merger or old corporate networks that host critical business functions that you can't yet decommission, there is always some vulnerability within corporate infrastructures. It is the CISO's responsibility to understand these issues, have visibility into the risk they pose to the company, and using tools such as threat intelligence feeds, prioritize the issues to remediate.

Indications Are, You've Been Compromised

Now that I have laid the groundwork for our discussion, let's define threat intelligence. Threat intelligence is a collection or grouping of information that is gathered from human and electronic sources that are both internal and external to the organization. This information is usually evaluated to verify its validity and can provide in-depth context about a threat, such as the motivations of the threat actor/group, the conditions necessary to exploit any vulnerability you have, and whether the threat is active. Other useful information that I have gathered from threat intelligence is whether there are variants of the threat, what type of after-effects a company could expect from a correctly exploited vulnerability, and what "indicators of compromise" (IoC) an organization could search for to verify if they have experienced a compromise because of this threat.

I have used IoC lists in the past to search for specific types of malware to which I knew my organization might be susceptible in order to establish whether we had an active malware infestation that needed immediate remediation. I have also used IoC lists to verify that we had no pressing issues and then proceeded to remediate less urgent vulnerabilities. However, I would still periodically scan with updated IoC lists to make sure there were no new risks to our enterprise networks. Another part of threat intelligence reports that I have found useful is the list of defenses against specifically identified threats. Sometimes the defense is a software update if it's available, and sometimes there is no current defense because the threat is so new or unique.

I do like to read over the defense information and picture how I would incorporate it into my security program's controls and deployed infrastructure. Just don't be surprised by the fact that you may get alerts on new threats, and it can take time for vendors to patch the issue. You may have to think of secondary security controls to use until the threat is successfully mitigated.

As a CISO, you will typically subscribe to multiple threat intelligence data feeds. You will incorporate some of these data feeds into your endpoint solution or your deployed firewalls, and therefore get the advantage of using these feeds in your deployed security technologies. However, some of these data feeds will provide in-depth knowledge of threat actors and their tactics, techniques, and procedures (TTPs). I have found this information to be critically important in educating my teams about the threats facing our organization and providing context for the specific security controls and technologies we deploy to reduce our company's risk exposure.

The SANS 2016 Cyber Threat Intelligence survey (Shackleford, 2016) documents the growing importance of threat intelligence. This survey spoke to over 220 high-level security executives across all industry verticals, from IT to Government to Manufacturing to Banking and Finance. What I found startling in this study was that only 6% were not using threat intelligence and over 40% ranked themselves as having mature threat intelligence processes. I believe this survey makes a critical point: threat intelligence is maturing in organizations, and security professionals are viewing it as a crucial asset that they use to make more informed decisions.

Attackers today are sharing information about new attack methodologies and networks they have compromised, and they are evading static block lists to leverage compromised accounts/credentials to maintain long-term access to corporate infrastructures. In order to effectively manage and fight these threats, CISOs and their teams need to use multiple solutions to assess, scan, monitor, and remediate threats. I believe that threat intelligence is one of the more valuable assets they can use to assist them in this fight.

Sources of Intel

To use threat intelligence effectively, you need to make some decisions about which sources you wish to use. SANS recommends categorizing the sources available as either internal or external (Bromiley, 2016). _Internal threat intelligence_ is information that is within the organization. It is information that an organization's security and operations teams have from previous experiences with vulnerabilities, malware incidents, and data breaches. This information, if properly documented, can provide you with some meaningful insights into earlier compromises of your enterprise networks. It can also highlight recurring methodologies that worked against your security program.

For most organizations, this information will probably be collected in a log management system or SIEM platform. If this incident information can be obtained and used to accurately document a history of attack patterns, malware, and vulnerabilities, it can provide invaluable insight into security gaps that can be remediated or help the company identify business processes or legacy issues that need to be addressed to prevent further compromises.

External threat intelligence is threat intelligence that is available from multiple sources outside the organization. These external sources can be subscriptions or "feeds." These feeds can be consumed directly by your security appliance for a monthly fee. Alternatively, these feeds can be reports that you receive via email or from a threat portal where you can download the data that apply to your organization. Another type of external threat intelligence feed that you may have access to could be specific to your organization's industry.

One that comes to mind is the Financial Services Information Sharing and Analysis Center (https://www.fsisac.com/), known as FS-ISAC. FS-ISAC is an industry forum for collaboration on critical security threats for the financial services sector. As a member of such a collaborative body, you can get alerts on current security issues, access to existing threat white papers, and network with peers that you can speak with about best practices for remediating identified concerns. Another type of external threat intelligence feed that you may have access to is from law enforcement or government entities such as the FBI or the Department of Homeland Security (DHS). Some organizations may operate in industry verticals designated as part of the critical infrastructure.

With this designation, CISOs can request access to threat intelligence feeds and security services not commonly available to public companies. See DHS Enhanced Cybersecurity Services (ECS) for more information[14]. The last type of external intelligence feed that CISOs can use are crowdsourced services. In these feeds, data is provided by members anonymously and can be helpful to organizations that are looking for specific information but don't want it known that they require it.

Now that you know where you can obtain threat intelligence, remember that these threat intelligence data sources are only as good as the data provided. You and your teams will need to spend time verifying the information you receive, which is why I recommend that you have several sources of threat intelligence, so you can compare the data. Another issue that you will need to understand in order to manage your data feeds is context. Does the data apply to your organization, its assets, and your security program? If you are paying for a data feed and you find that most of the information doesn't apply to you, then consider changing to a different threat intelligence provider.

One of the last points I want to make about threat intelligence is that your data must be in a format that can be easily consumed by your teams. If you have to reformat the feed to accurately ingest the data into your security suite, then you should consider using other threat intelligence sources.

I want to reiterate that you should view threat intelligence as a valuable tool, and you should aggregate both your internal and external data sources to give you a complete picture of the threats facing your organization and their potential impacts to business operations. I believe that this threat picture will be critical in helping the business make decisions involving enterprise risk, which leads us into our next question for discussion: "*What are the business scenarios for incorporating threat intelligence services into an enterprise cybersecurity program?*"

The business environment we operate in today is constantly changing. Technology is moving at a speed that most organizations struggle to adjust to and the threat space is evolving even faster. It is this

---

[14] https://www.dhs.gov/enhanced-cybersecurity-services

challenging climate, with numerous new attack surfaces, that we CISOs must adapt to. We must make contextual decisions to reduce our organization's exposure to risks that previously were unknown.

I believe threat intelligence becomes a strategic benefit for security teams. In the 2016 SANS Threat Intelligence Survey (Shackleford, 2016) it was documented that 73% of the 200+ security professionals surveyed believed they made better-informed decisions through the use of threat intelligence and 58% thought it assisted their teams in providing a faster, more accurate response to security incidents.

Unfortunately, many organizations today spend much of their time scanning and remediating vulnerabilities, believing they are plugging all of their security holes. In fact, I have found peers who were focused on newly discovered vulnerabilities but let legacy vulnerabilities remain unaddressed. At times I think large portions of the security industry and corporations as a whole are focused on zero days, APTs, and ransomware but are forgetting one of the fundamental rules of cyber hygiene – do the basics first, do them correctly, and do them consistently.

When you do cyber hygiene with threat intelligence, you take your security program to a different level. The threat data provides context to your teams about your deployed architecture and helps prioritize the use of limited resources on security gaps that have an impact. This educated view enables a better understanding of why cyber hygiene is essential and how foundationally these necessary security processes/controls allow the company's security program to be more innovative.

It is with this in mind that I want to look at several business reasons for using this type of information to assist a corporate security program. One of the first points I want to make is that you and your teams are always striving to identify and protect your organization's critical assets. I believe threat intelligence assists you with this task by providing insight into the methods and vulnerabilities that would be leveraged to target your business' critical assets. This information can be used to provide an attacker's view on what security controls and solutions you currently have in place, and then provide the context on why you should make specific recommendations to improve.

Threat intelligence also provides you with critical information that can be used to look back through your logs and look at past security or network issues with a more discrete eye towards attackers' TTPs. This analysis will help you determine if you have been targeted in the past, with which exploitation methodologies, and if the attacks were successful, which controls, or processes may need to be implemented to prevent future compromises. Threat intelligence data provides a wealth of knowledge on groups that are targeting your organization, so use it to educate yourself, your staff, your executive team, and your company.

Using this detailed information, corporate security teams can become aware of new techniques or methodologies that are evolving and be proactive in reviewing current defenses and initiating projects to mitigate issues before they become the latest incident. A CISO can make a good business case that he or she should invest in incorporating threat intelligence into their security program.

However, we need to answer some questions to use threat data effectively. The decision to incorporate threat intelligence feeds into your security program is not something to be taken lightly. You want to make sure this information is current, vetted, applies to your organization's deployed architecture, and is in a format that can be readily ingested by your program. However, there are some questions that a CISO must consider when evaluating which threat data feeds to subscribe to for his or her security program.

Some fundamental questions that I believe are worth discussing when reviewing a threat intelligence offering are as follows:

1. How many data feeds are available and what is the information comprised of, i.e., URL/IP block lists, IOC lists, domain reputation lists?

2. What are the possible file formats of the data feeds?
    a. Are they available in CSV, XML, or compatible in STIX/TAXII format?

3. Are they available via an API?

4. Do you have the capability to process and incorporate these feeds into your deployed security suite?

5. What are their sources?
    a. Some will probably tell you they are using a deployed sensor network, or they might say its confidential information. Be careful about taking the "confidential" explanation at face value.

6. How current is this data and do they provide analyst reports?
    a. Is the data in real-time or near real-time?

7. Do they offer high-level reports or report summaries that can be used to educate executive staff and provide awareness training?

8. What is the cost structure of the offerings?

9. Do they have a tiered structure where the more you pay, the more services are available to your team?

10. Do they provide subscriptions over several years such that purchasing a multi-year subscription is cheaper?

11. What kind of customer support do they offer?
    You will find that as you use threat intelligence, you will at times find false positives or issues with your data feed files. You will be required to reach out to the threat intelligence provider for support, and you need to know if they have 24/7 support. What is their response time for trouble tickets? If you require escalated support in the event of an incident, what are their prices, and do they provide any services?

I hope I have brought up some valid points in this discussion about why threat intelligence can be leveraged to improve a security program and provide benefit to an organization's strategic business operations. I also hope I have given you some helpful questions to ask so you select the correct threat intelligence feeds that will provide value for your organization. I genuinely believe threat intelligence is a strategic asset that CISOs need to incorporate into their security programs and train their teams on how to effectively use these information sources.

Chapter 13 Key Point and Action Item 4

You can easily be overwhelmed with threat intelligence data. The data you use has to be data you trust because you're going to make daily priority decisions based on that data.

You should conduct an assessment of the threat intelligence data you are receiving by validating which feeds are accurate and timely and which are not. Eliminate the untimely and inaccurate data feeds. This step alone can dramatically improve the fidelity of your threat intelligence program.

How to Incorporate Open Source Threat Intelligence

There is one last topic for discussion, and that is the use of open source threat intelligence and how to use it in combination with your paid subscription feeds to improve your security defense profile. Our last question for discussion is as follows: *"Which Open Source Threat Intelligence (OSINT) resources should a CISO consider for enhancing their threat vulnerability management program?"*

Open source threat intelligence refers to publicly available threat intelligence sources, tools, frameworks, and sites that a security team can use to assist them in understanding the current perils facing their organization and predicting potential future threats based on that information. Within the open source threat intelligence realm, security teams can adopt numerous offerings from community sources. Examples of some these offerings are threat intelligence data feeds and open source software to create threat labs for testing malware.

There are also threat intelligence frameworks for cataloging and reporting threat data and, finally, open source software for developing threat intelligence analyst platforms that security analysts can use to manage their organization's threat response portfolio. Regardless of whether the CISO purchases a commercial offering that has all the above or the CISO has staff with mature skillsets that can build a threat intelligence platform, I believe the CISO needs to be proactive and start a threat intelligence program as soon as possible.

To me, open source threat intelligence gives CISOs another source of data and solutions, at minimal cost, that can be used to educate their security teams. I look at OSINT as an opportunity to get the resource-constrained CISO some tools and data feeds they can use to make the case that CTI is a strategic resource that is crucial and as the use case matures, purchase commercial feeds or tools where required.

So as the question for this final discussion states, let's look at some OSINT resources that are available for the CISO to use for improving their security program. The information that follows is not an all-inclusive list. Instead, I will organize resources that I have used in the past into several categories. I hope these resources provide value to you and your teams. The OSINT resources are as follows:

Sources – these are typically lists of information, whether in spreadsheet, API format or formats specific to deployed hardware/software within the users' environments:

- C&C Tracker – feed of known, active, and non-sinkholed C&C IP addresses:
  http://osint.bambenekconsulting.com/feeds/c2-ipmasterlist.txt
  (C&C Tracker, 2017)

- Cymon – good aggregated website of threats, feeds, and intelligence: https://www.cymon.io/ (Cymon, 2017)

- ExploitAlert – listing of the latest exploits released http://www.exploitalert.com/ (ExploitAlert, 2017)

- Spamhaus Project – contains multiple threat lists associated with spam and malware activity https://www.spamhaus.org/ (SPAMHAUS, 2017)

- VirusShare – repository of malware samples to provide security researchers, incident responders, and forensic analysts access to samples of malicious code https://virusshare.com/ (VirusShare, 2017)

Threat Feed Formats – formats for sharing threat intelligence data, typically for indicators of compromise (IoC) data:

- CAPEC – comprehensive dictionary and classification taxonomy of known attacks that can be used by analysts to advance community understanding and enhance defenses https://capec.mitre.org/ (CAPEC, 2016)

- MAEC – project from Mitre aimed at creating and providing a standardized language for sharing structured information about malware https://maecproject.github.io/ (MAEC, 2017)

- OpenPhish – site to identify zero-day phishing sites and provide comprehensive, actionable, real-time threat intelligence https://openphish.com/ (OpenPhish, 2017)

- STIX – now managed by OASIS, standardized language used to represent cyber threat information https://oasis-open.github.io/cti-documentation/ (STIX, 2017)

- TAXII - now managed by OASIS, TAXII defines concepts, protocols, and message exchanges to exchange cyber threat information for the detection, prevention, and mitigation of cyber threats: https://oasis-open.github.io/cti-documentation/ (TAXII, 2017)

- VERIS – set of metrics designed to provide a common language for describing security incidents in a structured and repeatable manner http://veriscommunity.net/index.html (VERIS, 2017)

Frameworks/Platforms – solutions used to collect, analyze, create, and share threat intelligence:

- AIS – Department of Homeland Security's (DHS) free Automated Indicator Sharing (AIS) capability enables the exchange of cyber threat indicators between the Federal Government and the private sector https://www.dhs.gov/ais (AIS, 2017)
- ATT&CK – model and framework for describing the actions an adversary may take while operating within an enterprise network https://attack.mitre.org/index.php/Main_Page (ATT&CK, 2017)
- MindMeld – An extensible Threat Intelligence processing framework that can be used to manipulate lists of indicators and transform and/or aggregate them for consumption by third-party enforcement infrastructure https://github.com/PaloAltoNetworks/minemeld/wiki (MindMeld, 2017)
- MISP – open source software solution for collecting, storing, distributing and sharing cyber security indicators and malware analysis http://www.misp-project.org/ (MISP, 2017)
- OTX – open access to a global community of threat researchers and security professionals. It delivers community-generated threat data, enables collaborative research, and automates the process of updating your security infrastructure with threat data from any source – there are costs https://www.alienvault.com/open-threat-exchange (OTX, 2017)
- Threat Crowd – browser designed for the finding and researching artifacts relating to cyber threats https://www.threatcrowd.org/ (Threat Crowd, 2017)

Tools – tools are either sites that can be used to analyze information or actual software that can be used by an analyst to parse, create, edit or publish threat intelligence data:

- Automater – tool to do analysis of IP Addresses, URLs, and Hashes: http://www.tekdefense.com/automater/ (Automater, 2017)

- Combine – tool to gather threat intelligence feeds from publicly available sources:

  https://github.com/mlsecproject/combine
  (MLSec Project (Combine), 2016)

- Cuckoo Sandbox – open source automated malware analysis system https://cuckoosandbox.org/ (Cuckoo Sandbox, 2017)

- LOKI – LOKI is a free and simple IOC scanner https://www.bsk-consulting.de/loki-free-ioc-scanner/ (LOKI, 2017)

- Machinae – tool for collecting intelligence from public sites/feeds about various security-related pieces of data: IP addresses, domain names, URLs, email addresses, file hashes, and SSL fingerprints https://github.com/HurricaneLabs/machinae (Machinae, 2017)

- Malwr – site is a free malware analysis service and community https://malwr.com/ (Malwr, 2017)

- OSTIP – a threat data platform project https://github.com/kx499/ostip (OSTIP, 2017)

- Virus Total – free service that analyzes suspicious files and URLs and facilitates the quick detection of viruses, worms, trojans, and all kinds of malware https://www.virustotal.com/ (Virus Total, 2017)

Research, References or Books – reading material about threat intelligence including research and whitepapers:

- CAR – Cyber Analytics Repository, a knowledge base of analytics based on the Adversary Tactics, Techniques, and Common Knowledge (ATT&CK™) threat model https://car.mitre.org/wiki/Main_Page (CAR, 2017)

- Definitive Guide to CTI – document describes the elements of cyber threat intelligence, discusses how it is collected, analyzed, and used https://cryptome.org/2015/09/cti-guide.pdf (CTI Guide, 2015)

- NIST SP 800-150 – NIST document for exchanging cyber threat information within a sharing community http://nvlpubs.nist.gov/nistpubs/SpecialPublications/NIST.SP. 800-150.pdf (NIST SP 800-150, 2016)

- Intelligence-Driven Computer Network Defense – whitepaper on the use of cyber threat intelligence to break the intrusion kill chain http://www.lockheedmartin.com/content/dam/lockheed/data/c orporate/documents/LM-White-Paper-Intel-Driven-Defense.pdf (Intelligence Driven Defense, 2010)

- MWR Threat Intelligence – white paper discusses the processes of requirements elicitation, collection, analysis, production, and evaluation of threat intelligence https://www.ncsc.gov.uk/content/files/protected_files/guidanc e_files/MWR_Threat_Intelligence_whitepaper-2015.pdf (Chismon & Ruks, 2015)

Chapter 13 Key Point and Action Item 5

After you have validated your data feeds and uncluttered your life by eliminating untimely, inaccurate, and redundant sources, it's time to remediate the gaps that remain.

You should review the Open Source Threat Intel (OSINT) sources and match the structure and content to your gaps. This will allow you to quickly and inexpensively create a complete program to fit your needs.

As I previously stated, the CISO should use threat intelligence feeds as part of a broad range of solutions within their corporate cybersecurity program. With that said, there are three critical processes a CISO must have in place with threat intelligence to get the maximum benefit for their company.

1. First the CISO and his or her teams must select data feeds that are relevant to the organization, the industry it operates in, the technologies deployed in its business portfolio, and the geographic locations where it conducts business. This first process is all about understanding how the threat information relates to the organization, so that it provides maximum risk mitigation.

2. The second process is about aggregation. As I stated before, you should have multiple types of data feeds. No one data feed will meet all of the requirements of an organization, so you should look at a mix of sources from commercial, open source, vendor/industry specific, and internally created feeds. Again, select feeds that are relevant to your program, the organization, and the threats you face.

3. The last process you must follow, which I believe is critical, is after selecting your data feeds you must collect metrics. You need to collect metric data over time to verify the worth of the threat information, and this should help you demonstrate how it is helping the security program reduce risk and make better-informed decisions for the business.

The job of CISO is one of making decisions. These decisions will have wide-ranging impacts on the organization and its strategic business operations. Threat intelligence is there to assist you and your security teams in providing enterprise risk management as a service tuned to the needs of the organization and effective in responding to threats.

Summary

For Chapter 13, we began our discussion by asking these three questions:

- What is threat intelligence, and what types of external threat intelligence sources should the CISO use to augment their cybersecurity suite?
- What are the business scenarios for incorporating threat intelligence services into an enterprise cybersecurity program?
- Which Open Source Threat Intelligence (OSINT) resources should a CISO consider for enhancing their threat vulnerability management program?

There is a plethora of sources for threat intelligence, from free, open source to vendor supplied to proprietary add-ons. Something for every budget and every category of risk. The key is not what you consume or how much you spend, but the context in which the threat intelligence becomes actionable.

In closing, we would like to leave you with these five key points and next steps:

1. In addition to the cross over between threats that operate in the physical and digital worlds, the law enforcement community has enormous experience in gathering threat intelligence. **You should uncover all of the touchpoints between your organization and both the law enforcement and regulatory communities. Ensure that you have defined an appropriate two-way information flow in each case and develop a process to regularly utilize that information flow.**

2. The informal human network that you have been building serves as an invaluable source of threat intelligence, from pooled and shared feeds to side-channel discussion to a short list of who to call and who might warn you of impending threat. **You should review how the people in your human network prefer to interact and look for opportunities to join or organize your colleagues. Take advantage of existing communities or form your own if needed.**

3. Context is everything. All the threat intelligence available to you won't do you any good unless you know how it applies to your organization, in your industry, and in your region. **You should review each of the six keys to threat intelligence and make sure you have a complete understanding of how each affects you. Revisit this annually or as major changes occur within your business or when major seminal breaches occur.**

4. You can easily be overwhelmed with threat intelligence data. The data you use has to be data you trust because you're going to make daily priority decisions based on that data. **You should conduct an assessment of the threat intelligence data you are receiving by validating which feeds are accurate and timely and which are not. Eliminate the untimely and inaccurate data feeds. This step alone can dramatically improve the fidelity of your threat intelligence program.**

5. After you have validated your data feeds and uncluttered your life by eliminating untimely, inaccurate, and redundant sources, it's time to remediate the gaps that remain. **You should review the Open Source Threat Intel (OSINT) sources and match the structure and content to your gaps. This will allow you to quickly and inexpensively create a complete program to fit your needs.**

As Matt said, threat intelligence without context is just a laundry list of threats that create fear, uncertainty, and doubt in some scenarios and the "boy who cried wolf" syndrome in others. To build a good threat intelligence program, you need to understand what you are protecting. Specifically, know your industry, your employees and key stakeholders, your organization's processes, the applications that support these processes, and the underlying infrastructure (operating systems, hardware, and networks). With this in hand, you can make sure your human network, your connections to law enforcement, and your data feeds will fit your needs and help you protect your organization.

Chapter 14 – Continuity Planning and Your Approach to Backups

Introduction

In the next four chapters, we're going to do a deep dive into the entire process of preparing for, responding to, recovering from, and learning from cyber incidents. A passage Bill writes in Chapter 17 is worth previewing here: While it's helpful to break the entire incident response discipline into a series of discrete phases so that each can be described individually to assist with training and the command and control of response activities, it is rarely clear-cut when one process ends, and the next begins. There is often significant overlap, and as new information emerges, it is usually necessary to revisit a phase previously thought completed. For instance, while in recovery, monitoring activity may detect the presence of indicators of compromise identified for the current cyber incident and that may send you all the way back to the containment phase.

At times, the material we present over the 12 essays that make up these next four chapters, that overlap will become apparent not just within the activities of responding to the specific event, but over the entire set of disciplines we cover.

In Chapter 14 we look at the close relationship between business continuity planning and your strategy for becoming a cyber-resilient organization. Each of the three authors ties these two critical business processes together and emphasizes the importance of understanding what is fundamental to the business.

Bill discusses backup and recovery planning. He challenges the reader to factor into their backup planning the traditional elements of business continuity planning while considering vital new dimensions. These new dimensions include accommodating new service delivery models such as cloud computing and new attack methods such as ransomware in our models.

Matt emphasizes the importance of executive and board-level engagement. From understanding the organization's core priorities and tying those to the appetite for risk to making sure the board understands how the BCP / DR strategy seeks to manage and mitigate that risk, Matt shows how ultimately it is about business strategy. A key way that the CISO drives this engagement is by making sure that the security program and security architecture should be reflective of organizational priorities as captured in BCP tools such as the BIA.

Ensuring that the organization is a going concern is the ultimate responsibility of the board.

Gary reminds us of the impact that cyber incidents can have, including outcomes like disruptions to business continuity and reputation damage. Significant events can translate to disappointed customers, lost jobs, and hard monetary costs that can leave an organization reeling. He then helps the reader construct a plan by building on many of the lessons from previous chapters and showing how the pieces fit together.

Some of the questions the authors used to frame their thoughts for this chapter include:

- What is a Business Continuity Plan (BCP) and what are the steps to create one?
- What critical components should a Disaster Recovery Plan (DRP) include to be effective?
- What value does the CISO's security program receive from the organization's Business Continuity Plan and its associated Disaster Recovery Plan?

Backups and Planning – Bonney

In Volume 1, several chapters dealt directly with actions that the CISO or the Information Security organization should take to gain a thorough understanding of their environment. These included Chapter 3 on data classification, Chapter 4 on third-party risk, and Chapter 7 on risk management and cyber liability insurance. Now in Volume 2, Chapter 12 discusses monitoring and signals, and in this chapter, we're addressing backups and planning.

Looking briefly at the table of contents, you'll also notice that we go step-by-step through responding to and communicating about incidents (Chapter 15), recovery and resuming operations (Chapter 16), and forensics and post-mortem (Chapter 17). This chapter on backups and planning, provides the critical transition between the material covered in Volume 1 about understanding your environment and the material covered in Volume 2 about dealing with the constant onslaught of cyber incidents your organization will unfortunately experience.

What Business Processes Are You Trying to Protect?

Leaving the tired cliché of "it's not a matter of if, but when" behind, we can focus on the certitude that as economic value has migrated to the online world, all organizations are subject to fraud, vandalism, and disruption. In this reality, you would expect that we'd dedicate fully half of this two-volume set to preparing for and then executing on remediation, recovery, and improvement activities, and you'd be correct. It is half the job; the other half is working with management to create the safest possible technology environment for your organization.

Another interesting aspect of both volumes is that we spend a fair amount of time discussing areas of focus traditionally reserved for the CIO. These include the entire chapter on data classification (Chapter 3), the data focus in third-party risk (Chapter 4), along with the parts of measurement and reporting (Chapter 5) and tools and techniques (Chapter 8) that focus on your process inventory.

We did this because it is vitally important to know what business processes and data you're trying to protect and because this is critical information for planning and executing your backup and recovery strategies. Like data classification and process inventory, backup and recovery were once the exclusive provinces of the CIO, but the emerging role of the CISO, beyond expertise in cyber risk, policy, and data protection, is the continuity of business operations.

As we wrote in Chapter 1, this requires that you integrate your information security function into your organization's business continuity planning process. To do this, you must partner with your colleagues to understand what you are helping protect, and then you must assist in prioritizing the recovery of the assets and defining the strategy for their recovery.

As you begin to dig into your organization's business continuity plan, there are a few fundamental concepts that are especially important. We first mentioned the Business Impact Analysis (BIA) in Chapter 5 as the possible subject of metrics: do you have one, how recent is it, what are the high-impact business processes? As input for the planning process, the BIA becomes critical. At a minimum, you'll need to know operational impacts (the impact on customers, the impact on back-office functionality), financial impacts (lost revenue, expense impact), and technological dependencies (systems, networks, sequencing, etc.) of each business process you identify.

As you develop your recovery plans, you need to keep in mind the recovery objective and the recovery time. The recovery objective, expressed as "Recovery Point Objective" or RPO, defines the exact state to which you must recover the process. You'll need to decide if you must record every transaction or if you can simply determine the current known good state and continue.

The recovery time, often expressed as the "Recovery Time Objective" or RTO, defines how long the organization can withstand the process being unavailable. The RTO gives you the timeframe during which the process must be recovered in the primary site or made available in an alternate location. Digging deeper, once you have your inventory of business processes and have prioritized that list, you can begin to build your BIA.

Your next step is to identify and communicate your most critical systems and the sequence of recovery. Depending on the interdependencies, you may need to re-establish enabling processes before recovery can be attempted or even started. After you have developed and communicated your prioritized and sequenced list, then you can map out the tasks required for recovery. You'll also document the criteria for declaring a switch to alternative sites or services, and the departments and individuals responsible for those decisions. Each system will have a different set of checklist tasks based on its distinct operating system and configurations. It's also important to note the time it takes for each step required to restore operations, and test full system backup and full system recovery while you're documenting each checklist. There should also be specific steps listed for testing and verifying that any compromised systems are completely clean and fully functional.

It is helpful to use a scale for the criticality of business processes to allow you to allocate appropriate resources for recovery. One suggestion is to use the FIPS 199 availability impact levels:

- Low (outage has little impact)
- Moderate (disruption would cause a moderate impact on the organization)
- High (mission critical – the damage or disruption would cause the most impact)

Your first task with your colleagues is to agree on who makes the tie-breaking call on any business processes about which the team doesn't agree. One option is to have the CIO make the tiebreaker calls, with active input from the business line representative for that process.

Your Backup Strategy

With your processes so labeled, you can begin to plan your backup strategy. Perhaps you'll use tape backups for low, (optical, WAN/LAN) replication for backups with a cold or warm site for moderate, and mirrored systems with disk replication and a hot site (active/passive to active/active) for high. Your organization determines the criteria for what constitutes low, moderate, and high. After you have a preliminary model, cost it out and make sure the organization can afford what you've scoped. Conversely, understand the impact of what you classify as moderate and low and determine if the business can live with that.

Note also where your organization is on its cloud adoption journey. Distinguish between your maturity levels for utilizing cloud storage in an operational (or transactional) mode versus as departmental backups or file archiving versus as a formal part of your availability or resilience strategy. In other words, do you just use the cloud to store some non-critical files or do you do transactional work in the cloud and can you/should you use cloud storage as part of your recovery strategy? Do not mistake informal departmental usage of cloud storage for a well-integrated cloud utilization strategy.

When you have completed these tasks, you should have in hand a detailed list of recovery objectives. It is from this list of objectives that you can begin to identify the required redundancy you'll need to guarantee recovery to your agreed upon RPO within your agreed upon RTO. These requirements allow you to fill in the details for what to back up on tape (virtual or physical, with the associated differences in procedures), what to replicate across your data centers, what to back up to cloud storage, and what to mirror between active/passive and active/active sites. They include personnel, facilities, network access, processing (bare metal, virtual, and cloud), storage, applications, and data. Each of these must be described in depth and tested to make sure you have accounted for all necessary components.

Along with these complexities, you need to factor in both new technologies that have already had significant impacts on how you deliver technology to the user, and the rapid rate at which technology is changing. It would be a mistake to dismiss the unique characteristics of cloud computing. It can be fashionable among senior leaders to demonstrate mastery by trivializing current trends.

Yes, certain aspects of cloud computing have been around for years and yes, one can find articles written in 1997 about the history of cloud computing. But several things about modern cloud computing are so drastically different from your father's cloud computing that they warrant special attention to make sure you can truly meet your recovery time objectives. In addition to detailing the business processes and technology dependencies, you need to make sure you can replicate (or rebuild) the virtual CPUs, storage, and network environment in use, and that means you must invest the time to understand it, at the discrete virtual component level. Here is a sample of the questions you need to answer:

- Virtual Technology Assets
  - How are your virtual components configured and how are they orchestrated?
  - What unique backup and recovery challenges does this present and how do you account for them?
  - What are the regulatory, contractual, or policy implications associated with their configuration and orchestration? For instance, do you have configuration requirements to meet PCI-DSS standards?
  - Besides CPU and storage, how are other virtual components, such as networks, routing, and connectivity allocated, built, orchestrated, and backed up?

- Data Assets
  - One of the compelling value propositions of cloud computing is inexpensive but durable storage – do you have a data availability/redundancy/replication strategy that accounts for the orders of magnitude more data you are generating and collecting? While it is tempting to assume that your "cloud team" has taken the necessary steps to replicate cloud data using cloud assets, it is still imperative that you formally consider appropriate recovery objectives. For instance, do you need replication at the storage unit, data center, or region level?
  - What are the regulatory, contractual, or policy implications associated with this data? For example, do you have geographical boundaries you must respect for personal data or regulated sensitive data?

- Micro-Services and "Appification"
  - Applications are delivered using many more models than before, including more single-function applications, more interlaced single-function applications, and more reusable components and services that originate or are accessed both inside of and outside of your organization. Do you understand the interdependencies between these services and how to restore functionality in the case of an outage?

This is not an exhaustive list, but by working with your colleagues you should be able to review process documentation where it exists and is current and interview process owners where documentation is absent, out of date, or incomplete to ensure the inventory of essential components is complete. Incorporate virtual asset inventory into your organization's configuration management process by extending your configuration management database (CMDB) to accommodate cloud components using native cloud tools. Do not try to retrofit your legacy CMDB; it will not likely scale. If your organization doesn't utilize a CMDB, now is a great time to establish one, at the very least for your virtual assets.

Given the rapid rate of technology change, you'll likely also want to revisit your plans more often than you might have in the past. Where a biannual review of the overall BCP might still suffice, you might review inventories of critical components quarterly, or when making significant changes. It all depends on the needs of the organization.

To assist with this planning, I recommend you start with the NIST standard for continuity planning, "800-34: Continuity Planning Guide for Information Technology Systems."[15] SANS also has an excellent (though older, it was written in 2002) online document in their reading room, "Disaster Recovery Plan Strategies and Processes."[16]

After you have discovered, documented, and verified the components you'll need to recover and built a recovery strategy to restore needed functionality within the timeframes required, you'll want to be directly involved with the vendors your organization uses to provide various services. Assuming the role again of chief resiliency officer, you'll want to test continuity plans and ensure that each vendor plays their appropriate role and is integrated smoothly into your recovery team. Along with facilities and technology partners, this includes your backup vendor(s).

Plan to Defend Your Backups

In more mature organizations with depth in the various disciplines in information technology, most CISOs, until recently, did not have to

---

[15] See: http://nvlpubs.nist.gov/nistpubs/Legacy/SP/nistspecialpublication800-34r1.pdf for an online version of this publication or search for the "800-34" standard.

[16] See: https://www.sans.org/reading-room/whitepapers/recovery/disaster-recovery-plan-strategies-processes-564 or search for appropriate key words.

take a personal hand in designing or implementing a data backup strategy that would allow organizations, or individuals, to recover from simple mistakes and mechanical failures. Their role was more focused on continuity planning to address major disruptions, such as natural disasters, pandemics, or wide-scale cyber-attacks. Most backup software and process implementations for these mature organizations do adequate planning around the expectations for recovery, including issues such as:

- Whether to include all files for all users?
- Whether to include only files placed on departmental drives?
- Whether to restrict the use of backup resources to data used for critical business processes?
- The approach to backing up virtual assets
- How quickly should backups be available?
- Whether to encrypt backups?
- Which backups to store off-site?

However, I would be remiss if I did not mention the particular case of ransomware. In addition to ensuring that backups are complete, routinely tested, and kept secure, you'll also need to address the growing phenomena of cybercriminals holding your data captive.

Ransomware began emerging in the first decade of the twenty-first century and by midway through the second decade has become one of the most potent and virulent forms of malware. The premise is simple: the person or entity that values your data the most is you or your organization. You created it; you use it every day, you are responsible for it. Why go through the trouble of stealing your data and then figuring out how to offer it for sale to someone who may not know how to value it when the criminal can just sell it back to you?

The approach is simple as well. Infect the target system with malware that stealthily encrypts files that are accessible from that system and then hold the access to the encrypted files for ransom, requiring the owner to pay the criminals to regain access to their data. Of course, there is no honor among thieves, and there is no concern over whether the files are indeed recoverable. There is only concern that the method used to hold the data captive is at least effective enough to cause sufficient disruption to motivate the owner to pay for its release.

Because of this new form of attack, the CISO has two new problems to address. First, you must now become familiar with and take part in the planning around day-to-day operational backups. In the past, you only had to focus on continuity in the face of significant disruption. Second, you must now focus on protecting your backups from direct or indirect attack. Whereas in the past only large-scale vandalism brought your backups into the line of fire, now the ability of cybercriminals to render your backups unavailable through corruption or destruction is an emerging capability of various families of ransomware.

While the mechanics of addressing this attack-vector will vary from organization to organization depending on the protected data, the system and network topology, and the deployed technologies, the planning is relatively straightforward. You'll want to use the same calculus you used for determining which files should be backed up in the first place.

It is doubtful that your organization chose to take centralized responsibility for all files on all storage devices anywhere within your network or on any systems that have a role in your operations. You likely decided that specific data fell within your backup and recovery objectives, some did not, and the file owners themselves would address some. When designing your anti-malware strategy, you likely considered possible contagion between end nodes, from end nodes to server nodes, and from server nodes to end nodes.

The difference with ransomware is that you now need to defend against deliberate attacks on the backup copies. That means that the best practice of routinely checking backups for validity becomes paramount, and that you must maintain the ability to physically or logically separate backups from operational data.

Willful attacks to hold data hostage by (in part) attacking backups and duplicate copies reinforces the requirement (also a well-accepted best practice) to minimize the number of trust-by-default connections that you allow from process to process. You should strictly enforce access privileges, especially for the highly-privileged access to critical processes such as backup servers and backup processes. You should strictly impose user and department data segmentation. Finally, this also highlights the need to patch and upgrade systems and scan for and close vulnerabilities. While entry into your network is usually through attacks that manipulate users to take unwise actions, exploiting unpatched systems and relaxed permissions enables lateral movement within systems.

While individually these steps may seem trivial, taken together lack of proper access controls, untested backups, and unpatched systems form the unholy trinity of poor system hygiene. When implemented effectively, the same preventive measures that help prevent cyber-attacks and unintended downtime also protect your backups.

To summarize this section, a vital part of the CISO's role is to leverage their detailed knowledge about business processes, data assets, and threats to the organization to help the organization develop a solid contingency plan that will allow recovery as swiftly as needed in the event of a disaster, whether natural or human-made. Planning recovery efforts based on the identification of critical business processes and involving the business process owners in decisions about the appropriate recovery point and recovery time objectives are crucial to developing an effective plan with high-level buy-in. And finally, while these planning approaches have matured over many years, it is essential to remain flexible and integrate new technology delivery models and threat vectors into your planning process.

> "The objective of business continuity management is to make the entity more resilient to potential threats and allow the entity to resume or continue operations under adverse or abnormal conditions."
>
> (Association of Contingency Planners)

Let's face it – cybersecurity is exciting. Our profession is in the crosshairs of the media, with reports related to high-profile attacks frequently covered on the nightly news. We even have popular TV shows. For new entrants to our profession, this focus on cybersecurity may seem to be the norm. For those of us who have been in the industry more years than we'd like to admit, we recognize that the current focus on cybersecurity is a relatively new phenomenon. It may come as a shock to some that there was a time when cybersecurity (and before that, information security) was the forgotten stepchild of IT, overlooked from a resource and budget perspective. Security was the department – let's be honest about this, the individual – that would get the table scraps from the IT budget once leadership addressed all other "priorities."

I bring up this historical perspective to acknowledge our profession's debt of gratitude to our colleagues in the business continuity and disaster recovery (BC/DR) community. Historically, our two disciplines shared similar common neglect. Like security, everyone knows and recognizes that business continuity and disaster recovery are important elements to an organization's overall resilience.

Despite this recognition of the importance of BC/DR, most organizations only pay lip service to this critical discipline with incomplete and untested BC/DR plans. Furthermore, our colleagues in BC/DR frequently have their budgets and projects undermined by higher priority efforts within the organization. The result is that organizations are less resilient and subject to significant interruptions to their operations. Kind of sounds like the risk factors associated with inadequate and poorly-resourced security programs.

While the current focus on cybersecurity is beneficial, we should not overlook the contributions from our colleagues in BC/DR, especially in the context of resiliency. Our respective professions both focus on resiliency. Resiliency is at the heart of cybersecurity. No organization is immune from being attacked. In fact, our organizations are subject to ongoing and in many cases highly persistent attacks. Our jobs are to ensure that our organizations remain resilient when confronted with risks, be they cyber or natural disasters.

We can learn and have learned much from our colleagues in BC/DR. First and foremost, let's not overlook one of the great tools that our BC/DR friends leverage to evaluate their continuity programs – the business impact analysis (BIA). BIAs are powerful tools that should be leveraged to improve our security programs. They convey detail related to organizational priorities, expressed in terms such as maximum allowable downtime (MAD), recovery-point objective (RPO), and recovery-time objective (RTO). Further, well-crafted BIAs highlight key dependencies on applications, staff, infrastructure, and vendors.

Collectively, the detail resulting from the review of a BIA provides essential context related to the organization's risk landscape. We don't have cybersecurity for cybersecurity's sake. Cybersecurity must be focused on the business and not just cool and innovative technology. Ultimately, a business consists of distinct processes and protecting these processes from cyber risk is our raison d'être.

The BC/DR community has also done an excellent job of looking at mitigating strategies to improve organizational resilience. Strategies related to fault tolerance of components, fail-over, and high-availability architectures including active/active and active/passive configurations have their roots in approaches designed to improve RPO and RTO. In the aggregate, our BC/DR colleagues have produced a body of work that can inform how we look at our cyber programs with the ultimate goal of improving the operational resiliency of organizations.

Let's take a look at how cybersecurity can improve resiliency. I'd like to recommend we spend a bit of time on the following:

- Defining, documenting, and mitigating risk
- Tying risk to the organization's core priorities and organizational objectives
- Keeping executive management and the board of directors appropriately informed

These three practices will help us to position our cybersecurity program in a manner that improves the resilience of the organization.

Defining, Documenting, and Mitigating Risk

CISOs would be well served to bring risk management front and center in their security programs. We cannot protect every system equally. Not all business processes, applications, and infrastructure are created equal. Similarly, not all employees have the same value to the organization. This inequality may seem obvious, but our security programs frequently don't reflect this reality. Too many security programs attempt to apply ubiquitous security to all systems, infrastructure, and employees.

The consequences of a blanket, cover-all approach to security are challenging. Unless the organization benefits from an ever-expanding budget and nearly unlimited resources, the reality of a protect-everything-equally security program is watered down security. Critical systems are under-resourced and under-secured while we effectively overprotect non-critical systems. The root cause of this disconnect is fundamentally a lack of alignment with organizational priorities. A discussion that is risk-focused is the most effective means to avoid this dynamic.

Key to a successful risk discussion is for the CISO to capture and understand the organization's overall risk appetite concerning the impacts on the confidentiality, integrity, availability, privacy, and even the safety of material business processes. These impacts, however, need to be more formally aligned with enterprise risk management and specific risk considerations for the organization related to financial, reputational, operational, and other higher-level risk considerations.

When done correctly, a risk-focused discussion translates detailed technical risk into business terms which senior executives and the board can more readily consume and act upon. Executive management and the board are concerned about the impacts of an adversary on the organization, its reputation, and its finances, even if they are not well-versed on the tactics, techniques, and procedures (TTPs).

CISOs should continually ask themselves: "What is it that I don't know that I should know about this business process or initiative that could impact the confidentiality, integrity, availability, privacy, and safety of the process?" This open-ended question keeps the focus on considerations that could materially impact the organization. Returning to our colleagues in BC/DR, the BIA can facilitate this line of questioning. What dependencies and risk factors – notably from a cyber perspective – could negatively influence those processes that are most critical to the organization? Knowing these factors will help align your security program and architecture to those processes that the organization values most – as noted in the MAD and RPO/RTO.

Another, more direct but less structured approach to understand risk appetite across the organization is to simply ask colleagues in various departments and lines of business to clarify their areas' priorities and key functions (e.g., business processes). This insight will facilitate the alignment of your security program to the organization's core focus, effectively, what the organization values most. For the good of their security programs, CISOs must excel at understanding this business context.

Tying Risk to the Organization's Core Priorities and Organizational Objectives

Far too few CISOs align their security program with their organization's mission and strategy. One reason is that too many CISOs are buried deep inside their organization's structure. Not viewed as a key member of the executive team, the CISO simply is not engaged nor participates frequently enough in organizational strategy. When they do engage, their input is largely too technical to resonate with business and executive counterparts. This must change.

CISOs should ensure that they are well-versed in the organization's core strategy. Part of the CISO's role is to ensure that cyber risk that could impact the strategy or mission of the organization is understood, documented, and treated in a manner consistent with the entity's risk tolerance. If the CISO is not sure what the organization's risk tolerance is, he or she needs to ask questions until it's clear. Equally important, validate this understanding with other stakeholders in the organization. Don't let too much time go by without asking again. Risk tolerances change.

In Volume 1 of the CISO Desk Reference Guide, my colleagues and I touched upon the role of the board of directors and executive management. As I noted, you should avoid blindsiding senior management and the board. CISOs can and should help these constituencies know the risk related to the organization's strategy. CISOs should document and align cyber risk to the entity's strategy, highlighting the consequences and potential impacts associated with the organization's objectives. To facilitate this, CISOs and their teams should evaluate the effects on confidentiality, integrity, availability, privacy, and safety related to the organization's operations and critical initiatives. This alignment needs to become second nature.

To conduct these assessments, the CISO will need to take a full-stack view of the infrastructure supporting these activities as well as a broader view of the initiative to include critical vendors, stakeholders, employees, and other dependencies. The assessment should include gathering or preparing necessary documentation, including a context diagram (i.e., a subset of a data flow diagram) to look at the critical components of the strategy – notably data flows.

Where are the trust boundaries? Are there key vendors or suppliers that are part of the strategy? What type of information is required to execute the strategy (e.g., PII, PHI, credit card, and intellectual property) and where is this information stored and protected? What type of IT infrastructure is required to operate the strategy?

The CISO and key members of the security team can offer crucial technical due diligence on the strategy. As the components of the strategy become evident, the CISO can oversee threat modeling and risk assessments of the various parts of the program. The result will be a more informed understanding of the risk environment related to the strategy and business function. This knowledge should form the basis for how the CISO informs executive management and the board about the suite of cyber-related risk that the organization confronts.

Keeping Executive Management and the Board of Directors Adequately Informed

As noted above, the CISO should play an integral role in overseeing and informing risk management activities. Given the near-constant news about the compromises of companies and government agencies, executive management and the board will want to know just how secure the organization is. In the preceding two sections, I noted how important it is for a CISO to align his or her security program to the organization's core functions, processes, and strategy. This alignment, ultimately, serves as the foundation for ongoing discussions with executive management and the board about the risk profile of the organization.

CISOs will have a more receptive audience for their recommendations if they adopt this approach: review and assess threats and risks to the organization's core functions and strategy as opposed to risks to the infrastructure. Furthermore, convey the risks to the organization in business terms that highlight the potential impact on reputation, financial exposure, regulatory compliance, contractual obligations, and operational considerations. Effectively, the CISO conveys critical risk insights to executive management and the board. Informing these insights are the CISO's previous efforts to analyze the impacts on confidentiality, integrity, availability, privacy, and safety to core business functions.

Returning to our colleagues in BC/DR, the CISO function shares some of the same challenges that our colleagues in BC/DR face. Namely, how do we mitigate risk and improve resiliency for our organizations and express our strategies and programs in terms that executive management and the board will understand and act upon in a manner consistent with the organization's overall risk appetite? At the heart of our profession is our goal to protect our organizations. That sounds straightforward, but it's nuanced. Knowing the organizational or business value of what we're protecting and aligning our security programs to this value requires context and an understanding of our organization's strategy and core functions. Those CISOs who efficiently capture this organizational context and are also well versed in describing cyber risk in business terms and aligned to the organization's strategy and core functions will see their security programs better understood and funded by executive management.

Business Continuity Planning: A strategic Process That Must Include the CISO – Hayslip

"The growing awareness of cybercrime and its impact to the balance sheet puts the role of today's modern CISO center stage as a corporate partner who must be involved in their organization's efforts to establish and manage a BCP program."

For today's businesses, it is no longer a matter of if they will experience a cyber-related criminal incident. Instead, it is a question of whether the organization has business continuity and disaster recovery plans in place to reduce the incident's impact on corporate operations. In 2016, IBM sponsored a research document, conducted by the Ponemon Institute, titled "2016 Cost of a Data Breach: Global Analysis" (Ponemon, 2016). This report found that the costs organizations face for managing the fallout of a data breach continue to rise, and now average **$4 million per incident**, up from $3.79 million in 2015. This number equates to average triage costs of $158 per data record and depending on the company's industry the price could go as high as $355 per record (e.g., in the medical industry).

So, how do these numbers relate to business continuity and CISOs? Mature companies, focused on managing their risk exposure, should have established a Business Continuity Plan (BCP) and a resulting Disaster Recovery Plan (DRP). These plans are unique to each organization and are developed to assist the business in responding to events that can have significant negative impacts on strategic operations. Historically, organization-wide impacting events were considered to be issues such as earthquakes, fires, supply chain failures and bankruptcies.

However, cyber-related incidents are now becoming a new class of events that can have far-ranging impacts on a company's ability to create and collect revenue. It is this growing awareness of cybercrime and its impact to the balance sheet that I believe puts the role of today's modern CISO center stage as a corporate partner who must be involved in their organization's efforts to establish and manage a BCP program and its DRP process for recovering IT and cybersecurity services.

In typical organizations, the CISO is tasked to develop the Security Incident Response Plan and to manage the Security Incident Response Team. However, in today's dynamic threat environment, the modern

CISO is also considered to be a strategic peer to their organization's business units. It is this partnership that requires the CISO to understand the company's BCP and its disaster recovery procedures, both of which provide value to the CISO and their enterprise security program. Keeping this in mind, the three questions and discussion to follow will explore the importance of the BCP and DRP programs to the organization and the CISO.

Cyber Incidents Have Far-Ranging Impacts

In November 2013, cyber criminals hacked Target (Daly, 2016) using a vendor's account credentials to gain access to the company's network. Over a 30-day period, the hackers stole 110 million credit card and customer records. The cost to Target for this incident, almost four years later, is still ongoing. Due to this breach and the critical data it involved, Target has spent over $200 million to reissue new credit cards, upgrade their networks, notify affected consumers, and engage third-party forensics teams to investigate how this breach occurred. These costs do not take into account the brand damage they suffered, the resulting 46% drop in revenue, nor current ongoing lawsuits and regulatory actions.

This one example makes the point that cyber events can cause a shock to the corporation's strategic initiatives and if companies expect to be resilient and absorb these types of incidents, they need to develop and implement robust BCP programs, plans that contemplate the impacts of a cyber-attack. We are now ready for our first question, *"What is a Business Continuity Plan (BCP) and what are the steps to create one?*

Businesses recognize that some crucial services they deliver to customers must be available continuously. This requirement is changing the focus of business continuity operations from resuming business operations in the shortest time possible to one of ensuring that critical operations continue to function even during a disaster. In one word, resiliency – to deliver services to the client and have a BCP program that when activated can still deliver a level of service in which the client is not even aware of the disaster's occurrence. To begin, some definitions that will provide insight into our discussion are as follows (NIST 2010):

1. *Business Continuity* - the activities required to keep the company running during a cycle of interruption to business operations.

2. *Business Continuity Plan (BCP)* – an organization-wide collection of procedures that are managed by a coordinator. These procedures consist of actions to be taken by specific personnel and business units in the event of an emergency or disaster. This plan is activated

by a senior member of the executive team who has specific authority during the event to take actions protecting the business.

3. *Disaster Recovery Plan (DRP)* – a collection of processes, plans, and procedures for restoring the company's IT operations or infrastructure to full functionality during and after the event. The DRP is usually an addendum to the BCP and many organizations use these names interchangeably to refer to similar processes.

Business continuity is organization-wide whereas the DRP is more focused on IT and cybersecurity.

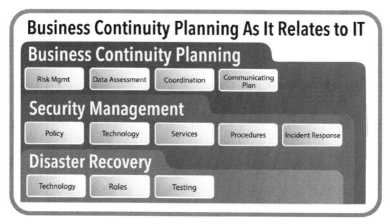

Figure 14.1 BCP Security and DRP

The goal of business continuity is to continue business operations through uncertain times until reaching a level of normalcy. It is not always necessary to activate your BCP during an incident. However, disaster recovery procedures do get activated during a business impacting incident. The focus of the DRP is on re-establishing corporate IT networks and cybersecurity controls to return operations, assets, and services to normal. The BCP and DRP programs will encompass processes that will require the use of emergency assets such as standby data centers and public cloud resources or partnerships with third-party service providers to provide expedited service.

These processes incorporate additional inherent risks by potentially superseding, at least temporarily, your cybersecurity controls. Activating emergency standby systems or granting third-party service provider's emergency access to systems and data sometimes circumvents standard controls for system configuration, identity and access management, storage management, and backups. It's this pervasive operational risk that provides the call for the CISO's involvement in the development of their organization's BCP program. Your participation is essential to ensure that as the organization activates emergency operations to manage a disaster-level event, it doesn't expose itself to new unseen risks that could significantly interrupt recovery operations.

Developing an effective Business Continuity Plan incorporates multiple planning steps and objectives including:

- *BCP Program Steering Committee*– during this phase of building a business continuity program the structure of the management committee is decided and a member of the executive team is selected to champion the program. All team members should have a level of authority sufficient to make decisions and ensure team members receive training.

- *Business Impact Analysis (BIA)* – during this process a significant amount of information will be collected on the services and procedures the organization delivers to its customers. This analysis will require stakeholders from all business units to identify critical services that must be delivered even in the event of a disaster. It is also during this portion of the BCP process when you conduct a risk analysis of the impact on discovered services. That information should then be used to select an overall strategy and develop a budget for the BCP program.

  The BIA will generate an enormous amount of data specific to risk, revenue, and operations for selected assets. Some of the critical data-sets the BIA provides CISOs includes a list of assets that have strategic importance to the business and the amount of revenue that can be lost over a given time if a cyber-related incident impacts the asset or service. This relationship of revenue loss to a cyber disruption event is crucial; it can be used to help quantify risk baselines for each asset and assist you in justifying the chosen level of security protection to mitigate these identified threats to revenue.

- *Developing the BCP* – in this step of the BCP process, the response team members for business recovery are identified and assigned their areas of responsibility. A plan structure is developed incorporating procedures to protect and provide the critical services identified in the BIA. During this step, identify the backup and recovery requirements and work with stakeholders to develop and agree to the scenarios for the plan's activation. Several important BCP steps to validate in this phase are escalation procedures, communication/notification requirements, and plan activation conditions.

- _Plan Creation_ - during this part of the BCP planning process team members and essential stakeholders walk through and document emergency response procedures. It is also in this step that the business must decide how they will orchestrate their response to an emergency, i.e., activate a command center, designate a specific location as the new headquarters, or disperse and operate remotely.

This decision will impact how the communications response matrix must be implemented and will also influence detailed recovery procedures. One of the last areas to cover is contracts, which will need to be reviewed to document the service levels the business is obligated to provide. Also, contracts for recovery services should be prepared and be available for immediate execution as required.

- _BCP Testing and Training_ - by this step the BCP has been created but the company must test it, and the best way to do this is to use a scenario, one that is possible and could have an actual impact to the business. Run this scenario and at the conclusion develop a report to evaluate the response of team members and the business units and identify areas that need improvement.

Once completed, use this report to schedule training for team members and schedule the next BCP scenario event. What is critical in this step is that the BCP gets exercised on a regular ongoing basis to increase awareness in the organization and provide team members with the experience they need so that when the emergency is real their response is coordinated and efficient.

- _BCP Maintenance_ - create the program, implement regular testing for the plan, and insert different scenarios to flex team members' abilities to work together and triage responses to selected disaster events. However, even though the BCP plan is now operational, it still must be periodically reviewed to ensure it stays current with the company's business operations. Once the BCP is updated, distribute the new plan to recovery team members and schedule a scenario to test the new plan's validity.

As you can see, the BCP process is quite extensive, there are many stakeholders involved, and it will cross all organizational units within a business. There are critical components of the BCP and its disaster recovery plan (DRP) that make this program an essential function of the organization. These processes and the identified data to support them combine to make this program an operational platform to direct the organization in times of crisis. Now for our next question: "*What critical components should a Disaster Recovery Plan (DRP) include to be effective?*"

At the start of creating the BCP, team members from across the organization were identified to assist in collecting and vetting data on assets (e.g., software, hardware, and data) that were deemed crucial for business operations. This data was received and reviewed by the team's stakeholders and executive leadership through the performance of risk assessments and business impact analysis (BIA) studies. These BIA studies were conducted on the identified assets to provide context to those that were considered critical and begin to identify and create restoration procedures that would be required to recover these assets in a time of crisis.

It was also in the beginning stage of the BCP where stakeholders helped identify the Recovery Time Objective (RTO) and Recovery Point Objective (RPO) for each critical asset. These two metrics define the maximum duration of downtime that can be accepted before unacceptable business losses occur and the maximum amount of data loss permitted due to a business-impacting incident. Note, that the RPO metric will be affected by the criticality of the data type, especially if the data has compliance or regulatory requirements for availability or retention. The DRP document contained in the following table provides an excellent example of how to use this data.

Disaster Recovery Critical Assets & Recovery Procedures (High Level)

Critical Asset	RTO/RPO	Threat	Prevention Strategy	Response Strategy	Recovery Strategy
ERP System	4 Hours / 2 Hours	Server Failure	■ Secured Server Room ■ Secondary Server ■ UPS	■ Switch to backup server ■ Validate UPS operational	■ Repair primary server ■ Transistion back to primary connection or server
Web Portal	2 Hours / 1 Hour	Loss of online sales portal	■ Failure Alerts ■ Redundant Internet Circuits ■ Redundant Web Server	■ Switch to backup internet connection or web server ■ Verify database and payment connections	■ Repair internet connection or web server ■ Transition back to primary connection or server

Figure 14.2 High-Level Procedure View

As noted in the above table, we segment the collected information by specific critical systems and vet and enter their respective RTO/RPO times. This depiction is just the beginning of creating a mature Disaster Recovery Plan and consists of listing critical assets,

RTO/RPO times, business-impacting current threats and the strategies for prevention and for responding to and then recovering from the event. This high-level table is light on details; more in-depth procedures come later when each one of these assets and their threats is broken down, and we identify the specific steps for recovery and managing the asset during a continuity event.

Once you create this first stage of the DRP, business stakeholders need to review each identified critical system and think about what is required for the asset to be available during an emergency. Ideally, these dependencies are captured and understood during the BIA process. Consider these dependencies:

1. People – Which staff and contractors are required for the system? If you find there is a shortage of a specific skill set or system knowledge, you may want to look into training staff.

2. Facilities – Can the identified assets be ported into the cloud or do they need to be in a datacenter? Another issue to consider is where will the emergency staff that are part of the BCP and DRP process operate from?

3. Supporting Technology –Which supporting technologies will be required for critical assets to work such as room for the emergency equipment, HVAC, sufficient primary and secondary power, availability of rollover, and the list can go on and on. In creating this list, look at your current configurations and then think of the bare minimum that would be required for operations.

4. Data – Are there issues with the data (e.g., where the data is located, how it is backed up, and on what media)? Another requirement around data that I would suggest needs to be identified is who requires access to the data and for what purposes. Do the same people have data requirements during an emergency as during normal operations?

5. Supply Chain – Will there be a requirement for alternative suppliers for services? Identify supplier requirements and if new contracts are required, put them in place to enable the BCP activation process to be smooth and efficient with no interruption to third-party services.

After documenting and reviewing the elements listed the above, stakeholders must create the second stage of the DRP. Take the strategy of each identified critical asset and develop step-by-step procedures to recover the assets during a business continuity event. Data from the tables developed during the asset strategy sessions will be required to create the disaster recovery procedures. I will use the two assets identified in the above table and provide more in-depth information for recovery procedures.

Disaster Recovery Procedures (In-Depth)					
Critical Asset	Threat	Response Strategy	Response Action Steps	Recovery Strategy	Recovery Action Steps
ERP System	Server Failure	▪ Switch to backup server ▪ Validate UPS operational	▪ Verify server is down ▪ Verify data has been backed up and available ▪ Test backup server ▪ Roll to alternate server ▪ Load backup data ▪ Test apps and databases for accuracy	▪ Repair primary server ▪ Transition back to primary server	▪ Verify cause of server outage Install new server ▪ Test new server ▪ Install image from current server to new server ▪ Make new server the primary and put into production
Web Portal	Loss on online sales portal	▪ Switch to backup internet connection or web server ▪ Verify database and payment connections	▪ Verify web portal server down ▪ Verify backup internet connection available ▪ Test backup server ▪ Verify sales databases backups are available ▪ Transition to backup Internet connection ▪ Transition to backup web portal server ▪ Load sales databases into backup server ▪ Verify Internet connection	▪ Repair internet connection and/or web server ▪ Transition back to primary connection or server	▪ Verify cause of internet outage - speak with ISP and network team ▪ Repair internet connection ▪ Obtain new server ▪ Install new server ▪ Test new server ▪ Install image from current server to new server ▪ Make new server the primary and put into production

Figure 14.3 In-Depth recovery Procedures

The recovery procedures noted in the above table document the "response" steps to a specific threat and the "recovery" steps to return to normal operations. This stage of the DRP is the most time consuming, and the organization's IT and cybersecurity teams will be required to assist in documenting the recovery steps. Once this process is completed and reviewed by BCP and DRP team members, the overall DRP plan can be updated to include this information. The structure of the DRP plan itself will be very similar to the CISO's Incident Response Plan and will contain:

- *Introduction* – the purpose and scope of the disaster recovery plan

- *Roles and Responsibilities* – including contact information for team members

- *Incident Response* – summary of the incident response plan and reference to the full document

- *Plan Activation* – activation and communication matrix, including specific guidelines to activate the full DRP or BCP.

- *Procedures* – typically a RACI matrix to break out who will respond to recover specific critical assets and the documented procedures for these assets

- *Addendums* –include inventories, network maps, contracts, service-level agreements, and any other supporting documentation that may be needed by the team to execute the DRP

> **Chapter 14 Key Point and Action Item 4**
>
> The adage is that the devil is in the details. This adage has never been truer than when you are preparing the detailed runbooks needed to recover processes and systems after a significant disruption. You are often executing procedures rarely if ever run in combination and by people who never witnessed the small tweaks needed to launch successfully.
>
> **You should add recovery strategies and detailed step-by-step recovery instructions for processes and assets in your recovery repository.**

As we finish the discussion on the disaster recovery plan, I believe it is evident that much of the data and processes here will aid the CISO in developing a contextual view of business operations and assets that are considered essential to protect. In assisting the Business Continuity Program Manager with the development of the BCP and DRP, the CISO will have access to much of the required business unit data they will need for their risk management and security programs.

The BCP and DRP programs that reach throughout the business are like the CISO's enterprise security program. All three programs can profoundly influence operations and strategic business decisions. I feel having a mature BCP and DRP initiative within the company dramatically benefits the CISO, their security team, and their ability to address risk during critical cyber incidents.

Now to our final question: *"What value does the CISO's security program receive from the organization's Business Continuity Plan and its associated Disaster Recovery Plan?"*

Leveraging the BCP and DRP for Cyber Resilience

In our final discussion, we will look at the value a CISO can retrieve from the data contained in healthy BCP and DRP programs. In my own experience, I have found time and again that being part of the development process for these strategic functions was critical for me to understand what was needed by my company's business units to do their jobs and be successful. I used this insight to develop policies that directly supported my company's goals, and it influenced how I distributed my security suite and its controls throughout the company's enterprise networks.

To understand the worth of this data to a CISO, remember that the BCP is an organization-wide program that encompasses people and processes and their responses to an emergent event. The DRP, on the other hand, also contains data on people and processes, but it includes a third critical element. This third element is technology, and the DRP focuses on the strategic processes required to return this technology and its services to operational order. As you can imagine, these programs are intertwined, and many of their work-flows feed one another. From a high-level view, the BCP anticipates business disruptions and plans for the rapid restoration of business operations through the DRP process.

Both programs contain extensive information that can be used by the CISO to enhance security operations. The core element of the BCP program is the previously mentioned Business Impact Analysis (BIA). The business should have a BIA for each revenue-generating service or technology, and this analysis should focus on the people and processes for each critical revenue asset.

Some of the essential information the BIA provides is the list of assets that have strategic importance to the business, and the amount of revenue that can be lost over a given time if the asset or service is impacted by a cyber-related incident. This relationship of revenue loss to a cyber disruption event is crucial. I have used this information to make a case to include CISOs in the BCP and DRP process. This type of "impact to revenue" data can also be used to help quantify risk baselines for each asset and assist CISOs in justifying their chosen level of security protection to mitigate these identified threats to revenue.

Having a security program and its risk management controls focused at this level of granularity will include working closely with the business owners of these assets. The CISO's established relationships with their peers in the corporation's various business units will be crucial during the process of scrutinizing and understanding the BCP and DRP data. From personal experience, as I was vetting this type of data I would speak with my stakeholders and ask them questions from the BCP and DRP data-sets to see how current the information was and if anything had changed.

If I found discrepancies, I would report them to ensure the BCP and DRP were current because this data helped me and my security teams understand what hardware, software, data, work processes, sites, and intellectual property were essential to the company's business operations. After working with my peers, I would then use the network and data-flow maps to identify where the critical assets were in the overlapping maze of my businesses' sprawling network infrastructure. Once I had that understanding, I then proceeded to segment the networks into more-defensible sites and restructured my security suite and its associated controls so that I had visibility on how these critical assets were accessed.

I also used this data to build an addendum to my Incident Response Plan (IRP) that matched vital assets to the business unit owner. This addendum assisted my IRP team when responding to an intrusion event. We understood the criticality of the asset as well as the impact on revenue from a breach. We also knew who to contact for assistance as we triaged the incident.

Chapter 14 Key Point and Action Item 5

Business processes connect people to customers, tools, and outcomes and form the backbone of value delivery. Expertise matters and having the right people engaged in critical decision-making saves valuable time and can help avoid severe errors.

You should establish and then record in your recovery repository the owners and subject matter experts for all the processes and assets so that you can reach the right people when needed to recover your critical business processes.

I hope I have provided some insight into the links between the business continuity and disaster recovery operations and the enterprise's security programs. I recommend that CISOs be involved in the development and management of these programs, not only because the data is critical to them but because the modern CISO must develop business acumen to be successful. This contextual awareness of their company's business operations and cybersecurity's impact on it is better understood through the information and processes contained in their company's Business Continuity Program and Disaster Recovery Program.

Summary

For Chapter 14, we began our discussion by asking these questions:

- What is a Business Continuity Plan (BCP) and what are the steps to create one?
- What critical components should a Disaster Recovery Plan (DRP) include to be effective?
- What value does the CISO's security program receive from the organization's Business Continuity Plan and its associated Disaster Recovery Plan?

Various catastrophes, such as the bombing of the Oklahoma City Federal Building and the September 11, 2001 terrorist attack, have pushed us to make sweeping changes in national defense posture and pass legislation mandating redundancy in whole industries. But the rarity of catastrophes and the tendency for them to affect some disproportionally compared to others, perhaps geographically or by industry, often causes us to discount the potential for impact to ourselves. The indiscriminate nature of cybercrime has leveled the playing field so to speak. As the chief resilience officer for many organizations, it is the CISO's job to make sure recovery becomes a fait accompli.

In closing, we leave you with these five key points and next steps:

1. We have suggested various actions that are focused on learning about your environment at a deep level. We've asked you to complete a business impact analysis (BIA), learn about your critical business processes, take inventory of your critical assets, and assess your talent. All of this is in support of becoming a more resilient organization. **You should aggregate your BIA and your process, asset and talent inventories into a repository and add recovery prioritization and sequencing information that would be used in recovery operations.**

2. We have evolved from a time when hardware failures, coding errors and natural disasters were the only drivers of business continuity and disaster recovery plans. The means to disrupt, damage and profit remotely have added an important dimension to recovery planning. **You should add a strategy for protecting your backups and your recovery plans from a cyberattack. This strategy will help ensure both resilience for your operations and**

make your organization less susceptible to the ransomware family of attacks.

3. Risk is the business of the CISO. Risk informs how the CISO directs the security resources of the organization and risk informs how the organization prepares for adverse events to ensure resilience across the lines of business. **You should update and integrate the risk assessments you have done as part of your Chapter 4 third-party risk assessment and your Chapter 7 risk management actions into your process and asset recovery repository.**

4. The adage is that the devil is in the details. This adage has never been truer than when you are preparing the detailed runbooks needed to recover processes and systems after a significant disruption. You are often executing procedures rarely if ever run in combination and by people who never witnessed the small tweaks needed to launch successfully. **You should add recovery strategies and detailed step-by-step recovery instructions for processes and assets in your recovery repository.**

5. Business processes connect people to customers, tools, and outcomes and form the backbone of value delivery. Expertise matters and having the right people engaged in critical decision-making saves valuable time and can help avoid severe errors. **You should establish and then record in your recovery repository the owners and subject matter experts for all the processes and assets so that you can reach the right people when needed to recover your critical business processes.**

The key points and next steps we have outlined in this chapter are focused on building up your institutional knowledge about the core business processes of your organization. It is hard work, but we believe it will pay off as your organization becomes more resilient by being less prone to disruption and more rapidly recovers from adverse events.

Chapter 15 – Incident Response and Communication

Introduction

Incident response is the most visible function for a typical CISO. For good or for ill, it is the primary way CISOs are judged. Beyond the immediate impact of demonstrating the organization's resilience to customers, management and employees, how an organization deals with incident response says a lot about its culture. Does the organization recognize the challenges and opportunities of doing business in the twenty-first century? Does management invest in and support the security hygiene and preparation it takes to protect long-term value delivery while competing in a digital world?

Bill starts by focusing the reader on the training and preparation that must be done, specifically triage training for the security team and situational training for the whole organization. Quickly recognizing and responding to incidents can be the difference between a minor disruption and a major breach. Communicating effectively during an incident is also critical to maintaining the confidence of the organization's many stakeholders, and preparation is key to success here as well.

Matt reminds us of the ongoing yet still emerging convergence of information technology (IT) and operational technology (OT). The ability of errors in code or network misconfigurations to contribute to the physical harm done to a person or group adds a new dynamic to data protection. In addition to increased technical complexity, this now forces a level of due care that is new to many industries. Just as interactions between the physical and digital world are exploding in scope, so too are people becoming more aware of the peril of being an open book to merchants and criminals and demanding greater say over and greater protection for the use of their online identities.

Gary shows how organizations can demonstrate value in their incident response program by first understanding that the business must be the focus. Once the organization realizes that incident response is about staying in business, not playing spy-catcher and whack-a-hacker, investing in incident response becomes investing in the organization, its customers, and its people. He then walks us through building the incident response program and measuring its success.

Some of the questions the authors used to frame their thoughts for this chapter include:

- What is the business value of an Incident Response Program (IRP)?
- What are the processes to create an IRP?
- What are some methods to measures the effectiveness of an organization's IRP and why is it important to the CISO?

Incident Response and Incident Communications – Bonney

> "We've repeatedly discussed the importance of setting the right tone at the top and cannot overstate the case for incident response. People are busy. The people you will need to ensure the continuity of operations are in the highest demand."

Throughout Volumes 1 and 2, we have moved back and forth between what we consider to be the entire lifecycle of cybersecurity activities and the individual constituent processes that make up that full lifecycle. We've tried to give readers a holistic view of a comprehensive cybersecurity program. We have also done several deep dives into specific important processes, describing at length the steps we recommend you take along with the reasoning behind those actions so that new and aspiring CISOs might have a blueprint for how to build a functioning cybersecurity program for their organization. In the last chapter, I outlined how some of the chapters in Volume 1 and Volume 2 fit together and established the prerequisites between the various processes.

Here in Chapter 15, we're covering incident response and incident communications. Experienced CISOs understand that response and communications go together like a hand and glove and they also understand how the preparation we've been describing provides the essential foundation to enable the organization to detect, respond to, and recover from cybersecurity incidents.

While responding to incidents is not the only thing we do in the cybersecurity discipline, it is critically important, and our management judges us based on how well we do it because it is so visible. The ability to quickly and correctly recover from cyber incidents has direct implications for the organization's resilience and may directly impact the balance sheet. So, with that as preamble, let's break incident response down into its discrete phases: prepare, detect, contain, eradicate, recover, and improve. Each phase has its corresponding communication requirements. The graphic below (15.1) depicts these steps as a familiar "virtuous cycle."

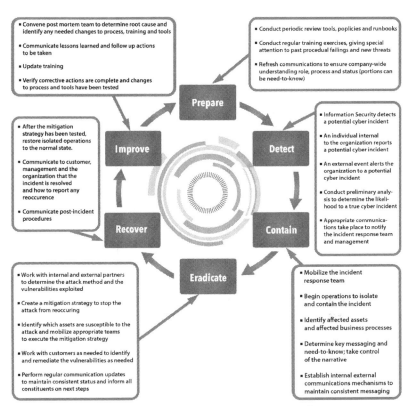

Figure 15.1 Incident Response Virtuous Cycle

Much of the previous 14 chapters have dealt with preparing for the inevitable incidents. Whether this means knowing what is in your asset inventory, knowing which critical business processes are most vital to your organization, or developing your human network, most of the chapters in our two books are designed to prepare you for this role. Here in Chapter 15, we'll tackle prepare, detect, contain, and eradicate; in Chapter 16 we'll deal with recovery and resuming operations ("recover" in the graphic above), and in Chapter 17 we'll address forensics and post-mortem ("improve" in the graphic above).

Preparation is Key

Specific now to the tasks directly associated with incident response, preparation consists of the following key activities:

- Create and train the response teams to recognize issues and to respond to the issues reported.

To be able to respond to incidents or potential incidents as they occur, the organization must identify and train one or more individuals and empower them to take appropriate action. This training includes how to triage potential incidents to determine the likelihood and potential severity and who to call (management, vendors and partners, law enforcement) to escalate incidents that they are not able to resolve on their own. They should know the key data elements to capture when cataloging or escalating an event as this information will be vital at later stages of incident response. As you are developing your full incident response plan, continually identify and update the requirements for data capture. The makeup of this team and how to contact them should be readily visible to the entire organization.

- Train the entire organization to recognize and report issues that may constitute a cyber incident.

This training is analogous to the security mantra: "If you see something, say something." Many people are afraid or at least hesitant to raise an issue because of the perceived risk that what they surface might turn out to be benign. They might wish not to distract precious resources from more critical tasks, or they might be embarrassed to raise a false alarm.

When training the organization to play the frontline role, make sure they know the basics, so they have confidence in what they report, but give them an easy way to raise the alarm without having to perform a technical categorization to submit the report. Asking a non-technical person to properly label what they have seen as malware or phishing or anything for that matter might be intended to help information security respond more rapidly, but it might have the unintended effect of scaring off the person before they even report the issue.

In addition to training for recognizing and reporting incidents, you should conduct regular tabletop exercises with representatives of the entire organization and the response teams to make sure that book learning and lecture can be put to use in real life scenarios. Make sure that representatives of the entire organization are rotated through training to avoid the trap of having departments "assign" the training to junior people who aren't truly representative of their groups.

In addition to testing process and ensuring that individuals know how to respond, maintain the tools you use in every aspect of incident response, and test the tools as well. Take corrective action for problems with the tools and processes.

- Prepare communications templates in advance of any incident.

  These communications templates should identify for whom the message is intended, what to communicate, who will publish, and under whose authority. This preparation might not seem critical to handle in advance, but when the user community is demanding answers via social media or some other public forum is being used to discuss or amplify the issue, your ability to respond rapidly can de-escalate the issue and allow your organization to regain the narrative.

  In addition to the value of pre-packaged templates with ready-to-go messages, identifying the authorizing party in advance can both save time and ensure the right messages are going to the right constituents at the right time with the full support of the team that needs to assist. Depending on the nature if the issue these activities could include handling the press, shareholders, customers, or employees.

To avoid giving you three complete breakdowns of the key steps in incident response, I'm going to focus the remainder of my contribution to this topic on two concepts: governance and communication.

Communication is Essential

I am going to frame this within the constructs of five key activities that will help the organization provide good governance for its incident response plans, including key roles for executive leadership and the board of directors, and the corresponding communication objectives within those activities. These key governance activities are:

- Adequately staff, equip, and train the organization to deal with cyber incidents.

  Balancing resource needs across competing objectives is a critical function of the board and a key requirement for effective governance. The board should take a lead role in ensuring that the organization is prepared to rapidly recover in the event of a disruption caused by cyber incidents and validate the preparations made to ensure business continuity. At the least, this would include allocating time on the board agenda to review plans and ask probing questions. For particularly complex organizations it may make sense to subject the plans to audit review. The point is not to be prescriptive about which steps the board should take, but to be clear there is a wide array of options and it is paramount that the board exercise its fiduciary duty to ensure the continuity of the organization.

- Provide guidance for the communication plans and escalation paths.

Avoid the temptation of a cursory review to ensure that you've merely checked all the boxes on the plan template. The audit team can do that. Management's job is to make sure that the communication plans are adequate to deal with the situation, that they involve the right people in decision making, and that they deal with key concerns for employees, customers, shareholders, and concerned public officials such as law enforcement and regulators.

The escalation path is critical to being able to bring the situation under control rapidly. Frontline personnel need to know who to call, and under what circumstances to make that call. Senior management must ensure that the escalation path includes people at the correct level and with the proper skillset to make critical decisions for responding. The early choices for containment and communications are the most important. At a crucial point, the skillset needed to make necessary containment decisions will give way to the skillset required to decide on appropriate recovery options, such as restoring in place or switching to alternate resources, such as a warm data center or temporary facility.

Public officials are also part of the escalation path. While there are regulatory conditions for breach notification that come with the threat of sanction for not meeting the requirements, there is usually enough time between the onset and conclusion of an incident and the close of the notification period. The more immediate need is to involve law enforcement at the right point if there is reasonable suspicion that a crime is being or has been committed and to involve regulators as needed depending on the nature of the incident and the industry. How do you know what the right point is to escalate to law enforcement or to notify regulators? Involve them in the preparation activities, discuss with your human network and your legal counsel, and consult resources in related trade organizations. The key is to plan for it in advance so that junior staff is not trying to figure out what to do in the heat of the moment.

One final thought on escalation deals with how and when to involve legal counsel in both the preparation and the incident itself. There are several reasons for having a representative from your legal group participate in the planning activities, developing communication plans, and being part of the escalation path. The primary objective is to minimize the organization's legal liability and maintain the organization's flexibility to participate in law enforcement actions or to pursue legal remedies. The legal group can:

o Identify the conditions that will trigger the notification of or escalation to law enforcement as well as the format of that notification
o Participate in crafting communications to minimize the organization's future liability
o Advise on contractual and regulatory implications and obligations of various containment and recovery options, such as the removal of files or the discontinuation (temporary or not, complete or not) of services
o Determine when it may be prudent to conduct deliberations about some or all of these options under the protection of privilege

It should go without saying that you will need to coordinate all communications to law enforcement or outside investigative agencies with your legal representative.

• Signal the importance of the preparation work to the rest of the organization by allocating time for themselves and their direct staff to participate in both the planning and the drills.

We've repeatedly discussed the importance of setting the right tone at the top and cannot overstate the case when preparing for incident response. People are busy and the people you will need to help ensure the continuity of operations are perhaps in the highest demand. It sends a positive signal to the organization if the senior leadership team is actively participating in and holding themselves and their peers and their respective teams accountable for ensuring the viability of the plans and making the identified improvements during the drills.

Besides the tone at the top, it is also imperative that the critical decision makers are aware of and trained in their role during an incident. For example, Sales and Customer Support are essential to decisions about service interruptions. They should be involved in establishing the criteria for decision making and be part of the escalation path as needed. Defining the role that each member of the senior leadership team will play during an incident is a crucial planning objective.

Each member of the senior leadership team should understand their role in preparation activities, communication plans, escalation paths, and decision making. Cross training is also essential. Just as team members in all disciplines get sick and take vacations, so too you should assume that senior leaders are subject to unexpected unavailability. Having a primary and secondary decision maker for each resolution that might require a decision by a member of the senior leadership team and training the secondary decision maker as well as the primary decision maker are critical.

- Marshal external resources from key partners and suppliers to make sure the preparation includes the entire ecosystem, including key customers.

Cyber incidents can involve assets associated not only with internal, back-office processes but often with customer-facing assets as well as assets that either require or contribute to partner networks and your supply chain or your customer's supply chain. For industries that are part of the nation's critical infrastructure, this could also involve government agencies and other partners in related companies.

The senior leadership team can help drive the engagement with partners and ensure that resources and priorities across organizational boundaries are aligned. For complex multi-partner integrations, leadership should consider information sharing and where appropriate joint drills between the organizations. This can prove vital to establishing the relationships necessary to respond appropriately to any incident.

It is also essential to work with key customers in preparation for any cyber incident. While some customers are more important from a revenue or reputation perspective, all customers should understand how you will communicate status, next steps, temporary service options, and expectations for service recovery. Larger, enterprise customers might have dedicated processes for informing them of incidents which may kick off formal response plans for them as well. Smaller customers or consumers may not be able to devote attention to your recovery plans until an incident impact them.

Your communication plans should take this into account and use all available options, from formal, designated points of contact to social media. Know your customers and know how to reach them. Involving your customers in your planning can also be an important part of their incident response plan and may be a requirement for them depending on the industry. In addition to helping them meet their regulatory obligations, you will be building their trust in you as a reliable partner.

- Dedicate the time and ensure the discipline to prioritize the improvements identified by testing.

Each time we conduct a drill or review a plan, we gain valuable insight into what we do well and where we might have issues. Every time there is a cyber incident, we become aware of how our current defenses are performing and whether there are gaps in our defenses. It is critical that we act on those insights and awareness and continue to make improvements to our incident response plans and our communication plans.

As we are conducting the drills, we need to evaluate whether the policies and run books reflect the current system state. Systems evolve, and we need to make sure our recovery procedures are keeping pace. We need to make sure that individuals who lack the same level of institutional knowledge as the people who wrote the policies and run books can follow the instructions, interpret the data, and make the right decisions. If not, the documentation must be updated, and the training repeated.

That last action is critical: once documentation is updated, repeat the exercise. Don't fall into the trap of relieving participants too early in the improvement phase. There is a lot of room for interpretation when responding to issues and gaps you've uncovered.

We can say the same for communication plans. Each time they are tested as part of drills or in live incidents, you should evaluate their effectiveness. Were the right people notified? Did they understand the notification and respond predictably? For example, if you informed your customers that they should switch to an alternate method for obtaining service and this caused a flood of customer support contacts, perhaps you were not effective in how you communicated the instructions to your customers. Subject internal communications to the same tests: did people respond the way you expected them to when you executed your communication plan?

When following escalation paths, did people respond in the manner expected within the time frame required? If not, why not? Were there staffing problems you didn't anticipate? Were the escalation paths bypassed because of a "heat of the moment" decision? What can you learn from that? Is there additional training that needs to be done? Do different people need to be empowered to make decisions? What can you learn from how the organization responds to an incident and leverage that in the future?

In addition to policies, run books, and communication plans, there are many tools (for instance, hardware and software) that the incident response team will rely on while working on an incident. These tools have specific purposes, and during drills and live events you should be continually assessing function and coverage. Function meaning you should determine whether the tools function correctly and whether they are up to date. Coverage meaning you should evaluate whether you have coverage for the entire infrastructure supporting your business processes.

To fix any gaps you discovered in the function and coverage will likely require prioritizing time to make any updates and may involve setting aside a budget for purchasing software licenses, hardware devices, or other technical capabilities, such as bandwidth or service plans. While it is always the case that cross-functional priorities need to be balanced, there are often more needs than there are resources. Without offering an opinion on whether any particular purchase should be prioritized over another, consider three additional points regarding gaps in your ability to respond to incidents:

- o Your ability as an organization to contain cyber incidents, recover quickly, and resume regular operations speaks directly to your resilience and business continuity
- o Cyber criminals are constantly improving their ability to penetrate our defenses and it is likely that at some point, probably sooner than you would like, they will discover the gaps you have in coverage and capability
- o A failure to respond to knowledge of gaps in capability and coverage may jeopardize your cyber liability insurance coverage or prove detrimental to your legal defense should you be subject to civil or government legal action

Chapter 15 Key Point and Action Item 1

It is difficult to predict how many challenges will be presented to you when a live incident is underway. What you do know is that time will be a precious commodity and resources will be severely limited. Key decision makers will be engaged on multiple fronts. Keeping your various stakeholders informed should be a high priority because not adding to the problem will be a critical concern.

You should create a list of the potential communication events that might arise during a cyber incident. These might include disruptions to product deliveries, closure of facilities, and estimated time of service restoration. Build a template for each potential event and obtain pre-approval so that in a crisis, fundamental messaging is ready for use.

In the next two essays on incident response, my co-authors will dive deeply into the tools and techniques necessary to respond to cyber incidents. Governance and communication are two overarching requirements for providing the correct mindset and posture to create effective programs that will allow you to quickly recover and resume operations, perhaps preventing some adverse events along the way.

Incident Response – It's All About Muscle Memory – Stamper

There are few, if any, security processes that will be more impactful to the CISO's success than incident response. I'm not in the habit of disagreeing with renowned physicists, but I will take exception with Niels in this instance. There are three things we can predict with certainty: death, taxes, and that our organizations will be the subject of cyber-attacks. If we have to anticipate one event that every CISO will confront, it is that he or she will be at the fulcrum point of a cybersecurity incident impacting their organization.

Our competencies in designing and overseeing our incident response practices will be one of the critical determinants of the success of our security programs. If there is one process that requires ongoing attention, oversight, and preparation, it is the incident response process. This focus is all about "muscle memory." The more attention and focus placed on incident response, the better.

IT and OT Convergence: The Game Has Changed

I believe we are entering a new era in our profession where the quality and efficacy of our security programs will have more critical repercussions than ever before. Specifically, given the convergence of traditional IT and operational technology (OT), the impact on safety resulting from our actions has never been more significant. We will see both physical harm and the loss of life resulting from cyber-attacks, if this has not already occurred.[17] Further, we will see liability claims against our organizations when we are negligent in our security and IT practices. Our world has fundamentally changed. Negligence and its implications are now part of our cybersecurity vocabulary.

Establishing negligence requires the following:
- **Duty**: Given the number of regulations – both domestic and international – that require comprehensive security

---

[17] Independent Security Evaluators were able to show a number of compromises resulting from cyber-attacks that could kill hospital patients: https://www.securityevaluators.com/hospitalhack/.

and privacy programs to be established, documenting a *legal duty of care* related to our security programs is all but guaranteed.[18]

- **Breach of Duty**: With frameworks and standards establishing specific functions, capabilities, responsibilities, and the controls required for security programs, we've effectively moved from the cover of discretionary practices to prescriptive requirements and obligations. The excuse that we did not know of or were not aware of an obligation no longer holds water.

- **Causation**: When an individual is harmed or injured as a result of a security patch not deployed timely, or a configuration setting provisioned incorrectly, there is likely causation.

- **Damages**: With the conditions mentioned above, establishing a case for damages, e.g., liability and settlement awards are likely.

Effectively, we are entering an era of increased liability and financial exposure resulting from the cybersecurity practices of our organizations and our programs specifically.

We will also witness other significant changes resulting from this OT and IT convergence. Historically, software manufacturers sold or, more appropriately licensed, their software with near-absolute disclaimers of warranty. The software is typically licensed "AS IS" and "WITH ALL FAULTS." The Disclaimer of Warranty clauses found in most licensing agreements will also likely convey that there is no warranty that the software is free of defects or is suitable for any particular purpose.

Grossly overstated, we license software with little to no product liability exposure for the manufacturer. Moreover, limitations on liability further reduce the software industry's financial exposure. At present, the software we use to run our organizations is laden with defects and flaws that challenge our efforts to secure our organizations. Worse, we have limited to no recourse. These conditions will change. And this change will produce huge impacts across multiple industries.

For manufacturers, product liability has been a significant risk and an impetus to focus on quality processes. As an example, manufacturers

---

[18] As we discussed in Volume 1 of the CISO Desk Reference Guide, we should not bury CISOs deep in the organizational structure. CISOs need to be able to convey the risks associated with the organization's security practices in everyday business terms to executive management and the board. Ultimately, the board and executive management are accountable for the "duty of care" over their organizations, including the funding and resourcing of the security program.

in the automotive industry are routinely sued based on liability claims. Japanese manufacturer Takata has been at the center of a massive airbag recall that ultimately resulted in the company filing for bankruptcy. Each year, the American Bar Association highlights some of the more prominent product liability cases, including a 2016/2017 case against Tesla related to purported software flaws in their Model X and Model S cars.[19] Tesla is claiming that it has no legal duty to create a fail-safe car. Nevertheless, Tesla actively solicits vulnerability reporting related to their vehicles.[20]

What we are witnessing is the significant, early change to "product liability" associated with software. It's my opinion that the software industry's ability to hide behind disclaimers of warranty will ebb in short order as cases surface where individuals have been physically harmed or killed due to poor quality software deployed on operational technology. One could argue, with techniques such as threat modeling and security by design principles, that these vulnerabilities could have been anticipated and addressed before being released to production.

In short, when someone dies because of poor code, the game has changed. If there's one thing the U.S. does well, it's that we sue. We sue with the best of them. We are likely entering an extremely litigious era where the manufacturers of products and software are in the crosshairs of class action attorneys. Our security programs could also be the target of these lawsuits.

These realities have a couple of important implications for our organizations. One is less dramatic than the other. First, when software manufacturers and organizations are held liable for software defects, there will be an inflationary event – software manufacturers will likely raise prices to address their financial exposure to product liability cases. Second, and at the heart of this chapter, how our organizations deal with security flaws – and the resulting incidents – will become the fodder of legal actions, media coverage, and the intense focus of the board of directors.

The bottom line is that if incident response has been a process you have put off until next quarter or delegated to other members of your team, it's time to bring incident response front and center and make it a top, if not the top, priority of your security program.

Let's take a look at the components of good incident response programs. To do this, we need to make some assumptions that will

---

[19] Here are details related to this case:
http://www.abajournal.com/news/article/tesla_responds_to_lawsuit_by_claiming_it_has_no_duty_to_design_a_failsa.

[20] https://www.tesla.com/about/legal#security-vulnerability-reporting-policy

provide meaningful context relative to our incident response efforts. First and foremost, an incident will happen, and it will happen when the organization is least prepared to address the consequences. Invariably, an incident will take place when you or key members of your team are out of the office either after hours or on vacation. Cybersecurity incidents rarely happen when you have your full team trained with appropriate resources and during normal business hours. Anticipate that incidents will happen at the most inopportune time.

Another critical assumption is that the incident will involve infrastructure that you do not directly protect (e.g., shadow IT or from a service provider) but you will be held accountable for the consequences. Lastly, assume that the incident will impact a high-value, material business process for your organization. Bottom line, expect and plan for the worse. Cybersecurity incidents can be life-impacting and career-ending if not handled well. Now that we've raised our anxiety levels, let's get to work.

Here are some critical elements of a successful incident response program that you will want to validate and document. As a general rule, you should prepare much of what is described below in advance. Stated differently, don't wait for an incident to occur to start this work.

Incident Response Is a Team Sport

Too frequently, we think of incident response exclusively as a cybersecurity or IT discipline. Nothing could be further from the truth. Incident response is an organization-wide process that impacts nearly all departments. The CISO and the IT teams will be focused on the technical elements of the response, but there are other key participants. It's important that these other stakeholders are aware of their roles and are trained to handle those functions that are their responsibility. CISOs should determine collaboratively with other stakeholders who should be engaged in the process and document their functions in a clear RACI matrix.

Some likely participants would include the following:

- **Human Resources**: HR may be required to deal with a rogue employee or other insider threats as well as communicating status to frontline employees if the incident warrants this level of communication. HR teams are also typically responsible for overseeing training programs for their organizations and will likely have a role ensuring that incident response training is adequately addressed and evaluated for effectiveness.

- **Legal Counsel**: Counsel may be required to notify regulators, law enforcement, or other external parties, notably when the incident involves the exfiltration or loss of personally identifiable information (PII), protected health information (PHI), or intellectual property (IP) that impacts national defense or other critical sectors. External counsel may be used to contract third-party resources, such as those that handle crisis communications or forensics, in order to invoke attorney-client privilege.

- **Corporate Communications / Public Relations**: Corporate communications may be called upon to draft and disseminate communications to the media and other external entities. Depending upon the circumstances, they may serve as the primary voice of the organization, communicating updates and status to consumers and other affected parties.

- **Line of Business / Department Heads**: Colleagues in various lines of business or departments are critical players in the incident response process. They are typically more aware of the impacts to operations than others and offer valuable insight as to what to base the response in this context. These colleagues will also be a significant source of ground truth, institutional memory on key participants in a process, as well as vendors and suppliers impacted and the cause of the incident. Many of these colleagues may have also previously contracted third-party services and other forms of shadow IT, bypassing traditional IT assessment and evaluation of these providers. Their engagement in incident response planning and defining response priorities should not be overlooked or underestimated in terms of its importance to this process.

- **Executive Management**: The executive team plays a critical role in establishing the tone at the top for the organization and ultimately what the appropriate level of risk tolerance should be. Executive management may be called up to authorize and fund additional resources should they be required and may serve as the core public communicator for external notifications (e.g., for those incidents that involve significant consumer-related data).

Clearly, given the pervasive impacts of an incident, it's imperative that the CISO widen the circle of the concerned relative to the process. Let's dig deeper into these impacts.

Know Your Obligations

Beyond building the team, the CISO should document and know both contractual and regulatory obligations related to incidents. The European Union's General Data Protection Regulation (GDPR) requires notification to the data protection authority within 72 hours of a breach. U.S. state-specific breach notification laws also mandate actions and timeframes.

CISOs need to be aware of the organization's obligations to notify regulators, state attorney generals, and consumers when incidents involving PII or PHI occur. [21] CISOs should meet with their organization's legal counsel to validate these obligations. Breach notification clauses are becoming more commonplace in service agreements, so the CISO should also be aware about whether their organization is required to notify clients as part of an existing agreement.

Oddly, these obligations may be a benefit to the CISO's program. In documenting these requirements, the CISO may determine that he or she does not have the resources or infrastructure to fulfill these breach notification requirements adequately. Surface this risk to legal as well

---

[21] Reference Article 33 of the GDPR for notification requirements: http://www.eugdpr.org/. See also the National Conference of State Legislatures summary of US state breach laws: http://www.ncsl.org/research/telecommunications-and-information-technology/security-breach-notification-laws.aspx.

as your executive team. Given these obligations, they may support or fund required resources – notably around those technologies that help to detect nefarious activity within our networks and applications and among our users. Should these concerns be surfaced, and the executive management team does not address them adequately, which is fortunately or unfortunately their prerogative, you have at least established accountability.

Determine and Validate Response Priorities

This is where collaboration with other stakeholders in the organization – notably executive management and department heads – is critical. No organization has unlimited resources, staff, and infrastructure to support comprehensive security. Effectively, the CISO cannot protect all processes, all applications, all infrastructure, and all users equally. We need to determine and validate which processes and operations are fundamentally most valuable to our organization. This validation is all about priorities. As a result of this review, there will be processes that we just cannot protect with the same level of attention and focus as others. You cannot love all servers and networks equally.

CISOs should review the organization's current business impact analysis (BIA) to determine which processes have the highest criticality and impact to the business (typically measured in MAD and RPO/RTO). The CISO should also validate this understanding with executive management and key line-of-business stakeholders to ensure this is an accurate representation of the organization's priorities and risk tolerances.

With these criticalities established and the dependencies associated with these operations and processes documented, the CISO should leverage one of the most powerful tools in his or her toolbox, threat modeling. CISOs should have their teams conduct threat modeling exercises on the more critical or high-priority operations, processes, applications, and infrastructure within their organization.

Threat modeling will indicate where there are inherent weaknesses in these systems that the organization values most. Further, threat modeling will also provide contextualized indicators of compromise (IOCs) that can inform the security and IT staff and make them more effective in their monitoring of this infrastructure. Threat modeling offers a common set of expectations and understandings related to applications communicated in STRIDE and DREAD assessments. Your team can leverage threat modeling to validate security requirements and expectations across those high-priority environments.[22]

Prioritizing incident responses is a nuanced effort. Historically, we think of incident response as an effort to contain and isolate a compromised device, server, application, or network. The reality is more intertwined, especially now that OT has come into scope. The operational context derived from the BIA and the discussions with colleagues across the organization will highlight this. For organizations that deliver healthcare or are involved in manufacturing or other operationally-intensive industries, isolation and containment may bring down a process where availability is frankly more important than the compromised state of a given component.

In the case of healthcare, a decision to contain or isolate a system could result in the loss of life. If an application is pulled that is currently in use for a procedure a doctor is performing, this may undermine the effectiveness of that procedure and place the patient's safety in jeopardy. Ransomware is another way to consider this nuance. Beyond the operational and financial impacts that ransomware presents, one of its more severe consequences is that our core systems are unavailable until they are restored, or we pay the ransom (something I would discourage). Knowing which of the following attributes takes precedence in response is key: confidentiality, integrity, availability, privacy or safety. Depending on the context at hand, these may need to be ordered and prioritized.

Based on input from key stakeholders of the organization, the CISO needs to understand and document the response priorities at the point when a compromise occurs for a given system. Some systems will be more impacted by integrity and confidentiality than others. Financial systems are a case in point. Responses focused on maintaining integrity are likely more in order. For other operationally-focused systems, availability may be the highest priority. CISOs and CIOs should not assume they know what these priorities are. Gather this information through assessment, discussion, and ongoing validation with colleagues outside of the security and IT departments. When in doubt, ask, and then document that understanding. Validate frequently.

The engagement of law enforcement may also impact response priorities. Many organizations will justifiably engage the FBI (or more likely, the Bureau will be the entity doing the notification) when they find an indication of compromise for their organization. It's important to recognize that the FBI's objectives may differ from those of your

---

[22] The Open Web Application Security Project (OWASP) as well as Microsoft offer valuable tools to help fast-track your threat modeling efforts if they are not already underway.

firm. Specifically, the agents assigned may be more focused on the observation of the tactics, techniques, and procedures (TTPs) of the adversary to support attribution and ultimately prosecution rather than the restoration of the system. CISOs should be prepared to understand this nuance and know the impacts on their efforts when law enforcement is engaged.

Chapter 15 Key Point and Action Item 3

The combination of integrating OT and IT along with increased regulatory and law enforcement activity and the added awareness of users of their own peril have added several new dimensions to decision making during incidence response.

You should document and communicate the intersection between OT and IT in your environment and conduct tabletop exercises to simulate the decision-making challenges across the three axes of service delivery, law-enforcement, and data protection. Repeat these drills often enough that making the hard calls between the physical, digital and regulatory realms becomes a discussion and not a point of paralysis.

Similar to the comments above about the value of knowing regulatory and contractual obligations, the CISO benefits from the discovery process required to understand the organization's response priorities. When done correctly, the CISO has a more contextualized view of the organization and a better understanding of what's deemed material and critical to the organization's operations and strategy. This knowledge produces a detailed picture of where in the organization's security infrastructure and processes there are inherent issues that require remediation.

Documenting and agreeing on response priorities for core operations, processes, and applications will also reduce ambiguity when an incident occurs. CISOs should anticipate conflict which they will need to address during this effort. Individual departments may have distinct priorities and expectations that will need to be arbitrated by senior management. Ideally, a security charter and the input of senior management, preferably the CEO, will clarify response priorities.

In many ways, and as was discussed in the previous chapter, CISOs can learn from our colleagues in business continuity. There's an ordinal relationship for system restoration when a natural disaster or other service-impacting issue occurs. Our response priorities to a cyber incident are no different. Document and validate priorities in advance. During an incident, there is rarely the luxury of time and the availability of resources to discover this detail.

Document the Obvious

It's the middle of the night, and you get one of those calls. You stumble to your home office, fire up the laptop and try to figure out what's happening. It is precisely the wrong time to look for fundamental information. CISOs and their teams should make a concerted effort to ensure that validated core documentation is readily available for all key participants in the process. There is specific information that should be readily available and agreed upon before an incident occurs, including the following:

- **Contact details of key participants**: Ensure that you and your team have the contact information (including more than just the office number) of these participants readily available. This means that your incident response plan should have embedded in it contact details including the home phone, mobile phone, alternative email, and other such contact information that will be necessary to reach key participants.

- **Contact detail and account numbers for key vendors**: If you needed to reach your ISP at 3:00 AM, would you have their contact detail readily available? Would you know your account number? Would you, or another member of your team, be authorized to request changes? During an incident is the wrong time to realize that you don't have this information readily available or that the vendor's authorized personnel and emergency contact list includes no one on your team, rendering them unable to make the changes you need to restore service or contain an issue.

  Draft a list of the most material vendors (those primarily associated with those high-priority systems described above or found in the BIA) and validate who is authorized to make changes and that all required account detail is readily available to them. Moreover, if your organization is using third parties to facilitate forensic analysis or crises communications, make sure to embed their information in your plan.

- **Escalation Matrices and Conditions**: Make sure that your incident response plan contains a clear escalation matrix that indicates the circumstances and contacts for escalations. Include alternate contacts in the matrix. If you are not reachable, who should your team contact?

- **Clarify Signal to Noise Issues**: Include a matrix that highlights the differences between events, alerts, incidents, and crises. Train your team on how to know when these conditions change (e.g., when alerts become a full-fledged incident).

- **Organizational Communications**: Your corporate communications team, assuming you have one, should pre-draft basic communiques for various potential scenarios (e.g., a data breach, or a DDoS attack that impacts availability). These drafts should be reviewed by the legal team to facilitate their finalization when an actual incident occurs. During the height of an incident, you don't want to be distracted by these requests.

- **Authorizations**: Ensure that required authorizations are pre-established and agreed to in advance. Think about scenarios that may require special approvals and validate the process to obtain these.

- **Process Workflows and Documentation**: Create a workflow diagram understandable by both your team and non-technical colleagues that shows the basic workflow in addressing an incident. Ensure that the process diagram is validated by all key participants in the process.

- **Runbooks or responses to certain types of attacks**: The threat modeling exercises that were part of your evaluation of your security operations will help serve as the basis for specific scenarios your organization may likely confront. Develop runbooks that declare what the response would be with some common attacks including:

  o Distributed Denial of Service / Denial of Service
  o Ransomware
  o Phishing / Spear phishing
  o Malware
  o Compromised Vendor or Supplier

These runbooks will become foundational to your ongoing stewardship of your incident response program. More on this below. As you and your team begin documenting the obvious, you'll find other factors and areas related to your incident response program that should be pre-determined. Your goal is to adequately document and validate as much detail as possible before an incident. Remember, during an incident, you will not have the luxury of time. *Time lost looking for information that could have been pre-determined and appropriately documented is for the benefit of the adversary and to the detriment of your organization.*

Once you collect and validate this documentation, set up a schedule to review these details and the incident response plan frequently. Ideally, this review should take place quarterly. Make sure that key members of the incident response program have both hard and soft copies of the plan available to them.

Muscle Memory is Key

As I noted at the beginning of this chapter, incident response is one of the most key processes that a CISO oversees. It's also a process that can make or break your career and have significant, even life-impacting, consequences. Incident response is serious stuff. It's critical that you and your team, including those other stakeholders and the participants in the process, exercise your organization's responses to an incident on a frequent basis.

While many standards suggest annual incident response exercises, I strongly recommend that you change the cadence to quarterly. Here is where the adage "don't let perfection stand in the way of progress" is appropriate. Incident response benefits from muscle memory. In this case, even high-level discussions about incident response will improve overall organizational preparedness and resiliency.

Charge members of your team with creating a response workshop tied to the likely scenarios addressed above. Ask them to document what the response priorities should be, who should be engaged in the effort, etc. Have them validate these understandings with other stakeholders within the organization. Your team may need to come up with this information if you and other key executives are unavailable. It's important for key members of your team to think about the impacts of an incident and what the repercussions would be on essential processes, applications, infrastructure, and users.

Bring up the incident response process in your day-to-day discussions with your team and other colleagues. One simple way to do this is to ask the following question: "What would happen if adversaries compromised this system?" These discussions, although not quite the same as a full-fledged exercise, have the benefit of raising awareness and they effectively facilitate muscle memory. The more frequent these discussions, the better.

Automate Key Functions

Don't let your team deal with complicated and detailed technical issues with manual and archaic tools and associated practices. Our teams lose too much time looking for forensic evidence during an incident. There are powerful new tools that can readily facilitate the incident response process, including the collection and evaluation of forensic evidence. Security incident response platforms should be evaluated based on the volume of incidents your organization typically faces. For many organizations, the number of alerts that go un-triaged can be alarming (no pun intended). The reasons for this dynamic are typically too few staff doing too much manual work.

Incident response platforms have important capabilities that ultimately raise the overall security preparedness of the organization and help ameliorate the orphaned alert challenge so many of us face. Specifically, many incident response tools facilitate the collection of and provide the context for forensic artifacts. They can, for example, determine if a given hash has impacted other systems, or assess the reputation of a given IP or DNS entry. This context helps to validate how extensive a given incident may be by using such artifacts (e.g., a known bad file or hash) to determine how expansive the compromise is.

These tools also provide workflows that facilitate escalation and case management. Newer incident response platforms leverage machine learning to provide guidance on appropriate next steps (including detail on specific command line actions to take based on the type of attack or the indicators of compromise that are present). Another reason to consider an incident response platform is that many of the applications include runbooks and other guidance that can dramatically improve the efficiency of a response. When evaluating these platforms, assess the level of integration the platform offers (minimally, it should integrate with your SIEM and directory services), the integration with threat intelligence platforms, and with other elements of your security architecture.

Given the importance of the incident response process to your security program, my recommendation is that CISOs for larger organizations prioritize and fast-track the adoption of an incident response platform. CISOs working at medium and smaller-sized organizations should consider these platforms as a complement to current staffing requirements or to using an MSSP that offers this functionality as part of their service. Not leveraging one of these platforms is analogous to flying without radar. The consequences could be extreme.

Incident response is seminal to security operations. Make sure that you and your extended team are well prepared to address incidents as they arise. In the next chapter, we'll discuss the implications of recovering from an incident and resuming operations. Returning to business as usual following a significant breach is typically more aspirational than reality. There are, however, strategies that can be implemented proactively to ensure that your organization is resilient when confronted with a significant breach.

Incident Response – a CISO's Best Friend – Hayslip

> "Incident response isn't about technology, it is really about business."

I want to set the stage for us. In the early morning hours, as the CISO for a global software company, you are awakened from a deep sleep by the chirping of an emergency number on your smartphone. As you proceed to talk in hushed whispers, you are informed by your managed security services provider (MSSP) that their SOC analysts are reporting an anomalous incident in your organization's primary datacenter.

The MSSP used the incident response communications tree and contacted the company network team and security liaison staff, who are now reporting they see suspicious network traffic and upon investigation have found evidence of a malware outbreak in several production servers. As you wake up and shift into troubleshooting mode, you receive more troubling information. This issue doesn't affect just a couple of servers but has manifested itself as ransomware on critical production databases. With this information, as the CISO, it's time to transition into your role as the Incident Response Team Manager and begin the activation of the company's Security Incident Response Plan.

Cybersecurity leaders today know their roles have matured and they must align their departments and security programs to the business and support its strategic goals to be successful. However, one area many organizations and CISOs still need assistance with is incident response. In 2016, SANS surveyed 591 security professionals about the state of incident response in their organizations (Bromiley 2016). There was some good news – 76% of those security professionals had dedicated internal IR teams, an increase from the SANS 2015 survey.

However, there is still much work to be done. Approximately 21% said that their time to detect malware in their networks, or "dwell time," was two to seven days, while 40% indicated that they could detect an incident in less than one day. Some other bleak statistics: malware remains the underlying cause of most reported breaches, at 69%, with unauthorized access seen as a rising menace due to attackers taking advantage of weak, outdated remote access and authentication mechanisms. This report noted that 65% of the security professionals surveyed were still dealing with a shortage of skilled personnel, and only 58% of organizations admit to regularly reviewing and updating their IR processes.

The report demonstrates that incident response, as a program, is in a state of change in organizations today and when there is a security incident, many lack the ability to lead a coordinated response to the event. I am sure there are reasons why organizations do not have formal incident response policies or documented incident response methodologies. Some companies focus on purchasing technology in the belief that when an event occurs, the purchased hardware and software will save the day. Unfortunately, they are missing a critical point – incident response isn't about technology, it is really about business.

It's About the Business

At its core, incident response is about an organization's strategy and business processes, it is tactical and will incorporate stakeholders from many departments within the company as well as external partners. Incident response is an action plan for dealing with incidents like internal and external intrusions, cybercrime, disclosure of sensitive information, or denial-of-service attacks. In typical organizations, the CISO is tasked with developing the Incident Response Plan and managing the Incident Response Team. This is why the questions we will discuss focus on the business value of your incident response, the processes to follow for an effective program, and how the CISO can measure the effectiveness of their IR program.

Cybercriminals are successfully targeting and compromising businesses of every size across all industry sectors. This ongoing digital onslaught demonstrates the need for organizations to be prepared to respond to the inevitable data breach. They should guide their response with a methodical plan designed to manage a cybersecurity incident with the goals of limiting impact to business operations, increasing the confidence of external stakeholders, and reducing recovery time and incident remediation costs. These goals mean that organizations need to require their CISOs to create an incident response program tailored to the company's strategic operations.

However, many organizations lose sight of their incident response program's strategic value. Instead, incident response documentation describing how to act in the event of a breach is forgotten and soon out of date. The documentation quickly becomes ineffective for key decision makers; too generic, and unhelpful for making critical, informed decisions. I therefore chose the first question for our discussion to be about the business value of an incident response program. As CISO, there will be times when you will need to defend the resources needed for the incident response program, and you will need to be able to describe several business cases that demonstrate the value it brings to the company and its operations.

This leads us to our first question: *"What is the business value of an Incident Response Program (IRP)?"*

Cybersecurity incidents are on the rise and now frequently headline news around the world. Many of the recent attacks have brought severe damage to organizations of all types, including governments and international nonprofits. An organization with a mature incident response program would have a methodical course of action for responding to these attacks in a fast, effective, and comprehensive manner. However, many organizations do not see incident response as a mature process. Instead, they see it as a collection of disjointed practices and procedures, thus they prefer to contract it out to third parties.

How Incident Response Adds Value

To address this, I will discuss some of the issues companies see when looking at incident response and describe several cases that highlight how incident response can provide value to an organization. As we begin, some of the contention around investing in an internal incident response program is as follows:

- *There are too many common definitions of what constitutes a cybersecurity incident.* With this wide variety of interpretations resulting in organizations adopting different views on how to manage them. Many organizations consider it difficult to address this effectively and understand the level of incident response capability they require.

  - *Response* – That is true for many companies when they first start the process of addressing incident response and allocating resources for their CISO to build an IRP. However, there are amazing references from both NIST SP 800-61r2 (NIST 2012) and ISO/IEC 27035 (ISO 2016) to begin this process, so it is not unattainable.

- *There are different sources and types of cybersecurity incidents.* Some appear to originate from minor criminal groups and produce annoying disruptions, others from major organized crime syndicates that result in business-ending events. Plus, there are so many types of cyber incidents, such as hacking, malware, or social engineering. All of this generates confusion, and organizations just want something that is manageable. Given all this, why not outsource it to a partner who specializes in incident response?

○ *Response* – There are always some incident response services that can be outsourced to a third party. With that said, the business still has accountability for how it manages its assets during a breach and must be able to answer the questions of "reasonable care." For example, did the organization implement reasonable security controls and follow industry best practices to reduce risk exposure as much as possible? If a company doesn't have an incident response program, they are likely not meeting a "reasonable care" standard.

Even if a contracted third party does the primary work for the incident response program, the business still have an incident response plan. The plan will cover communication with its partners, what resources to activate for an incident, who has overall responsibility to manage the incident, and how and when to report its findings to executive leadership. In a sea of misinformation on how to deal with an incident, an incident response program provides the business clarity to reduce the incident's impact and return business operations to normal.

• *Many organizations do not understand their state of readiness;* they lack insight into how they would respond to a cybersecurity incident. In fact, many organizations are typically not well prepared in terms of having any personnel assigned to an incident response team or providing training to grow sufficient technical skills for team members. Even if they have an incident response program, they lack clear policies that provide guidelines on how to identify a cybersecurity incident, investigate the incident, take appropriate remediation action based on the incident, and recover critical business systems.

Many organizations also don't fully understand the location or use of their critical business data. They lack a complete picture of how their enterprise network topology is architected, and they don't know all of their egress/ingress points to the Internet. Finally, many of them lack information on the incidents themselves. Having no incident response program or an immature one at best, they respond to an incident after it impacts the organization and rarely collect internal threat intelligence on when, where, and how the incident occurred.

  o *Response* – An incident response plan, policies, and program provide a framework that enables quick decisions and provides a communication process to access critical third parties when needed. The IRP would have procedures to help team members know what they need to do, how to do it, and when to do it during a time-critical cybersecurity incident. The IRP process, led by the CISO, will also provide organizations with an understanding of the lifecycle of their data and how their networks are architected, and help in determining what event logs are considered appropriate for collecting and storage.

  During the remediation process, the collection of event logs will enable team members to understand when, where, and how the incident occurred. Finally, the IRP helps the organization define their business priorities; it provides understanding about its interdependencies between processes, support systems, and partners, such as cloud providers or MSPs.

- *Many organizations opt to purchase the services of properly qualified third-party experts.* Yes, this option can significantly help organizations. It can provide qualified personnel with the experience to handle cyber incidents more effectively and appropriately. However, the company must interface and work with these competent individuals because they need context into the organization's networks, its data, applications, and business practices to be effective. Even having the full IRP process contracted out, organizations will still have to participate in a cybersecurity-related incident. There is no sitting on the sidelines.

  o *Response* – Outsourcing to a managed security services provider (MSSP) to access more experienced, dedicated technical staff to respond to sophisticated cybersecurity incidents is prudent. If the organization lacks the resources to employ an internal IRP fully, then I would suggest a hybrid approach to augment those internal staff who will execute and manage the organization's response to an incident. A hybrid approach is one in which the company has an incident response program, created and managed by the CISO, with members from across the organization and trusted external partners. The program specifies in detail the business' response to particular types of incidents and documents when MSSP staff are required to assist in conducting technical investigations or performing post-incident analysis.

Typical business continuity/disaster recovery plans inadequately cover the impact cybersecurity incidents can have on organizations. These incidents can affect the ability to operate strategic business units and can lead to loss of reputation in a competitive industry and financial losses due to fleeing customers or third-party lawsuits. These are just some of the effects that a business can experience due to a cybersecurity incident if they have no IRP and are not prepared to defend themselves.

However, if an organization funds an incident response program they now have a platform to focus on upcoming security issues, facilitate the centralized reporting of incidents, and coordinate a response to those incidents. In fact, an IRP managed by the CISO can provide a platform to educate staff on security awareness, promote good cyber hygiene, and provide contacts to legal and criminal investigative units both internal and external to the business. I believe that all of these positive outcomes make the case that a mature IRP process provides value to any organization. Incident response is not about technology; it is about business and how the company responds using people, processes, technology, and data to defend that business.

Building Your Incident Response Program

As organizations begin to build their incident response capability, they will want to identify the best strategy for putting an incident response program in place. They will not only want to know what has worked well for others within their industry, but also want some guidance on the process itself and requirements they should follow to establish an effective incident response capability. With that, let us move on to our next discussion: *"What are the processes to create an IRP?"*

The primary objective of incident response should be to guide the incident response team members in a methodical process to respond to and remediate an incident. Focus this process on managing the cyber event in a methodical manner to reduce its impact on the company, reduce the recovery time for full operations, and minimize the costs to triage the incident. There are numerous questions that the CISO and the company will need to answer as they start the process of establishing an Incident Response Program (IRP). Typical questions to address are:

1. What are the basic requirements for establishing an IRP?
   a. It will be different for each organization due to industry, critical data, compliance, regulatory regime, etc.
   b. Use NIST SP800-61r2 as a foundation for the requirements your organization may need. Remember, the steps for IRP according to NIST: Plan, Collect, Normalize, Assign, Respond, Recover, Report, and Review.
2. What type of IRP should we establish?
   a. A full on-premises team
   b. A hybrid approach leveraging third party MSSPs
   c. A sharing model between multiple organizations
3. What types of services does the IRP need to provide?
   a. This is where you can decide which services can be outsourced because the security team lacks the expertise to provide it.
4. How big should the IRP be?
   a. Is it just security? Is it a mix of multiple stakeholder divisions, departments, organizations, or partners?
5. Should the incident response team be full-time, part-time? Should the team be housed in the security team?
   a. Big question here due to budget and impact on the organization; can potentially be a political nightmare if not managed correctly.
6. What are the costs to implement an incident response program and what are the long-term costs?
7. What initial steps should the CISO and organization follow to begin the process?

Understand, there are no standard answers to these questions. Incident response teams and programs are unique to each organization. It is critical for an organization to understand why it is building an incident response program and what it wants the incident response program to achieve. To visualize why these questions are important, I have included a graphic from NIST SP 800-61r2 (NIST 2012) that shows how the team managing the organization's response to a business-impacting cybersecurity event will reach across organizational boundaries and may reach outside the organization for assistance.

With Incident Response, Collaboration Is Survival

Figure 15.2 Incident Collaboration Candidates

During our discussion for each step in the IRP development process, I will also highlight specific issues you should be aware of that may slow down your project. With that in mind, let's begin with the first process step:

1. *Identify Stakeholders* – The CISO will need to identify who will need to be part of the overall planning, who will need to be part of the implementation, and who the IRP will serve once it is operational. The last component of this process, who will be served, is critical because it is not only internal business units that must be assessed but what external partners and vendors may need to be involved with this project.

    a. *Issues* – The biggest issue at the beginning stage of the IRP project is that the CISO will not get enough or the right stakeholders involved to make this program successful. If you miss business units within your organization, they will feel that they had no say in the planning of this project and will likely not assist the CISO once the IRP is operational.

2. *Obtain Executive Leadership/Management Support* – Obtain an executive sponsor who will champion the project and be a liaison for the CISO to other executive and business leaders within the company. Ask the executive sponsor to read the business case demonstrating the requirements for an IRP and the benefits it would provide the company

and request the resources to start this project. Once approved, ask management to announce the beginning of this program and request personnel to provide information and assistance when requested.

    a. *Issues* – One of the big problems with this step of the project is that we don't notify critical stakeholders, business leaders, and strategic partners of the IRP effort, and they remain ignorant of the resources expended.

3. *Develop a project plan for how you will build your incident response program* – Establish a project team made up of business stakeholders and assign a project manager to shepherd the IRP project effort. Use sound project management concepts for a project with organization-wide impact on the scale of an IRP. I would employ a project manager following an established framework like PMI's Project Management Body of Knowledge (PMI 2017).

    a. *Issues* – Project team doesn't have stakeholders who are involved in the project; the project's scope is unrealistic with regard to resource and time completion issues; project leader is not established in the organization and is not trusted to complete the project.

4. *Time for a walk-about, gather information* – The IRP project has identified who its stakeholders are and secured executive management sponsorship. It has a project manager assigned who is putting together the overall project plan. Now it's time to collect a lot of information.

Some information that will be required will be the types of incidents the business is currently remediating. Remediation information helps the project team decide what types of incident response services the incident response program will offer. Another component of this step is that we will need to understand who owns what data and how the organization is managing critical data such as intellectual property.

This information will also impact not only what services the IRP provides but also what critical regulatory or compliance reporting is required in the event of a breach. One final critical part of this step: as project members are out in the organization collecting information, make sure they collect data on legal, political, regulatory, business, or cultural issues that will impact providing IRP services to stakeholders. For example, if there are specific regulations or business contracts in place dealing with incident response, the CISO and project team need to know about it.

a. *Issues* – The project team misses speaking with critical stakeholders who can impact the types of incident response services the IRP offers the organization. Another issue may be disagreements around data and who owns it, who should have access to it, and whether or not an incident response team can access it to triage an active cyber-attack.

5. *Define the IRP Mission, Authority, Reporting Structure, and Organizational Model* – In this step of the process, the CISO will use the data collected and will need to include the executive sponsor and management to make some hard decisions. Make decisions about the overall mission and team structure for the organization's incident response program. Roles and responsibilities for IRP team members will need to be delineated, and the authority the team can exercise during an emergency will need to be approved. One of the last issues to cover in this part of the project is what types of reports will the IRP need, who will require them, and at what frequency?

a. *Issues* – Organizations' stakeholders don't understand the purpose of the IRP and its mission. This lack of understanding leads to degraded operations when non-IRP functions get assigned to the IRP staff, and the teams are not as effective in responding to incidents. One last problem you will see at this stage is about roles and responsibilities. If roles and responsibilities are not defined, there will be operational problems during an incident because team members will not understand their responsibilities.

6. *Decide on the level of services to be offered and if outsourcing is required* – This is another step where the CISO and IRP project team will need to discuss what level of service the organization can afford to provide during a cybersecurity incident. In deciding the services, the project team will also need to discuss how the organization's business units and personnel request to access these services and whether outsourcing makes sense due to talent or cost constraints.

a. *Issues* – Some of the problems I have seen in this phase of the project are deciding to offer too many services or having the incident response team commit to more roles than it can reasonably handle during an emergency (possibly an outsourcing opportunity).

7. *Define the internal and external communications interfaces* – In this step of the process, the CISO and incident response project team will identify key stakeholders, partners, and contractors that they will need to communicate with during an incident. The CISO will need to define how information should flow, what data should be released, and the methods of communication with external parties such as law enforcement, vendors, internet service providers, and other business entities.
    a. *Issues* – Data and communications not established in a secure manner as prescribed by the incident response policy which could result in a loss of trust in the IRP operating effectively. Missing communications channels and data sharing methodologies with critical stakeholders can lead to ineffective response times for the organization during a breach incident.

8. *Identify resources, create a budget and secure funding* – Analyze and document the resources for the short-term and long-term IRP. Look at the hardware, software, tools, cloud access, training, and facilities required for an incident response effort. Decide how to fund the plan, i.e., will it charge-back to the organization's business units or will you fund it centrally?
    a. *Issues* – One of the biggest issues here is not looking at how the program will be funded long-term and not budgeting for training program personnel. Incident response is a unique skill-set that requires ongoing training.

9. *Develop policies and procedures* – After the program has secured funding, stakeholders work with the project team to implement the incident response program. The CISO and team members will need to write the company's overall Incident Response Policy with procedures and guidelines detailing specific actions for team members and the communication process to be followed by the team with both internal and external stakeholders. Some references on writing an incident response plan are:
    i.   https://www.sans.org/score
    ii. https://www.sans.org/score/incident-forms
    iii. http://nvlpubs.nist.gov/nistpubs/SpecialPublicati ons/NIST.SP.800-61r2.pdf
    iv. http://www.csirt.org/sample_policies/index.html
    v.   http://www.aicpa.org/interestareas/informationte chnology/resources/privacy/downloadabledocum ents/incidentresponse.doc
    vi. http://cdn.ttgtmedia.com/searchDisasterRecovery

/downloads/SearchDisasterRecovery_Incident_R
esponse_Plan_Template.doc

a. *Issues* – If the IRP program lacks proper definitions of terminology, policies, and processes there will be an impact on the response time of team members to incidents. There also will be general confusion within the team and stakeholders in supporting roles as to what methods to follow in responding to an incident.

10. *Executive Leadership evangelizes the new Incident Response Program* – Once the IRP project has concluded and the program is operational, it is imperative that the executive leadership of the organization make a formal announcement. This announcement will help stakeholders across the company understand its purpose and that management supports it. The CISO should also ensure that training on how to contact the incident response team and the services it provides are given to HR to be included in the annual information security awareness training and new hire training.

a. *Issues* – If the organization does not formally announce the creation of the incident response program, no one will understand its purpose or how to interact with it in times of an emergency. This can seriously impact the organization's ability to limit the damage of a cybersecurity breach.

11. *Define methods to evaluate the performance of the IRP* – Define what requirements will need to be met for incident reporting and use these requirements to establish a baseline. Establish a lessons learned process for after-incidents discussions and what reports will need to be collected. Implement a survey method to collect feedback from the organization's personnel to track the performance of the incident response program and establish metrics that can be used to demonstrate value (our next discussion).

a. *Issues* – No methods are created to track and evaluate whether the incident response program is providing value. Without any collected feedback or metrics, the CISO will not be able to implement effective continuous improvement with regard to the incident response program.

As you can see, to establish an incident response program the CISO will have to work with stakeholders across the organization to collect the information needed to write both the organization's incident response policy and the incident response procedures and guidelines. Once these are written and the program is funded and operational, the CISO will have to prove it is providing value to the company. Let's look at the types of metrics the CISO should consider for evaluating the incident response program and what information is crucial to ensure we collect data that will help the program continuously improve.

Chapter 15 Key Point and Action Item 4

We've been discussing runbooks in various contexts, but there is perhaps no area where a detailed and verified runbook is more important than incident response. Much like pre-approved communication templates, having a detailed set of procedures that comprise your incident response program is vital to allow you to keep cool and address the incident.

You should build an action plan based on the eleven steps outlined to develop an incident response program. The plan should have the specific objective of identifying and closing the gaps between your current state and your ideal state.

Our last question for discussion is as follows: *"What are some methods to measure the effectiveness of an organization's IRP, and why is it important to the CISO?"*

There is a statistic in the previously referenced SANS 2016 report, The State of Incident Response, (Bromiley 2016), that I believe is relevant to our current discussion. It was found that 63% of respondents don't know the costs of their IRP program. This to me is amazing. As a CISO you have the responsibility of creating and managing a program that reaches into every corner of the business and its sole purpose is to reduce the impact of incidents so that operations are not affected, and they don't know their costs – unbelievable.

Measure Your Performance

You may ask, "Why does this matter?" The answer is that we know nothing in the field of cybersecurity is static, including costs for services, technology, training, etc., and this also applies to incident response. As the CISO for a company, how do you go before the board of directors and request more funds for the organization's incident response program if you can't give them your current costs and help them see the value to the business of allocating more resources to the program.

This is one of the main datasets that I believe is critical for CISOs to track. It will help justify new requirements, it can be used to show how much specific types of breaches cost and their impacts to the organization, and it can be used to provide insight into why new security controls are warranted. Some metrics that can be used to better understand the costs of an incident response program include:

- The direct cost of having to hire a third-party forensics/IR service provider
- The travel costs to get a responder to compromised systems because the organization lacks remote access tools
- The loss of productivity for a department that is impacted by a breach
- The costs of having to train staff
- The costs for having incident response team members manually triage an event because they lack automated incident response tools

By tracking these costs and the impact to the organization, I believe the CISO can make a good case for the adequate funding of the incident response program. However, sometimes understanding your costs isn't enough and this is where I believe the CISO needs to collect another set of metrics that demonstrates the effectiveness of the IR program and the value it provides to the business. These metrics center on incidents and the response of the team and stakeholders to triaging the breach.

Remember, cybersecurity is a life cycle that includes inventory, assessment, scanning, remediation, and monitoring. Incident response is part of this life cycle. Team members should be making effective use of cyber threat intelligence and proactively scanning, threat hunting, remediating, and monitoring the after effects. Some performance metrics to track during this process:

- The time from initial compromise to detection
- The time from detection to containing the threat
- The time from containment to remediation of the threat

These times can be collected and used to show whether the team is improving, specific compromises that take more time and resources, and how the loss of resources can negatively impact a team and the incident response services it provides. One last set of metrics that I would collect for demonstrating the value of an incident response program:

- The number of reported incidents
- The number of incidents successfully resolved
- Benchmarking of the current incident response program with others to determine an effective baseline

Chapter 15 Key Point and Action Item 5

Most metrics the CISO tracks are valuable beyond the context of just the information security program, and this is particularly true for metrics about the incident response program. Routinely reporting on cyber hygiene, incident response and cyber awareness will help the organization align for success.

You should verify that your metrics program captures sufficient data points to allow you to measure your incident response program effectively. Use the metrics listed in this chapter as a starting point if needed.

As we conclude our discussion, a good reference for the management of an incident response program is Carnegie Mellon University's Handbook for Computer Security Incident Response Teams (Carnegie Mellon University 2003). The handbook is quite lengthy. However, I have found it to be a good reference for CISOs as they write policy, put together an incident response program, triage an incident, and manage an incident response team. I hope this chapter has provided some value for you as you embark on creating a crucial, strategic program for your organization.

Incident response is one of the key programs that a CISO will be responsible for managing. It can be time-consuming to get your incident response program operational, so collaborate with your stakeholders and share the workload. Once it is up and running, be patient and remember the cybersecurity life cycle. Follow your documented processes and train like there is a breach every day so it will be "muscle memory" when it's time to respond live.

Summary

In Chapter 15, we began our discussion by asking these questions:

- What is the business value of an Incident Response Program (IRP)?
- What are the processes to create an IRP?
- What are some methods to measures the effectiveness of an organization's IRP and why is it important to the CISO?

Over the last couple of chapters, we have asked you to build on work you have previously completed. We're suggesting that you add to this work in ways that will help your organization utilize the data and process knowledge you have accumulated to achieve your goal of resilience. In addition to helping your organization become more resilient to disruption from any source, your knowledge of the business, how it operates, the key processes and people, and the relationships with customers and third-party providers should hopefully make you a welcome member of the senior leadership team.

In closing this chapter, we leave you with these five key points and next steps:

1. It is difficult to predict how many challenges will be presented to you when a live incident is underway. What you do know is that time will be a precious commodity and resources will be severely limited. Key decision makers will be engaged on multiple fronts. Keeping your various stakeholders informed should be a high priority because not adding to the problem will be a critical concern. **You should create a list of the potential communication events that might arise during a cyber incident. These might include disruptions to product deliveries, closure of facilities, and estimated time of service restoration. Build a template for each potential event and obtain pre-approval so that in a crisis, fundamental messaging is ready for use.**

2. Knowing who to call, who to escalate to and who needs to be informed about incidents impacting and efforts to recover each asset is critical. This knowledge helps you make timely decisions and minimizes the impact on your critical processes. **You should add to your template**

repository the primary owner and escalation point, along with escalation criteria, for each message template. **Key people on this list are the business owners who manage the customer, supplier, employee, and law enforcement relationships so they are not blindsided and can manage any fallout.**

3. The combination of integrating OT and IT along with increased regulatory and law enforcement activity and the added awareness of users of their own peril have added several new dimensions to decision making during incidence response. **You should document and communicate the intersection between OT and IT in your environment and conduct tabletop exercises to simulate the decision-making challenges across the three axes of service delivery, law-enforcement, and data protection. Repeat these drills often enough that making the hard calls between the physical, digital and regulatory realms becomes a discussion and not a point of paralysis.**

4. We've been discussing runbooks in various contexts, but there is perhaps no area where a detailed and verified runbook is more important than incident response. Much like pre-approved communication templates, having a detailed set of procedures that comprise your incident response program is vital to allow you to keep cool and address the incident. **You should build an action plan based on the eleven steps outlined to develop an incident response program. The plan should have the specific objective of identifying and closing the gaps between your current state and your ideal state.**

5. Most metrics the CISO tracks are valuable beyond the context of just the information security program, and this is particularly true for metrics about the incident response program. Routinely reporting on cyber hygiene, incident response and cyber awareness will help the organization align for success. **You should verify that your metrics program captures sufficient data points to allow you to measure your incident response program effectively. Use the metrics listed in this chapter as a starting point if needed.**

We've made this point a couple of times already, but it bears repeating. People are busy, and the people needed to respond to an incident are often those in highest demand. Prepare templates and establish escalation paths in advance to reduce stress and ensure better outcomes.

Chapter 16 – Recovery and Resuming Operations

Introduction

There is a fine line between incident response and recovery and resuming operations. To some extent, that line is only academically useful. The authors have covered many of the discrete activities in resuming operations in Chapter 14. Nonetheless, there is some discipline that is helpful in the immediate aftermath, both to make sure the incident is really resolved, and to learn and improve for a better response to the next incident.

Bill highlights two discrete activities that can be thought of as specific to resuming operations. First, it is important to realize that outside of the family of ransomware attacks, a major objective of a modern attack is persistence. Verifying that the recovered asset is truly back to acceptable baseline takes planning and diligence. Second, as is the case while the incident is underway, communication during the recovery phase is also critical. All stakeholders, including customers, suppliers, law enforcement, and employees, need to know what is expected of them.

Matt takes the reader through a hypothetical situation that a healthcare provider, in this case a hospital, might face. He recognizes that for many people reading this book, you might not have been through an incident before and may not have inherited a mature program. He uses that hypothetical to challenge the reader to be capturing lessons while in the moment with an eye toward building the muscle memory that the organization will need to improve operational resilience.

Gary provides a series of planning guides to help the reader prepare for the inevitable and then walks the reader through the activities. The reader should find it helpful to see how the planning is put to use and benefit from the reminders about critical information to capture in the moment. As Gary has pointed out throughout his essays, the CISO can never stop learning. That learning discipline is what allows the CISO to continue to push their organization to improve.

Some of the questions the authors used to frame their thoughts for this chapter include:

- What steps should an organization take to prepare for a data breach?
- During a data breach, what operations should the CISO be aware of and possibly manage as a member of the organization's business continuity effort and leader of the incident response team?
- What steps should be followed to resume normal operations and resume data breach management efforts?

Getting Back to Business – Bonney

> "Your executive team should know how incident response works and that it is part of normal activity."

Now that the incident has been detected, contained, and eradicated, it's time to recover and resume operations. It's important to distinguish between recovering the business process and recovering the asset. Certainly, many business processes will be entirely dependent on the availability and integrity of a specific set of critical assets. But keeping the focus on the business process as your key recovery objective will allow you and your organization to make crisper decisions about when to use backups, alternative sites, or other options defined in your recovery plans.

As with other disciplines that we've discussed, some of the ground we're going to cover in this chapter has traditionally been within the CIO's purview. But as we've stated before, in today's digital business world the most likely cause of downtime requiring recovery operations are cyber-related events, and that's going to place the CISO front and center. It's important that the CISO can take responsibility as needed and is working with the same recovery objectives as the CIO.

Planning and Preparation

Here again, the planning you have done in preparation for recovery is critical. We have already established that incident response does not begin with the incident. It begins in the preparation phase when you are taking inventory of your business processes and systems and creating RTOs, RPOs, and the sequence of eventual recovery activities. Each business process should have a runbook, validated by the business process owner, that details how to recover the business process, including decision criteria for asset recovery versus switching to backup or alternative assets.

It is critically important that the business process owner is intimately involved in the creation of the recovery runbook and the execution of the recovery runbook. The business process owner will need to balance internal stakeholder and external customer expectations regarding service delivery and contractual obligations for uptime and service availability. They will do this by using the RPO and RTO referenced in Chapter 14 as guideposts for prioritizing recovery activities and deciding between restoring primary assets versus switching to backups.

Another key aspect of your preparation activities is making sure your executive team knows that you are constantly working on incidents. They need to understand that you are continually evaluating log files, investigating outages, and tweaking your monitoring tools. Your executive team should know how incident response works and that it is part of normal activity. You'll want to present it as a routine activity and a continual process that addresses high-level investigations and specific incidents and outages. Reporting on some amount of the activity on a regular basis will help familiarize them with the work that will be required while recovering from high-profile events.

Having the executive team receive these periodic reports, act on them, and participate in communications and recovery activities will prepare them for the more challenging high-profile events, when you will need their support and when it'll be vital for them to pitch in by working their human network.

The reason this is important is that when we are stressed we rely on habits; quick, easy-to-remember responses are best for stressful circumstances when we are under pressure. The reasons that airlines trust pilots with ever more complex aircraft flying more passengers over greater distances as they gain experience and the military drills continuously are to form habits that will take over in times of stress. For your executive team to react in a positive and supportive manner and not distract the team with knee-jerk reactions, they need to be part of the routine incident management process.

Recover and Resume

The recovery steps include restoring the assets, validating the assets, determining when to place the assets back in service, monitoring the assets, and communicating the status, both at the business process and incident level. Restoring the assets will be the responsibility of the business teams and the IT team, but the CISO and the Information Security team also play critical roles. As you bring assets back online, InfoSec needs to assist with validation and monitoring.

However, before any of these activities can take place, it is essential that your organization's process for determining the regulatory or contractual impact of the outage or disruption is executed to catalog and, if necessary, that you sequester all assets needed for forensics activities and follow-up analysis. This review can be required to assist with regulatory action (for instance, a record request for a high-profile breach or outage) or to help the organization with its defense against any litigation instigated by authorities, customers, or partners. It is more than a matter of convenience. In many cases, the regulatory obligations under which you operate or the contracts that specify the services you provide to key customers spell out the need to preserve records and evidence and the failure to do so can potentially subject the firm to additional legal jeopardy.

Here again, it is critical to work with your legal team to appropriately handle records and systems, make detailed notes of what, if any, compromise has taken place against sensitive records or systems, and ensure you can complete any subsequent analysis. At a minimum, copy all logs and all records involved in the incident, and preserve the state of any systems (do a snapshot of virtual machines, for instance) involved. Care must be taken to handle sensitive records according to the appropriate data handling policy, even (and especially) when systems are technically offline.

For example, a simple downtime event can turn into a breach notification event if recovery personnel inadvertently review restricted PHI records while reviewing for record integrity. Certain designated personnel are likely empowered to execute specific pre-approved record integrity validation routines. Make sure this is how the records are validated, so you don't run afoul of data handling regulations. Remember that when offline, the application safeguards you or the vendor designed into the system may not be functioning. Without these controls, you may inadvertently expose records to inappropriate personnel. Make sure to account for this with your incident response and recovery runbook to avoid adding to your list of problems.

Chapter 16 Key Point and Action Item 1

Don't make the problem worse than it is. When systems are partially disrupted, the application-level controls for access to data are easily to circumvent by mistake. This can escalate a routine service interruption into a privacy violation that triggers a breach notification.

You should catalog data handling procedures for recovery activities that adhere to regulatory and contractual restrictions.

As you begin your recovery procedure, it is important to verify systems in sequence, and that sequence must take into account parent-child relationships and order precedent. Make sure to recover systems that depend on other systems in the right order.

Proper sequencing can take time, and it is important that sensitivity to RTO requirements do not cause the team to short-circuit this process. Preparing the executive team by routinely reporting on incident management activities and outcomes can help provide "air cover" here to allow your team to complete this work.

Validation

Working together with the business teams and the IT staff, the InfoSec team should help ensure that the asset is functioning as required, that the data set is intact, and that the asset is free from malware or compromise. To accomplish this requires more than running a virus scan on the asset, though you should not skip that step. As you bring the asset up, connect to your suite of monitoring tools, look for indicators of compromise, and perform the health checks you will need so you can state with confidence that the asset is ready for use in the production environment.

Validation may not stop with the locally identified assets. You must also determine if the cause of the event has had or will have an impact on other assets. For instance, has file replication and propagation been affected for any adjacent processes? If so, the incident response plan must be executed for those assets as well. A product recall might be necessary for customer-facing or remotely-deployed assets.

Validation must also be thorough. Until you know the type of attack and the motivation (what was the target and why), you don't know whether the attack was meant to persist past initial discovery. It is especially important to be diligent on validation and the next step, monitoring, even with low-level, high-impact attacks that appear easy to fix but that cause significant disruption. As tempting as it may be to get the operation up quickly and declare the incident over, you must try to avoid leaving vulnerabilities still active while operations appear unaffected. The cybercriminals might be back, and you might be tired or complacent when they start round two.

It is not unusual to cycle back through the detect, contain, and eradicate steps if you either detect the same compromise on a system that was thought to be secure or you detect other malware or compromises such as inappropriate accounts or improper applications or exfiltration code. You will need to iterate through the process until you validate that all assets are operational and secure.

Monitoring

The wealth of penetration and stealth techniques available to cyber criminals makes it difficult to be positive you've closed every door and rooted out every shred of persistence. It is imperative that you immediately begin monitoring all systems you put back in service and assign a high priority to watching these systems until you are sure you have reestablished a normal baseline of activity. Increased diligence for some period and then spot checks over a more extended period are valuable to gain confidence that the impact of the attack is indeed over.

Here is another way that your human network can help. Ask your colleagues, and with appropriate advice from your legal team, ask your law enforcement contacts what telltale signs you should be watching for as a result of this attack. In return, be prepared to share, as much as is prudent and with the advice of your legal team, logs and other details to help the community at large combat this attack when used against targets outside your organization. It's not just the neighborly and cooperative thing to do. By decreasing the number of types of attacks that work against your community, you help make your common defenses stronger.

Communicating

The business process owners should communicate service availability and the InfoSec team should declare the incident closed when the CISO or designated individual has determined that all activities associated with the detect, contain, eradicate, and recover phases are complete. The incident response communication plan should be consulted and honored for all other communication activities, including the notification of customers, partners, and law enforcement. The communication plan, of course, will specify when the legal and corporate communications teams are to be involved in these activities.

Another key aspect of communications is informing everyone who needs to know how to recognize a repeat of the same attack. It is especially important if the initial attack vector relied on humans making mistakes. Make sure employees, partners, vendors and, if prudent, customers, can recognize and then appropriately report a reoccurrence, and make sure your incident response teams can quickly apply what they learned in combatting the attack the first time around.

As part of your planning process, you no doubt identified which internal and external communication channels to utilize, and as part of the recovery and resume phase you'll test procedures, train frontline responders, and ensure everyone knows their role. If necessary, consider bringing on extra shift personnel for helpdesk activities and establish regular updates or alerts to the larger team. While paying customers may be the priority, don't forget to arm your team with the knowledge necessary to be good partners to support personnel.

Finally, I'll make one more plug for the legal team. In Chapter 15 we talked about involving public officials in training activities and bringing them along, as needed, in the incident response. It is vital to do this if public safety is at risk and will often be prudent regardless. It would be wise to have legal drive these interactions, both to utilize the expertise of the legal team and to free up important time for you to focus on recovery activities.

Other areas where legal can be especially helpful are in adhering to contractual obligations for incident notification to third parties, notification on any breaches that may have occurred, records handling and preservation, public communication, interacting with industry regulators, and advising on the appropriate levels of engagement with industry trade groups.

> "The fallout of attacks on companies from Target Corp. to Yahoo Inc. and, most recently, Equifax Inc. has thrust more corporate bosses to the front line of cybersecurity issues and changed the way they work."
>
> (The Wall Street Journal)

The reality is that bad things do happen to good security programs. How we effectively recover and resume operations in a manner consistent with organizational priorities may ultimately be our greatest test and challenge as CISOs. In the previous chapter, we discussed the importance of incident response as a security process that benefits from pre-planning and the frequent exercising of various scenarios (e.g., malware, ransomware, DDoS, and rogue insiders).

In this chapter, we'll deal with the consequences when our best efforts to prevent bad things from happening to our networks, applications, systems, and data fall short. Similar to incident response, breach response and recovery is a discipline that requires pre-planning and, frankly, anticipating the worse. If you plan for the worst, responding to and recovering from attacks and breaches will not be easy, but it won't be a fatal blow to your security program, the organization it protects, or your career.

Hypothetical Healthcare Provider

To highlight some foundational concepts of breach response, let's think about a particularly nasty scenario and how the response and recovery may look in order to facilitate pre-planning. Assume you are the CISO for a large hospital that has patient records numbering in the millions. Your organization is under significant cost pressure, there's been turnover both at the executive level and among the broader security and IT teams, and the level of shadow IT and third-party vendors is significant. Business associate agreements and mandated risk assessments of these vendors have been spotty at best as the organization has not truly defined the governance model for vendor oversight.

In short, organizational accountabilities are ill-defined, there's an expansive application portfolio that is not under the direct control of IT and security, and assessments do not occur for many material vendors for their potential impacts to security and operations. These "hypothetical" dynamics likely resonate with a number of us who have worked in healthcare or provided services to this sector. Just to add to the tension, you've been in your role less than a month. The former head of security left under less-than-ideal circumstances. It's now your department. You own it.[23]

You arrive to work early, and there are two agents from the FBI waiting to speak with you. It's victim notification time. It's bad. Nefarious circles are trading the protected health records (PHI) for over 25,000 of your patients. More records may also be at risk. What's the response, and how do you recover?

Addressing a breach of this nature should be anticipated with key next steps, priorities, and draft communications established in advance (see Chapter 15). As you are new to the organization and this work was not completed by your predecessor, you don't have this luxury. It's time to invoke the incident response plan and call to action the cybersecurity incident response team. Unfortunately, this team and key elements of your incident response documentation are also lacking. You're effectively starting from ground zero. Welcome to your new role!

Benefitting from Your Planning

The ability to triage and deal with multiple, conflicting priorities on your time will be one of your most important skill sets. Understanding legal obligations, organizational priorities, and escalation to critical stakeholders, including executive management and the board of directors, will be center stage as you think about what the agents are conveying. This scenario is why the planning efforts addressed in the previous chapter become so important. Time is not a luxury you will have during a breach.

Let's think about what the high-level response and recovery efforts should be and the best way to move forward when you are operating with high levels of uncertainty, incomplete information, and with teams that may not be aware of their responsibilities and key next steps in the effort to restore operations. Bottom line, your first exercise is not an exercise.

First things first. You'll need to widen the circle of concern and get help to support the triaging effort. You will need to designate someone from the team to serve as the primary technical point of contact and designate another individual to serve as the incident response coordinator who will help manage the broader response and

---

[23] For many new CISOs, the luxury of a well-crafted incident response program as we discussed in Chapter 15 may be just that, a luxury. Your first experience with incident response could be a significant breach under less than ideal circumstances.

serve as an interface to communicate with affected departments and parties. Get these key members on the phone to start the effort and effectively authorize their actions.

Your technical lead needs to quickly determine the nature and extent of the breach (e.g., the type and number of records affected, the systems compromised, and based on feedback from other stakeholders, when and how the system will be isolated if that is possible). Unfortunately, given other investigations, the agents from the Bureau were not able to provide much additional detail other than their notification that the breach was ongoing. The agents were not authorized to describe any of the TTPs or how they became aware of the compromise. Technically, you and your team are on your own.

Your security team needs help to deal with the breach. Determining how the compromise took place will require some assistance for forensic analysis. You decide to call in external support and leverage a third-party forensic / incident response firm. Fortunately, before joining your current organization, you had already worked with a couple of firms and are familiar with their work and their capabilities. You are also going to need the help of your colleagues in IT. The CIO is also aware something is amiss. His team has received a large number of help-desk inquiries in the past couple of hours. He preempts your call and reaches out to see if you are aware of anything going on.

You spend the next fifteen minutes with the CIO benefiting from his knowledge of the organization, his relationships with and understanding of key stakeholders and their priorities, as well as his more in-depth system knowledge.

Your designated incident response coordinator should be instructed to initiate the incident response plan but like you, she's also new to the organization and the previous team did not have sufficient documentation available. You and the incident response coordinator huddle up and sketch out a quick thirty-thousand-foot view of a plan.

The plan contemplates the following swim lanes:
- Define key stakeholders
- Validate contractual and regulatory obligations
- Communications
- Technical response
- What to tell executive management
- Remediation and lessons learned
- Moving forward

The Breach Scenario Unfolds

For the next fifteen minutes, the two of you quickly sketch out what needs to occur across each of these functions while trying to keep distractions to a minimum. You bring in a few senior members of the security team and start hashing out the response. Here's what surfaces under these less-than-ideal circumstances.

Define Key Stakeholders: Breach response is not just a cybersecurity and IT domain. It requires the participation and insights, including decisions, from key stakeholders throughout the organization. You and the incident response coordinator open up a spreadsheet and build a quick RACI matrix to highlight the key functions and roles associated with the breach response. You highlight the roles and engagement of human resources, legal counsel, your counterparts in IT and the help desk, the hospital's communications team, and other stakeholders. You recognize that once you complete this response, these stakeholders need to be part of incident response training and tabletop exercises. Right now, their role in the process will likely come as a surprise.

Validate Contractual and Regulatory Obligations: You know, given the limited details provided by the agents, that the compromise includes PHI. It's time to get your legal counsel engaged. You contact your legal counsel to arrange a meeting in an hour to let him know that you're dealing with a breach that will require notification to various state attorney generals as well as, potentially, federal regulators. Whether or not to notify federal regulators will be the legal counsel's call.

Once the two of you have met, your legal counsel will run

regulatory responses. He'll need information from you that you'll want to have ready – number and type of records as well as basic details associated with the breach. You agree that legal counsel will coordinate with the corporate communications team and handle media-related matters when the breach is made public. Your incident response coordinator will be a shared resource to help facilitate the legal counsel's efforts.

You also ask that legal counsel provide a designated resource to help facilitate the fast-tracking of contract reviews that will be required to bring in third-party resources to help with forensic analysis and remediation. You note that given the lack of detail about the breach, you are going to need to contract with a third-party forensic / breach response provider to facilitate and provide back-of-the-envelope estimates of the costs. There's no budget for these services, and your legal counsel cringes when you convey an estimate likely to be over six figures – including notification services. Legal counsel is also working with the CEO and other senior executives to convey detail on context on required notifications, essentially the various regulatory obligations required for the breach.

Communications: Your legal counsel and the corporate communications team, fortunately, are well-versed in dealing with issues impacting regulatory requirements and reputation-protecting activities of the organization. They are generally prepared and simply need the fact pattern of the breach to start their crisis communications plan. Once the fact pattern becomes known (effectively, what happened, what information was involved, what are we doing, what the affected parties can do, and contact details),[24] they will move forward.

Notifications to regulators have been pre-drafted and validated based on several scenarios. This type of breach, unfortunately, was not adequately contemplated so there's some legwork required to address the required communications. Your incident response coordinator is quickly working to provide legal counsel and the communications team with as much accurate information as is available. She is also taking great pains to avoid interfering with the technical work of other members of the security team

---

[24] State breach notifications vary somewhat in requirements and timing. This URL provides an overview of these requirements:
http://www.ncsl.org/research/telecommunications-and-information-technology/security-breach-notification-laws.aspx

– she knows that every interruption as they do their analysis creates a distraction and significant delay on the technical triage.

The team is doing their work effectively, and all that's required is to establish an appropriate cadence for updates and communication. You agree that you will provide them with updates every four hours unless something material arises as your triaging and investigation work continues. The reality, however, is that the requests for updates will be continuous and ad hoc, coming from multiple stakeholders as they learn of the breach.

Technical Response: Your technical lead is a star. Fortunately, she's worked in security and IT for healthcare for a while and knows how most electronic medical records systems are compromised. One promising thing that your predecessor did accomplish was to implement an incident response platform that helped to quickly assess the details from logs as well as network and user behavior. The story is becoming more evident. There appears to be a rogue systems administrator (or at least someone using the admin's credentials) that gained access to and stole medical records. Why this wasn't detected by your security team is another issue.

Given the exceptional work from your technical lead, you and she have outlined a course of action for how to address the rogue insider. You've contacted human resources to explain the situation. The VP of HR is adamant that the individual in question is not a rogue employee. She's worked with this individual for over 15 years and vouches for his dedication to the organization. Being new, you accept her perspective and go with the theory that credential harvesting likely occurred.

Upon further discussion with members of the broader IT team, you discover that the sharing of credentials is commonplace, even among admin accounts. Could things get much worse? The CIO confirms that this has been standard practice given skeleton shifts and high turnover. Security has taken a back seat to expediency. He too vouches for the individual whose credentials were used to affect the data breach. Regardless of whether it was a rogue employee or truly compromised credentials, at least there is an understanding of what took place.

You and the technical lead make plans to coordinate with the selected forensics firm. They will facilitate a more in-depth review of how the compromise took place, validate the number of records impacted, and which IOCs the respective teams missed that could have helped to preclude the breach.

What to Communicate to Executive Management: Almost immediately upon speaking with the agents, you placed a call to the CEO to let him know of the breach. He was at an off-site meeting and called back twenty-five minutes into the breach response effort. These twenty-five minutes proved invaluable as you started to get a better sense of what took place and what the response plan and requirements will be. Your talk with the CEO highlighted the known items, the compromise of 25,000 records, with more potentially at risk, and that you've notified legal counsel (who also called the CEO as did the CIO) and your team is working on the triage and containment efforts.

You let the CEO know that you and the CIO are working collaboratively to address the breach and while your team is working on specific technical matters, the CIO is ensuring that organizational priorities, notably those of the CEO, will be addressed. You agree that you will provide hourly updates to the CIO and that you and the CEO would speak again by 10:30 that morning. Hanging up, you know that the CEO will be calling again in short order as pressure on him for further details mounts. The circle of concerned is now wide, and multiple stakeholders are asking for details from both you and the CIO. What's worse, they are trying to see if there are discrepancies in what you've conveyed. As a new CISO, you don't have the same institutional knowledge as the CIO, and he's frankly a known asset. You, on the other hand, were an expensive new hire and the jury is still out.

Your focus with the CEO is to be very explicit on what is known and what remains to be determined. Equally important, you know that you will need to put together a comprehensive incident response plan to deal with these types of scenarios moving forward (this is likely not an isolated incident), and you will need to prepare the CEO and other senior executives for the fact that there is likely significant security debt to pay. You let the CEO know that there will be a detailed report, once you conclude the breach analysis and report on the state of the overall security program. You discussed this during your interview with him but did not anticipate that you would need to meet the requirement so soon. You will accelerate the timeline for building your security program.

Remediation and Lessons Learned: This incident highlighted significant issues with the security architecture and practices of the organization. You will accelerate your phased efforts for the security program. There is effectively no luxury of time to address some of the more compelling items. Credential management, something you had hoped had been already locked down, is a clear and present danger to the organization's information assets and systems. After speaking further with the CIO, you realize that the breach that took place is not an isolated incident. There have been other issues, over the years, where smaller compromises took place.

You bring your team together to debrief on the current status and what requires immediate attention. Implementing multi-factor authentication for admin credentials is a top priority. You also recognize that you did not focus security monitoring on the right indicators and that egress traffic was effectively a blind spot. Together with your team, and with the commitment from the CIO to adjust current practices, you outline your plan to start remediating the existing security architecture. You give instructions to your team to work closely with your technical lead and conduct a threat modeling exercise not just on the EMR platform but also on other key areas of the organization's infrastructure and across the more critical applications within the organization's portfolio of high-impact processes.

Moving Forward: This incident highlights just how impactful a security breach can be for an organization. There will be regulatory fines, likely by both the FTC as well as the Department of Health and Human Services' Office of Civil Rights (focused on HIPAA-HITECH compliance with the security and privacy rules). The board is going to want a detailed explanation of what took place and why it happened. There is significant security debt to pay.

Your role as CISO will require you to develop a comprehensive security budget – likely larger than anticipated based on past security spending – and which will likely result in significant challenges to obtaining funding. You will tax your political skills as you coordinate with the CIO to effect meaningful changes to monitoring, network segmentation, identity and access management, and overall infrastructure hygiene. There's a bit of a silver lining though – you've discovered some great latent talent within your new team. Your technical lead's ability to quickly discover the TTPs of the attack and implement mitigating controls suggests she's a real star. Time to work with HR to ensure that she's not at risk of leaving and is well compensated. Your incident coordinator has also shown some tremendous soft skills in managing the crisis and coordinating with other departments.

For many CISOs, breach response is a watershed moment. You are held to account for infrastructure and business practices that are mostly out of your control, and breach response can be a nightmare. We must proactively manage this component of our roles. Specifically, as an extension of incident response, breach response requires coordination with key stakeholders, notably the organization's legal counsel, senior executives, human resources, corporate communications, and potentially external stakeholders and regulators.

Chapter 16 Key Point and Action Item 3

Helmuth von Moltke the Elder famously said: "No battle plan survives contact with the enemy." Moltke was coming to understand that with modern weapons and larger, better equipped armies, resilience was far more important than drilling to achieve perfect battle formation. Resilience, in his mind, was achieved through what-if exercises that exposed his leaders to as many realistic scenarios as possible, so they could adapt to changing conditions.

You should build a table-top exercise using similar circumstances to those outlined by Matt for the hospital to allow your management team to simulate a breach response and recovery, so you can begin to develop your muscle memory.

Prepare your teams for a breach. Specifically, they need to be well versed on the specific indicators of compromise, ideally contextualized to your applications and systems from your threat modeling exercises, and nuanced and detailed for your specific systems and applications. Look at new tools that can help validate the impacted systems and which records were accessed, and that help your security analysts remediate issues in a timely fashion. Make incident management and breach and recovery training and preparedness central to your security program. We'll talk about the overall components of a security program in Chapter 18.

> "The CISO should also have agreements in place
> with third-party vendors that can provide
> emergency services during a breach."

A data breach is "a security incident in which sensitive, protected or confidential data is copied, transmitted, viewed, stolen or used by an individual or group that is unauthorized to do so" (ACF 2015). As this definition notes, a data breach is a security incident and organizations expect the CISO to manage the company's response to this event. In previous chapters, we spoke about business continuity and incident response and how the CISO supports these critical services and is responsible for the program that initially triages data breach-type critical events. In the discussion that follows, we will look at how organizations prepare themselves for a data breach, how they should respond to a breach, and the actions to be taken after a violation occurs.

Much of what I will discuss will not only pertain to how the CISO should respond but will also apply to the organization as a whole. As a CISO, you have a role as a strategic business partner to your organization, and you provide value through the insight and experience you have in managing risk and reducing its impact on business operations. I'm taking a more comprehensive view of how the organization should set itself up for success when managing an actual breach.

Your role as the CISO, in this scenario, is to understand your company's overall strategy for managing business-impacting incidents like data breaches. This understanding will enable you and your team to be more efficient in providing incident response services and provide context into not only how your teams need to respond, but how your peers, who are members of a larger effort, should operate in this time of emergency.

For organizations to efficiently recover from a data breach, they need to first plan for it and train their staff on how to respond. We know that in our current aggressive threat environment there is no one connected to the Internet who is not a target. If you operate in a climate where you are susceptible to exploitation, and we all do, it is common sense and good business practice for the CISO to plan early for how the organization will respond when it experiences a breach incident. Now to our first question: *"What steps should an organization take to prepare for a data breach?"*

Preparing for a Breach

Let's look at the recommendations from the Department of Justice (Department of Justice 2015) on eight steps companies can take to reduce the impact of cyber intrusions on their business.

1. *Data Classification/Governance* – To begin, one of the most significant challenges the CISO and stakeholders will face is understanding what to protect – typically this is data. Unfortunately, not all data is created equal, so one of the first demands the CISO and peers within the business must face is the requirement to identify which information is sensitive and needs protection. I look at this process as an opportunity. It is the chance for the CISO and team to work with all business units within their organization and inventory what applications, procedures, and data is critical to the company and required for operations. If by now you are having a feeling of déjà vu, well that's because you are; we have discussed inventory numerous times throughout various chapters.

    What is essential now in this process is identifying what data is critical and conducting a review of this data's criticality. Validate the cost to protect it, along with contracts, laws, compliance, or regulations that pertain to this data. Then decide whether the organization needs to collect this data or not. After this part of the inventory is completed, determine who to contact for assistance and who you must notify in the case of a compromise to this data. As you can imagine, this process is quite intertwined with incident response and business continuity. I view both of those programs providing input into the overall management of how an organization conducts its data breach mitigation effort.

2. *Have an Actionable Plan* – As discussed in depth in Chapter 15, the organization must have an incident response program (IRP) with a plan that has specific, focused workflows for team members on how they will respond to particular types of incidents and their responsibilities during an event. Here are some minimum components that the IRP should contain. It should specify who will lead the response to the incident; this person will not only lead the incident response team but will also represent the company in communicating with both internal and

external parties. There should also be criteria for when the plan should be activated and a list of critical stakeholders with their respective responsibilities and how to contact them.

The IRP should contain not only the guidelines for responding to specific types of breaches but also guidance on forensically preserving data for possible legal proceedings and advice on how to methodically document all processes taken by team personnel during the breach event. I have written these types of plans numerous times. The primary thing to remember is it needs to be flexible, and it should be continuously reviewed and used to train the incident response teams.

3. *Have the Technology, Security Controls, and Services Required* – This is one of the leading jobs for the CISO. They must champion the business value that a mature security program and a well-prepared incident response team provides to the organization. The CISO must ensure through the security program that all hardware, software, and network devices are up to date at their current patch levels and that the organization implements the correct configurations and recommended security settings. The CISO also must ensure that the necessary personnel, technology, and training for the company's incident response program have been acquired and used to train team members in preparation for responding to a variety of events. However, even with both of those in place, the CISO should not just focus on organizational personnel. The CISO should also have agreements in place with third-party vendors that can provide emergency services during a breach if required. Having these contracts beforehand will allow the CISO to move quickly in response to a breach incident and reduce the breadth of impact to critical business services.

4. *Have Real-Time Monitoring/Logging in Place* – The business will need to have real-time monitoring and network logging activated during a data breach. This control will significantly assist the forensic efforts during breach triage and remediation. However, there are many municipal, state, federal, and country requirements that require informing employees that they are subject to monitoring. Telling them can easily be implemented when users are given their accounts at the time of hire.

Typically, they sign a user consent form which notifies them they are subject to monitoring when using corporate network assets. You can also provide notification by having splash screens and user log-on banners to notify personnel they are on corporate networks and subject to the organization's information security regulations and acceptable use policies (AUP). Other efforts, like employing automated tools such as intrusion detection/prevention systems, firewalls, anti-virus, and threat-hunting platforms, can also assist security teams in monitoring for anomalous behavior and prevent incidents before they significantly interrupt business operations.

All of these solutions should have logging collection enabled. Combined, they will provide real-time network monitoring and also give the incident response team a repository of data from which to retrieve information for analysis. They can use this data to look for shifts in behavior that could be signs of anomalies to investigate. Note, this logging will require storage, so the CISO will also need to coordinate with the CIO and storage teams to ensure room is available to support these efforts.

5. _Make Legal Part of Incident Response Efforts_ – I highly recommend that you have a legal representative as part of your incident response/data breach response efforts. If they lack experience in technology, retain outside counsel with that knowledge. Cyber incidents are unique and have their own sets of circumstances around data privacy, data breach reporting laws, and possible liability issues from third parties. The business should have legal representation that understands these unique issues. Having representation as part of the team during a breach event will assist executive management in making critical decisions promptly. It will also help the CISO make decisions that are within legal bounds and more likely to hold up under court review.

6. _Review and Align Organizational Policies and Security Policies_ – The next thing I would recommend is to periodically review organizational policies against security policies to make sure they are aligned. If you have a security policy that states that system administrators who leave the organization must have their accounts suspended within three hours and Human Resources has a policy that says 12 hours, there is the potential for a mistake. Policies from different departments should support each other. It is this continuous review of security controls which the CISO should use to understand the security program's impact

on other departments and ensure the correct intent by all employees.

With that said, the CISO should also be aware of any adverse issues caused by a security control or policy that is too stringent and be willing to work with the business to reach a suitable compromise. If the CISO does not address these problems, they will become the seeds for shadow IT and eventually a doorway for a security incident.

7. *Establish Relationships with Law Enforcement Partners* – I have found from experience that it is helpful for CISOs to know their points of contact with law enforcement and any other regulatory organizations that can assist their response to a data breach if required. I believe it is very beneficial to be involved with institutions like the following and establish relationships with these organizations:

   a. https://www.infragard.org/ – InfraGard is a partnership between the FBI and members of the private sector. The program provides a vehicle for seamless public-private collaboration with government relevant to the protection of Critical Infrastructure.
   b. https://nfcausa.org/ – The National Fusion Center Association works to represent the interests of state, tribal, and major urban area fusion centers; encourage capable, efficient, ethical, lawful, and professional intelligence and information sharing; and prevent and reduce the harmful effects of crime and terrorism on victims, individuals, and communities.
   c. https://www.nationalisacs.org/ – Sector-based Information Sharing and Analysis Centers collaborate with each other via the National Council of ISACs.

8. *Establish Relationships with Information Sharing Organizations* – Finally, it is essential for the CISO to establish partnerships with peers and other cyber information sharing organizations. These agencies can be industry-specific Information Sharing, and Analysis Centers or they can be professional trade and industry groups. As a member of many of these organizations, I spend time collaborating with my peers. I learn from them about attacks they have seen or threat intelligence on methods that are being used to perpetuate fraudulent

activities that pertain to my organization's business operations. Security does not thrive in a vacuum. However, in a community, it will succeed. Be willing to get involved with your community and talk to your peers.

If you are concerned about what you are allowed to discuss, you should speak to legal counsel and understand your boundaries before you engage with others. I have had times where I needed specific information, and the peer I needed to speak with was willing to sign an NDA to protect both of our organizations. Be creative if required but establish these relationships and don't be afraid to ask for assistance. And just as important, be willing to provide help if it is requested.

Chapter 16 Key Point and Action Item 4

During an incident is the wrong time to reach out to establish a relationship with law enforcement, your regulators, your vendors, or anyone upon whom you will rely in a crisis.

You should perform a gap analysis of your state of data breach readiness as defined by the Department of Justice's eight steps a company can take to prepare and build action plans to close the gaps.

These are some foundational elements that CISOs can have in place that will assist them as they build their incident response program. Hopefully, with these measures in place, should the need arise to activate the incident response program the resultant breach remediation will be less complicated.

That leads us into the next phase of our discussion. One of our departments has notified us about some anomalous behavior they noticed in an email with a third-party vendor. Upon investigating the original ticket for support, a security analyst finds emails apparently spoofed from the organization's email server and customer support portal.

As the CISO, you start to look into this issue, noting the steps your team has followed as they pursued a digital trail that your instincts tell you isn't normal. Trust your instincts. It's time to get more eyes looking at this issue. You can always activate your incident response plan in stages as the event develops. That brings to mind our next question for discussion: *"During a data breach, what operations should the CISO be aware of and possibly manage as a member of the organization's business continuity effort and leader of the incident response team?"*

Putting the Puzzle Together

So, even with all of your hard work, you get notified by one of your business units that something is wrong with a code repository that the development team uses. In fact, when your team looks into the access logs, there is a discrepancy in the accounts that accessed it. Data in the repository seems to be out of place and jumbled. You want to think one of the developers, in a late-night caffeine-induced spree of coding, made a mess not following procedures.

However, your instincts tell you this is not normal and honestly, as a CISO, follow those instincts. It is better to explain later that you erred on the side of caution versus missing a significant breach of your company's intellectual property. You activate the incident response team and proceed to start collecting information. As you move to activate your procedures other processes will begin to unfold in parallel. These business continuity efforts are designed to position the organization to manage this incident and reduce its impact on the business and its customers. Let's talk about some of these operations that are activating, both under your effort as the incident response team leader and under the organization's designated leader for business continuity operations.

As you activate your incident response team, some of the first steps you will need to take include:

- Validate that this is a data breach event. Your team will need to examine the initial information and available logs to verify that it occurred, and if possible identify what type of information may have been accessed and by what methods, i.e., internal/external attack, or accidental disclosure.

- Activate the team once verification has occurred. Have the team start documenting their processes as they triage the event and seek to isolate the damage. Report your initial findings to the Business Continuity Team Leader and establish a methodology for providing updates.

- As your incident response team begins investigation and remediation, you will need to make a decision on which members to activate. As the team leader, you should have representatives from Management, IT, Legal, Public Relations, Risk, Finance, HR, and Audit on your team.

You will know as the investigation progresses how you need to activate. With that said, you should be communicating with them, so they are informed, and if you require assistance, they are ready to provide their help.

- As the incident response process proceeds, you will need to collect information on the scope and type of breach. You will need to report to executive management and the Business Continuity Team Leader information such as whether you believe this is criminal activity; what data, IT assets, or employees may be involved; and the current progress in preserving evidence for later forensic examination.

- Now that you understand which assets were affected by this breach, you will need to notify the Business Continuity Team Leader what data owners (internal/external) may have been impacted by this event. Having Legal as part of the team and involved in the remediation process is critical. Legal can help make recommendations as to which laws or contracts dictate if breach notification is required and what that looks like to the business. Legal is also essential if you suspect the commission of a crime and it appears that you need to activate the incident response communication plan and request law enforcement assistance.

You should also discuss with Legal what provisions in the company's cyber insurance policy can be activated if needed. If this is an extensive incident, you should consider bringing in third-party personnel to assist with the investigation and collecting evidence. Having agreements in place saves time and having provisions in the cyber insurance policy to pay for it makes it even better. Just make sure you understand those requirements and understand the extra costs, so you can speak with your procurement team about emergency funding.

Building Your Own Audit Trail

One of the workflows that begins when initiating an incident response process is the documenting of every task, decision, and step that is taken by team members. On another level, the CISO must also document the costs associated with this breach. During this event cycle, you should remember to record all of the employees and contractors who were involved and the hours they worked on this incident. You should also document costs such as forensic services, the purchase of new tools or hardware, and hours of lost productivity for the affected employees. This information can be used during the "lessons learned" phase after the breach has concluded to understand better what changes need to be made in the organization's plans for future events.

Let's now shift our focus and look at what is happening in the organization as the CISO leads the incident response team to investigate and counter the impact of this adverse event. The CISO has reported to executive management that an incident is ongoing, and the incident response team is activated. At this time, organizations will typically enable their business continuity process. This process is unique to each business. Some may initially convene just their crisis communications team and later activate the full business continuity team if required. For the sake of our discussion, let's look at some of the realities of the impact a breach has on an organization and discuss how the business continuity team interacts with the CISO.

It is hard for an organization to keep the fact that they have suffered a significant data breach quiet. Incidents are often leaked to the press, even before the incident response team has completed its investigation. Couple that with the ebb and flow of the media trying to get information from the organization and customers and employees on social media discussing the incident, and it can quickly turn into a critical business-impacting issue. The organization must have a plan. This plan should have a trigger similar to the incident response plan.

As the CISO activates the incident response team, the crisis communications plan should also be triggered. In the beginning, there will be limited information as you are in the initial stages of understanding the scope of the breach. However, as the CISO is busy behind the scenes, the business continuity team should be active in directing the crisis communications plan and proactively thinking ahead. Specifically:

- Do we know who was affected by this breach yet? If so, who do we need to notify first? If it was internal employees, we need to look at how we handle the situation to avoid a loss of trust in the organization due to the data compromise. If it was external partners, was it customers or vendors? If customers, we need to consult legal representation to understand what breach notification laws apply. If it was vendors, we need to talk to our legal representation to understand what contract clauses may apply that require notification, and what format that should take.

- Now that we understand who is affected, as the investigation continues the business continuity team should be looking at which assets can be prepared for a more substantial response if it is required. I would suggest they review the organization's cyber insurance policy to see what services are available. There will be a need for a dedicated web page to put out information, the business may need to activate a call center to handle irate customers' questions, and finally, there will be a need to address the media. Some cyber insurance policies have a rider to pay for emergency Public Relations assistance. Either way, whether it is in-house PR, or it's contracted to a third party, there needs to be a focus on what statements will be released and what information they should contain.

- As we develop our statements for the press, we also need to be monitoring social media and the press for leaks. Currently, we are fighting the incident, and there has been no word released of the breach. We know this is only a matter of time, so we want to focus on what we can issue at this time and control the story based on the data we have. What we plan at this stage is critical, because when we do address the media and our customers, we need to be transparent and honest when we communicate with them. We need to make sure our message expresses remorse, shows that we care deeply, and demonstrates that we are taking the remediation of the incident seriously. We need to communicate to the affected parties that the situation is fluid and we are answering questions with the information we currently have available.

We need to convey which individuals are affected and the impact of the breach. We should explain what the affected individuals need to do to protect themselves immediately, and then disclose to all parties when and where the crisis communications spokesperson will provide them with their next update. As we are planning all of this, we need to make sure Legal reviews the information we will release and tells us what questions we are allowed to answer. We want to be as transparent as possible and focus on maintaining our relationships with the affected stakeholders. With that said, an investigation is ongoing, and the information we currently have can quickly change, so we need to take care not to make promises or state facts until authorized to do so.

- News of the data breach has been disclosed and is now public information, but the business continuity team has prepared, and we have crafted our first statement. The focus of the report is on the investigation, and it mentions who the organization is working with, steps taken and being taken, and ends with the promise to provide future updates. The web page is now active for affected parties to get information and we have developed scripts for the call center, which is handling questions from those individuals.

  On the social media side, we are answering questions and monitoring social media for rumors that could impact the business and its ability to manage this incident. At this time, it's all on the CISO and the incident response team as they continue to remediate the breach incident. The business units should approach this as an opportunity to show leadership, and they need to be the primary face of the company to the customer.

  We need to be careful about claiming the issue is being resolved or giving any numbers until the CISO closes the incident. We instead should focus on the steps being taken to protect the customer and on using our communications avenues and present a consistent message. The business will also need to focus on regulators or compliance investigators if the breach included regulated data and should work closely with the CISO to provide data required by regulators as soon as possible.

The breach investigation has concluded. Usually, by this time, media coverage has subsided but as an organization, we still have customers that need assistance. The organization and the CISO must now embark upon the next stage of breach remediation, and that is "lessons learned." All parties should submit their notes and what went well/what needs improvement recommendations to the CISO and Business Continuity Team Leader. Then the organization should review the impact of the breach and what can be improved to assist in responding to the next event. It is this discussion for continuous improvement that will lead us to our final question: *"What steps should be followed to resume normal operations and improve data breach management efforts?"*

Never Stop Learning

As the CISO, you will be leading some of these discussions. You will have first-hand knowledge of how the breach occurred and the damage that was done and can make recommendations to reduce the risk exposure to the organization from future events. I use Section 3.4, *"Post Incident Activity,"* of NIST's Special Publication 800-61r2 revision 1 *"Computer Security Incident Handling Guide"* (Cichonski, Millar, et al., NIST SP800-61 rev2 2012) as a reference for post-breach activities and lessons learned meetings.

This guide describes the benefit to the incident response team and all parties that assisted with the incident. These lessons learned meetings are to bring closure concerning the work just completed and seek to improve security measures and help assist all teams to evolve and be ready to respond to future threats. I recommend that these lessons learned meetings take place within several days of the incident to ensure team members' thoughts, decisions, and notes are still fresh and accurate. This information and the team's recollections will fade over time. Address specific questions in these meetings, such as:

- Precisely what happened, dates, times?
- How well did the teams and management perform?
- Were documented procedures for managing an incident followed? Were they adequate or are there recommendations to improve them?
- What information was needed by the crisis communications team first?
- Were there problems with getting information from the CISO about incident activities? Are there recommendations to help that communications path flow more smoothly?
- Were there any steps taken by the teams that inhibited the recovery process?
- Is there anything the team members or management would do differently next time?
- Are there any information-sharing processes with internal or external stakeholders that can be improved?
- What can cyber-hygiene processes be put in place to prevent similar incidents in the future?
- Were there any indicators of compromise in the collected threat intelligence from the event that can be used to detect similar issues in the future?
- What are additional resources required by the CISO to help mitigate future incidents and reduce their impact on the organization's business operations?

As the CISO, you will have much of the information required to help answer these questions, and it is imperative that you maintain plan these meetings so that all parties can come together to provide contextual data to make improvements. You will use this information to prepare a post-incident analysis report that you will contribute to executive management.

This story should have a chronology of the event from beginning to end, issues discovered, and metrics on how the team performed and the management of the incident. The report should conclude with recommendations for improvement and the breakdown of costs and impact on the business. Once you complete this report, you are still not done. The company will be in the process of recovering from the breach, and the CISO needs to assist.

Chapter 16 Key Point and Action Item 5

Each network is different. Each attack, while often of common origin, mutates as obstacles are encountered and countermeasures are deployed. While difficult to do in the moment, learning to take notes about how the attack is unfolding and the measures you are taking is invaluable as input for training and process improvement.

You should build a narrative that describes the anatomy of each breach you experience, giving specific attention to the recovery efforts and what went wrong during recovery so that subsequent recovery efforts can evolve. Repeat this process for each subsequent security incident that involves a service disruption and measure the performance of recovery efforts over time.

From a business perspective, the company will be looking to protect and reestablish its relationships with those affected by the breach. The company will need to project its commitment to securing data that has been entrusted to it and cite new changes to security that allow it to tell a credible story of the business' strengths and where improvements are needed. As CISO, you will be an instrumental partner in this process as your organization begins recovering from the damage done to its brand and reputation.

SANS conducted a study on the costs associated with cleaning up a breach and the post-breach impact to an organization (Fogerty 2015). In this survey, at least 12% of the organizations reported after-effects of a breach, and post-breach operations were ongoing long after it was over. Some of these operations included dealing with potential fines and lawsuits, ongoing cleanup of recovering compromised data, and loss of customer trust and confidence in the business.

Don't Forget to Document the Costs

This survey also documented the costs to the company for a breach. Interestingly enough, it found that 81% of organizations that had classified their sensitive data before the breach and had prioritized their resources and security controls to reduce risk to their data had much lower costs associated with cleanup. It also found that of the 64% of those surveyed whose breaches did not receive media attention, over half had little to no impact on their business brand. Those receiving substantial media attention suffered significant loss in brand reputation. Be aware of these costs and understand that your security program and its controls can be a major factor in protecting the organization. The following table is from the SANS survey (Fogerty 2015), and depicts the costs for a breach of fewer than 1,000 records.

Expense	Amount
Controls Acquired	
Admin Policy Development	<$25,000
Training and Awareness	<$25,000
Additional Staffing	$100,000-$500,000
Managed Services	$25,000-$100,000
Technical Tools	$25,000-$100,000
Physical Controls	$25,000-$100,000
Customer Support	
Information Hotline	$5,000-$25,000
Credit Monitoring	$25,000-$100,000
Customer Notification	<$5,000
Brand and Reputation	
Drop in Revenue	$5,000-$100,000
Drop in Sales	$25,000-$500,000
Customer Churn	$500,000-$1,000,000
Public Relations	$25,000-$100,000
Brand Conference	$25,000-$100,000

Figure 16.1 Accounting for the Cost of a Breach

As you can see, there are some substantial costs associated with data breaches, and this is for a data breach of fewer than 1,000 records – imagine if your organization had lost one million customer records. You can use this type of information to help your organization understand its risk. I have found that when you address executive management on this subject, it is best to frame the discussion for the audience. Have a business discussion on impact to services and costs associated with remediation. Stay away from using scare tactics and discussing threats and vulnerabilities unless you are specifically asked a question in that regard.

As we finish this chapter, remember that your job as the CISO, Incident Response Program Manager, and Incident Response Team Leader is to understand the broader impact of a breach on the organization and the stakeholders involved during an incident response event. With this broader understanding of the impact to the business, you should have more insight into the controls and policies you select to build your security program and train your staff.

I have personally used this information to educate my incident response personnel and help them understand the shock to a business and its operations that a data breach entails and the impact to the company and customers that a breach can have over time as the remediation efforts wind down to completion. Having this greater insight into the business helps the CISO understand the context of the decisions they need to make during an emergency and the services their team must provide to be useful during an incident.

In closing, for those of you beginning the process of planning for an incident and building your program, I would recommend a good check sheet for data breach response (CISO Executive Network 2010) to review what your organization currently has in place and then have a discussion with management and begin to prepare. Don't be afraid to reach out to your peers in the cybersecurity community who have experience in this area. All of us CISOs had to start at one time or another with no program or limited resources, and we should feel free to ask for help and collaborate with each other. In the end, doing this makes all of us safer and matures our security community.

Summary

In Chapter 16 we began our discussion by asking these questions:

- What steps should an organization take to prepare for a data breach?
- During a data breach, what operations should the CISO be aware of and possibly manage as a member of the organization's business continuity effort and leader of the incident response team?
- What steps should be followed to resume normal operations and resume data breach management efforts?

To say that the CISO has a broad set of responsibilities is the definition of understatement. Add to the technical scope the responsibility of avoiding regulatory missteps and breach of contract while making the tough calls to prioritize triage and then recovery of critical information assets. While you're at it, please make sure the vast list of stakeholders is kept informed of the status of recovery efforts. Chapter 16 shows the culmination of all the preparation the CISO has asked the organization to do. Was it enough? Probably not for the first incident, but if you stay in learning mode, you'll get there.

In closing, we would like to leave you with these five key points and next steps:

1. Don't make the problem worse than it is. When systems are partially disrupted, the application-level controls for access to data are easily to circumvent by mistake. This can escalate a routine service interruption into a privacy violation that triggers a breach notification. **You should catalog data handling procedures for recovery activities that adhere to regulatory and contractual restrictions.**

2. While many large organizations have experienced dozens to hundreds of incidents that have forced them to develop mature incident response programs, smaller organizations, and inexperienced teams do not have that collective muscle memory upon which to rely. **You should develop a management response checklist to drive the initial role assignments for the executive team, including at least you and the CIO and your incident manager. The initial response steps should seek to triage the damage and bring calm to the response teams.**

3. Helmuth von Moltke the Elder famously said: "No battle plan survives contact with the enemy." Moltke was coming to understand that with modern weapons and larger, better equipped armies, resilience was far more important than drilling to achieve perfect battle formation. Resilience, in his mind, was achieved through what-if exercises that exposed his leaders to as many realistic scenarios as possible, so they could adapt to changing conditions. **You should build a tabletop exercise using similar circumstances to those outlined by Matt for the hospital to allow your management team to simulate a breach response and recovery, so you can begin to develop your muscle memory.**

4. During an incident is the wrong time to reach out to establish a relationship with law enforcement, your regulators, your vendors, or anyone upon whom you will rely in a crisis. **You should perform a gap analysis of your state of data breach readiness as defined by the Department of Justice's eight steps a company can take to prepare and build action plans to close the gaps.**

5. Each network is different. Each attack, while often of common origin, mutates as obstacles are encountered and countermeasures are deployed. While difficult to do in the moment, learning to take notes about how the attack is unfolding and the measures you are taking is invaluable as input for training and process improvement. **You should build a narrative that describes the anatomy of each breach you experience, giving specific attention to the recovery efforts and what went wrong during recovery so that subsequent recovery efforts can evolve. Repeat this process for each subsequent security incident that involves a service disruption and measure the performance of recovery efforts over time.**

Let's come back to the expanding scope of the CISO and the obligation to keep the company clear of legal and regulatory jeopardy. Matt mentioned in this chapter that incident response is a team sport and Bill pointed out that the legal department is on your team. Preparing the legal team to run point with law enforcement and your regulators, as well as be on the lookout for contractual obligations during breaches and suspected breaches is a prudent step worth taking.

Chapter 17 – The Aftermath: Forensics and the Value of Post-Mortem Reviews

Introduction

Although we are covering them in one chapter, forensics activities and post-mortem activities for cyber incidents are entirely different. We're going to repeat a passage from the introduction to Chapter 14: while it's helpful to break the entire incident response discipline into a series of discrete phases so that each can be described individually to assist with training and the command and control of response activities, it is rarely clear-cut when one process ends, and the next begins. There is often significant overlap, and as new information emerges, it is usually necessary to revisit a phase previously thought completed. For instance, while in recovery, monitoring activity may detect the presence of indicators of compromise identified for the current cyber incident and that may send you all the way back to the containment phase.

Bill draws the distinction between forensics for law enforcement versus what an organization might do for internal investigative value. Depending on your industry and the specific details of a breach, preserving evidence may be essential. Regardless of your organization's desire to use the courts, regulatory and contractual obligations may force you to preserve evidence and establish the chain of custody. Bill goes on to discuss how to incorporate post-mortem reviews into your process for continual improvement.

Matt helps the reader prepare for forensic activities, including working with your legal team, law enforcement, suppliers and anyone else who will need to know in advance what actions they can and cannot take and what assets, physical and digital, need to be sequestered. He then reviews the lifecycle of forensic analysis so that the organization can be prepared to conduct such an analysis by pulling together the right combination of internal and external resources.

Gary begins his discussion with a review of forensics methods that apply to all layers of the stack, including the network, system, software, mobile, and IOT. He then guides the reader through the decision-making process and the requirements for both building a forensics capability in-house, including a build-out of the lab, and staffing a forensics team. The caution to the reader is that this can be expensive, and the needs change continually, so be prepared for an ongoing investment.

Some of the questions the authors used to frame their thoughts for this chapter include:

- What is digital forensics and what value does it bring to the business?
- What resources are required to develop a digital forensics lab and should the CISO build one?
- What roles and resources are needed to field a digital forensics team?

Forensics and Post-Mortem – Bonney

> "The post-mortem is most effective when pairing findings with actions. It might be cathartic to identify the root cause, but you must be just as forthcoming about the behaviors that need to change to avoid a repeat occurrence."

There is a more pronounced overlap between the activities in the forensics phase and the activities of four other phases: detect, contain, eradicate, and recover. In many cases, the awareness that there is a cyber incident underway that will have a sufficient impact to warrant a forensic investigation doesn't occur until the eradication or recovery phase. This delay can be quite detrimental to good forensics outcomes. But before we dive too deeply into these activities, let's take a step back and define what we mean by forensics in this context.

The Purpose of Forensics

There are other texts and many training opportunities that guide organizations and practitioners operationally integrated with law enforcement, national defense, or cybersecurity service delivery. For individuals in those roles, digital forensics consists of using various techniques to seek to understand, at a deep level, how code, systems, data, processes, and organizations were targeted, penetrated, and affected. They use that knowledge to prosecute crimes, provide for the common defense and, in some cases, develop new offensive cyber capabilities.

For our purposes, we're going to recognize that you are not likely to be conducting the types of in-depth forensics typical of law enforcement or intelligence. These would include:

- Cross-drive analysis – correlating information across multiple hard drives to create a composite of activity)
- Live analysis – allowing various code snippets to execute in a controlled environment to determine their purpose
- Chip-off analysis – removing chips by de-soldering or chemically removing the adhesives holding the chip in place on the board to connect it to extraction devices

Instead, you will have two primary purposes for your forensics activities: preserving evidence for potential criminal investigation or civil litigation discovery and understanding your organization's vulnerabilities so that you can take additional preventive actions as warranted.

Understanding these two goals, you can start to design a process for the forensics phase of your cyber incident response. Let's take them in order: first, preserving evidence and second, identifying vulnerabilities.

Preserving evidence for future criminal investigation or civil litigation discovery will require you to capture at least the following:

1. Copies of log files for activity (including data extraction and alteration) on associated network devices, servers, and applications

2. Copies of log files for access to associated network devices, servers, and applications

3. Copies of configuration settings for all associated network devices, servers, and applications

4. Copies of log files for network, server, and application protection systems, including intrusion detection, anti-virus, intrusion prevention, firewall, SIEM, and access management

5. Copies (snapshots) of virtual machines and virtual containers for all associated servers and applications

6. Physical hard drives and bare metal servers for the non-virtualized infrastructure of systems and applications that were forced offline or deemed necessary to replace due to malware infection, configuration damage, vandalism, or tampering. This includes personal devices, such as mobile phones, tablet computers, and other personal technology.

Identifying the vulnerabilities for your organization will require you to analyze the following:

1. The attack vector(s) that were used to gain access

2. The nature of the lateral movement within your organization

3. The network assets and information assets that were compromised, including infections with malware, altered configurations, vandalism, and other tampering

4. The data that was extracted (or the harm that was done if the purpose was more vandalism than exfiltration)

5.   The business processes that were targeted and perhaps impacted

Rules of Evidence

Notice that in both cases, the items you will analyze or preserve as evidence come from the same root. How you handle these items is critically important. Without getting too deep into rules for admissibility of evidence in legal proceedings, suffice it to say that two fundamental forces impact how evidence is gathered.

The first is that courts, aided by governments at the local and national level, have requirements for admissibility that have been evolving over centuries in some cases. The second is that the digital world has been changing at a much quicker pace. In the 1960s, the discovery of an instance of cybercrime would merely require the seizure of tapes, hard drives, and (if necessary in rare cases) mainframes. These items would be preserved and analyzed in due time, providing a complete reconstruction from the evidence at hand.

Cybercrime was called computer crime back then because criminals needed physical access to the computer and cybercrime, which requires network access, was still a fantasy of the future. In other words, you could physically put your hands on all the available evidence.

That is not the case today. First networks dramatically increased the number of devices that participated in any business process's digital value chain. Then remote access altered the very concept of jurisdiction over cybercrime. Finally, virtualization blurred the relationship between an asset and a business process. As a result, we can no longer rely solely on physical evidence.

With these changes, though, new issues arise in demonstrating to the court that the evidence provided is both admissible and what the court considers to be "best evidence." "Best evidence" is a legal term that seeks to address the evolving nature of introducing "copies" into evidence given advances in printing, photocopying, and now, copying a computer file.

In the past, when copying was purely a manual transcription process, admissibility rules sought to limit the negative impact on proceedings due to imprecise or forged copies. Now, there is additional focus on the ability to establish the authenticity of a copy, perhaps using an unalterable watermark or, where necessary, establishing a chain of custody, such as by showing the generation and demonstrating that the copy has been stored in an unaltered state using a WORM disk.

With all of this complexity, now more than ever it is vitally important that you engage with your legal department or appropriate outside counsel. Start early in the planning and process documentation phases to establish methodologies for establishing the authenticity of evidence and chain of custody to meet the courts' rules and preserve the evidence your organization will need to meet its legal obligations. Please recognize that this chapter does not constitute legal advice.

It is also critical to work with your legal team during incident response activities so that decisions about potential liability, potential legal redress, regulatory enforcement, and other considerations that might suggest evidence that you need to preserve are made promptly, i.e., before evidence is lost or destroyed. Your legal team can also play a key role in communicating with law enforcement and regulators to make real-time good-faith decisions about requirements for future deliberations about the incident.

Keep in mind that it is not just about failing to give your organization the right evidence to defend itself or enforce a judgment on another party. Preserving evidence is also required due care that organizations must take, and courts can summarily rule against your organization or sanction (fine, impose a consent decree on) your organization due to egregious errors in this regard.

Finally, you will certainly do your best, working with your legal team and law enforcement, to anticipate the needs of evidence preservation associated with any one incident. But, in the unfortunate circumstance that legal action does result from the impact of this incident, there is a decent likelihood that this will require additional discovery activities. It will be difficult to execute these activities manually or with the staff on hand.

Discovery demands might include documentation of procedures, evidence of complying with procedures, internal memorandum (including, for example, email, text messages, and voicemail) that might shed light on management intention with regard to enforcement of compliance, funding to levels of due care, prioritization of various tasks, disposition of assets, obligations accepted, agreements entered into, copies of files recovered from backups, copies of files recovered from damaged disks, copies of files recovered after deletion, and a host of other options too numerous to list and impossible to predict given the unique nature of any incident and the business processes it might impact.

Given all of this complexity, you'll probably want to augment your capabilities with software or by contracting with a cyber forensics firm to assist you with the planning and execution of forensics practices. Here again, work with your legal team to make sure that any software or services you sign up for will meet your needs. Include the use of these tools and collaboration with service providers early in the planning process. Some decisions simply cannot be made too late in the process, and you should not overlook the risk of losing or destroying critical evidence because of poor planning.

Chapter 17 Key Point and Action Item 1

The chain of custody for evidence must be established immediately, it is not something that can be done retroactively. You need to know ahead of time the circumstances under which you must preserve evidence, the exact items to collect, and the appropriate handling procedures.

You should work with your legal team to establish criteria for sequestering assets and build a checklist of all the items to collect when the criteria have been met.

Determine What Happened

At this point, you have preserved the evidence that you, your legal team, and your forensics service have jointly identified as required for this incident. It is now time to turn your attention to conducting your forensic analysis (again, possibly with the assistance of a cyber forensics firm) to make sure you improve your security posture as necessary. It is essential to keep in mind that within this process, you are not looking for evidence of a crime. You are seeking to understand the attack vector(s) used to gain access, how the attackers moved laterally within your network, the compromised assets, what was taken, altered or destroyed, and which business processes were affected.

In each case, you are interested in learning what was done to make sure you have addressed that vulnerability. Do not make the mistake of assuming that "if they never got access in the first place, this would not have happened" and focusing only on endpoint security. For the attack to be as successful as it was, the attackers had to be able to move laterally and authenticate to internal assets that are probably protected differently than your endpoints.

A useful tool to help you identify all the stages of the incident that you should seek to understand is known as The Cyber *Kill Chain*®

developed by Lockheed Martin.[25] The Cyber Kill Chain comes from a military concept related to the structure of an attack.

Many information security professionals routinely use the Cyber Kill Chain to help them design incident response plans and train to respond during an attack by identifying the stage in the kill chain that describes an adversary's activities and then counter those activities. The Cyber Kill Chain is also useful to provide a template for forensic analysis, inspiring you to address how the attackers accomplished each stage and how to deprive future attackers of the same avenues.

The Cyber Kill Chain, as published by Lockheed Martin (Eric M. Hutchins 2011), is as follows:

1. **Reconnaissance** – Research, identification, and selection of targets, often represented as crawling Internet websites such as conference proceedings and mailing lists for email addresses, social relationships, or information on specific technologies. [26]

2. **Weaponization** – Coupling a remote access trojan with an exploit into a deliverable payload, typically by means of an automated tool (weaponizer). Increasingly, client application data files such as Adobe Portable Document Format (PDF) or Microsoft Office documents serve as the weaponized deliverable.

3. **Delivery** – Transmission of the weapon to the targeted environment. The three most prevalent delivery vectors for weaponized payloads by APT (Advanced Persistent Threats) actors, as observed by the Lockheed Martin Computer Incident Response Team (LM-CIRT) for the years 2004-2010, are email attachments, websites, and USB removable media.

4. **Exploitation** – After the weapon is delivered to the victim host, exploitation triggers the intruders' code. Most often, exploitation targets an application or operating system vulnerability, but it could also more simply exploit the users themselves or leverage an operating system feature that auto-executes code.

5. **Installation** – Installation of a remote access trojan or backdoor on the victim system allows the adversary to maintain persistence inside the environment.

---

[25] https://www.lockheedmartin.com/content/dam/lockheed/data/corporate/documents/LM-White-Paper-Intel-Driven-Defense.pdf

[26] While a relatively competent list of penetration techniques from 2011, you should add recent entries into the toolkit of attackers for consideration.

6. **Command and Control (C2)** – Typically, compromised hosts must beacon outbound to an Internet controller server to establish a C2 channel. APT malware especially requires manual interaction rather than conducting activity automatically. Once the C2 channel establishes, intruders have "hands on the keyboard" access inside the target environment.

7. **Actions on Objectives** – Only now, after progressing through the first six phases, can intruders take actions to achieve their original objectives. Typically, this objective is data exfiltration which involves collecting, encrypting, and extracting information from the victim environment. Violations of data integrity or availability are potential objectives as well. Alternatively, the intruders may only desire access to the initial victim box for use as a hop point to compromise additional systems and move laterally inside the network.

Even though we're not talking about responding to an active incident in this chapter, the countermeasures described in this whitepaper are instructive in deciding how to address the vulnerabilities you discovered through your analysis.

	Detect	Deny	Disrupt	Degrade	Deceive
1 Reconnaisssance	Web Analytics	Firewall ACL			
2 Weaponization	NIDS	NIPS			
3 Delivery	Vigilant User	Proxy filter	Inline AV	Email Queuing	
4 Exploitation	HIDS	Vendor Patch	EMET, DEP		
5 Installation	HIDS		AV		
6 Command & Control	NIDS	Firewall ACL	NIPS	Tarpit	DNS redirect
7 Actions on Objectives	Audit Log			Quality of Service throttle	Honeypot

Figure 17.1 Disrupting the Lockheed Martin Kill Chain

Using this chart as an aid, you should ask yourself the following questions:

- How might you detect, deny, disrupt, degrade, or deceive the activities you discovered for the attack vector(s) that were used against you?

- How did the attackers gain access and move laterally within your network?
- What were the compromised assets, what was taken, altered or destroyed, and what business processes were affected?

Now think more broadly and ask yourself these additional questions:

- What else do you need to monitor?
- Who do you need to train and what training do they need?
- What do you need to patch, upgrade, or retire?
- Where should you exert greater vigilance over less vulnerable or important assets?
- What access and actions do you explicitly need to block?
- What technology gaps do you have and how do you fill them?

You should also seek to understand the business assets that were attacked and why. Understanding the value placed on these assets by the attackers might help you anticipate what other assets might currently be or soon be under attack as well.

For additional reading, I recommend another whitepaper by Lockheed Martin: "Seven Ways to Apply the Cyber Kill Chain with a Threat Intelligence Platform." [27]

Post-Mortem Review

Now that the evidence has been collected and preserved and you have conducted your analysis, it is time to conduct the post-mortem review with your organization. The post-mortem is not monolithic. You should be flexible in your approach and tailor it to the type and scope of the incident. At the least, you should share your findings with your immediate team, your direct supervisor, and your peers.

Some incidents require a wider audience for the post-mortem. These include incidents with a wide-scale impact to internal processes or customer-facing processes. Also include incidents that were the result of or amplified by multiple human failures, such as the ubiquitous clicking on links from suspicious emails, sharing passwords, leaving passwords visible, or other actions you train your organization to avoid.

27

http://lockheedmartin.com/content/dam/lockheed/data/corporate/documents/Seven_Ways_to_Apply_the_Cyber_Kill_Chain_with_a_Threat_Intelligence_Platform.PDF

The post-mortem is most effective when pairing findings with actions. It might be cathartic or provide a sense of closure to identify the root cause, but unless you are just as forthcoming with the behaviors that need to change and the required actions, your workforce is not likely to make the changes necessary to avoid a repeat of the incident. They will feel lectured and picked on if the post-mortem is exclusively about what mistakes they made, and they will be confused about how they can help or what they must do unless it is explicitly spelled out.

There are several questions that you should try to address with all audiences, but the exact framing you use will vary. In discussing how the organization prepares for incidents, you might share with the larger team that the curriculum will change to include more training on how to spot suspicious email and how to report it to the technical group. You'll want to include when to expect that instruction, what form it will take, and how you will measure success. With the management team, you would likely add details about how much it will cost.

Here are some of the questions you will want to address:

- Was the organization properly trained, and if not, what are the specific gaps to address?
  - o Did we detect the incident timely?
  - o Did we report what we found correctly?
  - o Did we take prompt action to respond?

- Were our communications appropriate?
  - o Did we communicate to the impacted workforce?
  - o Did we escalate properly for technical assistance and to inform management?
  - o Did we keep customers and media properly informed?
  - o Did we properly notify law enforcement and regulators?

- Are our technical capabilities, including staffing levels, staff skill sets, tools, and service providers, adequate to the required tasks?

- What was the total impact of this incident?
  - o What were the hard costs of damaged assets and lost revenue?
  - o What was the impact on contractual obligations?
  - o What were the intangible costs such as damage to the brand and lost opportunity?
  - o How long were business processes impacted?

o   What are the legal ramifications, including breach notification, customer "make good," and potential regulatory action?

- What corrective actions do we need to take?
  o   Have we addressed all the short-term actions, including eradication and recovery?
  o   For our other systems that might be vulnerable to this attack or similar attacks, what is the plan to address, how long will it take, and how much will it cost?
  o   Are there medium-term to long-term actions to consider, such as system upgrades, system replacement, or changing existing service providers or hiring new ones? How long will these changes take and how much will they cost?

- Did our analysis show that there were third parties that contributed, through inappropriate action or lack of action, and did we address that issue appropriately?
- How confident are we that the corrective actions we have taken give us reasonable assurance that we can prevent the same or a similar attack from occurring in the future?

In addition to the questions listed above, the post-mortem review should include the following summation of the incident:

- The chronology of the incident. Include here what is known about when the attack began (note: it might not be possible to ascertain when reconnaissance began). Also include when you detected it, when you contained it, what steps you took to recover, when you put systems back in service, and when you considered the incident closed
- The root cause of the incident
- The corrective actions you have taken
- The next steps that you will take
- The costs incurred
- The potential legal impacts
- The 30, 60 and 90-day plans for follow up, including training, repairs, legal, and changes to third-party relationships

Chapter 17 Key Point and Action Item 2

Learning from failure is essential as the likelihood of being attacked again is near 100%. Asking ourselves what we could do differently and what we experienced that we didn't expect are invaluable disciplines.

You should create your own template for conducting your post-mortem reviews to answer the questions laid out in this section, incorporating additions and changes based on your internal review and your repetition of the post-mortem review process.

Planning for Forensic Investigations – Stamper

> "Cutting edge digital forensic tools are not being created and driven by law enforcement, but by private companies who need them for regulatory compliance and incident management."
>
> (SANS)

Unless your organization and your security team are quite large, it's unlikely that you will have dedicated expertise and resources available to facilitate forensic investigations of security-related matters, notably breaches. Nevertheless, there will be scenarios where having access to forensic capabilities will be necessary. Similar to the incident and breach responses, planning for forensic analysis in advance should be an essential priority associated with the CISO's security program, even for smaller organizations. Let's take a look at some of the core planning required to prepare you for when a forensic analysis is needed.

Why do we need forensic capabilities as part of our overall security program? There are two principal reasons. First, forensics supports legal claims and actions. Essentially, we use forensic analysis to determine if a crime has been committed and, ideally, determine attribution and present evidence that is legally admissible to support our claim in a court of law. This analysis can be required when there are disputes related to intellectual property, rogue employees, or corporate espionage. Another reason we might need forensic analysis is simply the matter of determining what took place and how – documenting "packet truth."[28] Forensics provides a great set of capabilities to evaluate the "history" of our environment (what took place at each stage or phase of the kill chain) and how actors who were not authorized made changes to that environment.

While there is overlap between these two capabilities, there are certain conditions precedent that need to be defined. If a forensic analysis is going to be used to support legal proceedings, effectively legally-defensible analyses, the activities must be legally authorized. Few things are worse than having evidence of a crime that would corroborate your case only to have the evidenced determined to be not legally admissible because the forensic analysis was not

---

[28] "Packet Truth" is meant to imply the insight and knowledge we obtain while evaluating logs, packet captures, and other network detail. Not to overstate the obvious, packet truth is challenged when there has been spoofing, man-in-the-middle, or other tampering efforts – to wit my evangelism of using threat modeling.

appropriately authorized, or the chain of custody did not offer the right assurance. To ensure proper chain of custody practices, you need to plan how you will handle forensic evidence (more on this below).

Preparing for a Forensic Analysis

When preparing for forensic analysis, make sure that you speak with your legal counsel and outline some of the scenarios where forensic analysis would be valuable. As discussed in Chapter 15, we should anticipate certain types of incidents. Revisit the list of potential incidents that you have planned for and determine what kind of forensic analysis to use in these scenarios. Recognize that just like threats and risks, evidence can come from many potential sources.

Evidence can be left behind by perpetrators outside of your organization (such as APTs, criminal elements, corporate espionage, state-sponsored actors, in-laws, among other unsavory actors). It can originate from inside the organization (for example, disgruntled and rogue employees). And it can come from your supplier and vendor ecosystem (this could include third-party service providers, "vetted" independent contractors, and the manufacturers and suppliers of systems, software, and hardware used in your environment). Anticipate needing to collect evidence outside of your "four walls," and plan how you will get it. Further, with the advent of connecting more operational technology (IoT, ICS, and SCADA) to our networks, it's important not to overlook these systems as potential sources of evidence.

Once you've evaluated these potential sources, coordinate a discussion with legal counsel to understand the repercussions of gathering evidence from these sources. Work out a process that is consistent with your organization's priorities (e.g., attribution and prosecution when cases arise or – potentially in conflict with those two items – the restoration of services).[29] For scenarios that involve the collection of evidence used to determine if there was a rogue insider involved, engage both human resources and legal counsel in this process.

While in the United States there are limited expectations of privacy in the workplace, we cannot say the same for organizations that operate outside of the U.S. As a case in point, privacy in the workplace in a

---

[29] Specifically, there may be a conflict between the desire to obtain attribution and the need to resume operations. This conflict should be anticipated in advance and organizational priorities established – potentially system by system – such that the procedures and expectations for how an incident that may involve forensics will be handled are documented.

European context is expected by employees and legally enforced.[30] Knowing what can and cannot be collected in support of an investigation in advance is critical. Where legal privacy protections preclude the collection of the evidence systematically, you'll need to look at alternative approaches such as user analytics that anonymize activity that can be unmasked subsequently with appropriate legal justification (e.g., a search warrant).

Equally important, the collection of evidence needs to be legally authorized. This authorization requires that practices are consistent with applicable laws and regulations. In the United States, Federal Rules of Evidence [31] govern this process. Changes as recent as December 2017 to section 902, subsection 14 (902(14)) reflect the evolving nature of digital forensics and are focused on streamlining the admissibility of electronic evidence by standardizing certain practices and expectations.

Specifically, the hashing value to determine the integrity of forensic evidence (essentially a presumption of authenticity). Documented and strong chain-of-custody practices should be front and center in your forensics program. Bottom line, CISOs should proactively work with their legal counsel to pre-validate evidence collection procedures in a manner consistent with the organization's objectives, priorities, and legal requirements.

As noted above, it's important that your forensics program is also used to determine the fact pattern of incidents where the end game is not attribution and legal proceedings but rather improvements to the security practices and architecture of the firm. Under these circumstances, forensic analysis is used to make internal improvements to the security program and reduce the risk of a similar issue taking place in the future.

Beyond collaborating proactively with legal counsel and HR, a good investment in your forensic preparation would be to meet with your local FBI office or your local sheriff's or police department's cybercrimes units to validate their requirements when they are working a case. Learn what they would need from your organization. Many law enforcement cybercrime teams are real experts in forensic analysis and have learned to investigate many technically-distinct

---

[30] Organizations that operate in both the European Union (EU) and United States would be well-served to review their employee manuals and acceptable use policies (AUPs) for consistency with local or regional employment laws and practices.

[31] There are pending updates (as described above) that will have an impact on proceedings. At present, a good starting point is found at:
http://www.uscourts.gov/sites/default/files/Rules%20of%20Evidence.

scenarios – frequently with open source tools, given their budget challenges.[32]/[33]

While they are certainly not attorneys, you may also gain some insights from them around what you can and cannot obtain without authorization. In meeting with your local or regional law enforcement cyber teams, you may also learn more about the tricks of the trade and develop some valuable relationships with the agents and teams that may be called upon when you have a case. It's better to establish these relationships sooner rather than later, so be proactive.

Chapter 17 Key Point and Action Item 3

Our partners in law enforcement have lots of experience in collecting and preserving evidence. In addition, they are routinely made away by judges and prosecutors about what is required to collect and how it to protect what you have gathered.

You should, along with your legal counsel, meet with appropriate law-enforcement departments and update your list from action #1 to include items requested by law enforcement and cleared by your legal group.

Five Stages of a Forensic Process

Now let's turn to your environment. Knowing that you will need evidence at some point allows you to think through what type of collection points will be necessary for your infrastructure. I recommend thinking about a forensic lifecycle and what tools and capabilities to require at each stage of the process.

- **Identification** – I've discussed the value of threat modeling throughout this Volume 2 as well as in Volume 1 of the CISO Desk Reference Guide. Using threat

---

[32]. While a separate topic, Michael Bazzell's work on open source intelligence techniques (OSINT) is a great resource on how to obtain evidence from non-traditional sources such as social media and mobile devices: https://inteltechniques.com/experience.

[33] There are a number of great resources that speak to forensic analysis. Readers are invited to look at the following organizations for additional detail:

- Scientific Working Group on Digital Evidence - https://www.swgde.org/
- International Association of Computer Investigation Specialists - https://www.iacis.com/
- High Technology Crime Investigation Association - https://htcia.org/

modeling – knowing the components of the systems, applications, and infrastructure that you are protecting, coupled with their inherent weaknesses – provides invaluable insight. Threat modeling highlights which controls are necessary, which IOCs are likely to be evident when an attack occurs, and how to adapt your security monitoring to this context. If you haven't done threat modeling on your more critical systems and applications, find a way to fast-track this effort.

Know your network, gateways, network segments, applications, and infrastructure. Consider how and where you would conduct packet captures (PCAP) and make it easy for your team to do PCAP work should something indicate that there is a compromise taking place. Coordinate with your network engineers to think about where specialized tools can be placed to facilitate this effort.[34]

The planning exercises that were noted above, including thinking through scenarios (outside actors, rogue insiders, and vendors), will inform where you can pre-plan for forensic evidence capture. Depending on your organization and your industry, you may have a higher proclivity for dealing with forensic issues. When this is the case, take this planning to the next level and develop a forensics-by-design approach that incorporates all elements of the forensic lifecycle into security and IT infrastructure practices – including vendor engagements.

- **Collection** – Your team, or a pre-vetted and ideally already retained specialized forensic support vendor, should know how and be prepared to handle the collection of forensic evidence regardless of type (be it packet captures, system images, volatile memory, or other evidence). It's critical at this stage that there are documented practices to ensure appropriate chain of custody and integrity over evidence (notably creating a forensically-sound copy of the evidence with integrity that would be unquestioned by opposing counsel should litigation result).

---

[34] There are important considerations on how to monitoring network traffic. A network TAP (test access point) reduces the likelihood of lost packets (essentially full packet analysis) but is expensive. A switched port analyzer (SPAN) approach could have packets dropped. There are also scenarios where ongoing collection network metadata may be useful. Again, collaborate with your network engineering teams to think through the pros and cons of the best way to capture network analysis.

Your team should also be prepared to address more complicated evidence collection procedures, including dealing with mobile devices and volatile evidence (e.g., memory, network flows, or "social media" evidence), and that these procedures meet the legal requirements discussed above. A good way to validate collection practices is to have your team address some potential scenarios where forensic analysis would be required and to simply ask "How would we collect and preserve evidence under this scenario and which tools would be required?"

If your team does not have the answer, that's a call to action. One response would be to contract third-party forensic expertise. Equally important, in the context of "forensics-by-design," think about how to handle proactive evidence collection along with the desired retention periods. This collection will require the collaboration and support of other stakeholders including your network and backup teams.

- **Preservation** – Your team and your forensic support vendor need to ensure that forensically-sound copies of evidence are maintained, and that the integrity and the chain of custody can withstand legal review and challenges. You don't want to learn how to do this during the heat of an incident or when litigation holds, and other forms of e-discovery actions are in play.

  Creating forensically-sound duplicate images of the evidence is key. Forensic analysis will always be challenged by the Heisenberg principle if not addressed correctly.[35] Due care must be given to ensure that the observation (collection and preservation) techniques do not materially affect the evidence. Make preservation procedures a high priority for your team and vendor. Validate their understanding. Review these practices with law enforcement or external experts who can provide guidance on the efficacy of these procedures.

- **Analysis** – Analysis is all about creating a legally acceptable and technically accurate fact pattern based on the evidence at hand. The use of this analysis may vary: it may be focused on legal proceedings or used to

---

[35] Werner Heisenberg is one of the 20th century's most notable physicists who contributed significantly to quantum mechanics. Heisenberg's uncertainty principle implies that the mere act of observation may have unknown or uncertain impacts on the object being measured or evaluated.

decompose security failures. Regardless of which objective, the analysis must be technically competent and not engage in subjective or speculative practices. Where the picture is not clear, and the findings are uncertain, state so clearly in the report. If there are blind spots based on the evidence, indicate this explicitly.

This analysis will inform how your organization learns from an incident by investing in new training, tools, and techniques, and validating forensic analyses practices moving forward. Separate from the actual reporting, it's also important to convey to key stakeholders (be they law enforcement agencies, legal counsel, or senior management) an assessment of the cost of forensics. Don't spend $50,000 on forensics to solve a $10,000 problem. Forensics is a tool, not an end game. It should inform business decisions and be cost-effective.

- **Attribution** – Let's face it, attribution is a four-letter word. Unless we are dealing with a rogue employee where attribution can be more definitive, attribution is challenging when dealing with outside actors. Attribution requires context. If your forensic analysis is focused on a legal case with an outside actor, you will need to determine whether having definitive attribution is cost effective. In the absence of scenarios that involve employees and independent contractors, attribution is often costlier than its value, especially for smaller organizations.

  Litigation is expensive. If you can definitively determine that a foreign company or individual was the source of a specific issue, are their extradition treaties in place to facilitate prosecution? Are the costs of such prosecution appropriate? The answer is likely "no." There's a caveat here. When dealing with matters that involve critical infrastructure and national defense, attribution may be more a matter of national security than of criminal prosecution. This determination is beyond the scope of this chapter. You should address this in advance with executive management, legal counsel, and the board of directors.

Being prepared to address forensic analysis requirements in advance can make all the difference in the world. You will have vetted potential vendors, know the procedures for collecting and preserving different types of evidence, and understand the economics of forensics.

As part of this preparation, don't overlook the value of a simple RACI matrix – similar to what we recommended for incident response. Indeed, the RACI matrix drafted for the incident response process would help address the majority of forensic analysis requirements. Know who is consulted and informed in the process, who – based on findings – needs to be escalated to, and under which circumstances. CISOs who think proactively about forensics practices – notably how to collect certain types of evidence in a legally-defensible manner while protecting chain-of-custody – will be good stewards of their security programs.

Why Digital Forensics Is a Valuable Service to the CISO – Hayslip

"Digital forensics assists the incident response effort by helping construct the timeline of the intrusion event."

Digital forensics investigations seek to uncover evidence that, when properly analyzed, provides an understanding of how a breach event occurred, the possible motives of the criminals who perpetrated the breach, and if possible the criminal's identity. The techniques used for these investigations are not solely for dealing with cyber-crime incidents. They can also be used to help solve crimes like terrorism, organized crime, fraud, drug and human trafficking, and extortion.

In today's connected world computers, smartphones, wearables, tablets, etc. can store vast amounts of information. This includes email messages and email addresses, contact lists, family pictures with embedded GPS coordinates, business financials, corporate research, videos, Internet histories, and phone numbers. This information can be processed through various algorithms to provide insight into a person's habits or a company's next acquisition. It's the sensitivity of this critical information that has driven the creation of many of the new data privacy laws around the world, and it is also what attracts cyber-criminals who seek to acquire this data for financial gain.

Therefore, the field of digital forensics is increasingly vital because cyber-criminals are more than the average hacker. Many of them are professionals motivated by financial gain and targeted espionage. The Federal Bureau of Investigation (FBI) estimates the economic loss to cyber-crime in 2016 exceeds $1.6 billion per year (Masters 2017). This is a 24 percent increase from the previous year, and the trend is accelerating.

Businesses have incident response teams whose mission is to counter computer-network intrusions, minimize incident damage and, through a "lessons learned" process, strengthen a company's defenses. However, fighting these new breeds of cyber-criminals is not an easy endeavor. Both law enforcement and computer security professionals are literally in a digital arms race against tech-savvy criminals.

These criminals and their organizations have the funding to develop and use advanced technologies to obstruct forensic investigations through such actions as infiltrating corporate computers to install their malware or using anti-detection, anti-forensics, and other techniques to cover their digital footprints.

It's with this bleak backdrop in mind that I want to approach our next discussion on how digital forensics can be an asset for the CISO. I want us to discuss the importance of this field for the business, what resources it would take to build a lab for an organization, and what would be required to field a forensics team.

Digital Forensics Is Becoming a Strategic Service

In my twenty-plus years in information technology and cybersecurity, there have been numerous occasions where my organization or one of its partners had to respond to a cyber intrusion incident. In each case, it was data that we collected which helped tell a story of what happened, how we could better protect ourselves, and sometimes who was responsible for the incident. In each case, as the senior security executive, I would have to speak with my organization's leadership and explain the collected digital forensic evidence in business terms, so they could understand how the event happened and we as a leadership team could triage the event's impact.

What is important is that with the rise in computer-related criminal activities that businesses are seeing today, digital forensics is becoming a strategic service that many are now exploring how to incorporate into their incident response and business continuity plans. The first question we are considering is: *"What is digital forensics and what value does it bring to the business?"*

By definition, digital forensics is the collection, preservation, analysis, and presentation of digital evidence that, if done correctly, can be admissible in a court of law. We use this type of collected evidence when responding to a cyber-criminal incident, for internal disciplinary hearings, or as evidence to further other on-going investigations.

As I mentioned in Chapter 15 on Incident Response (IR), digital forensics assists the IR effort by helping construct the timeline of the intrusion event. This timeline can help security professionals build a picture of the compromised data, and it can provide insight into the infrastructure or services that were leveraged to provide access and potentially pinpoint the misconfigured policy or unpatched vulnerability that enabled the illegal activity. This digital timeline and picture are critical for creating a contextual awareness of why the incident occurred and will provide data for the executive decisions required to reduce this new-found risk exposure to the business.

Digital Forensics Methods

Forensics is a field of multiple specialties. Law enforcement developed the methodology, but just as there are numerous types of technologies, there are also different types of digital forensics. Some of the methods a CISO should be aware of are as follows:

- *Computer Forensics* – a branch of digital forensic science that examines evidence found on computers, hard drives, and removable digital storage media.

- *Network Forensics* – a branch of digital forensic science that relates to the monitoring and analysis of computer network traffic for information gathering, legal evidence, or intrusion detection. Network investigations deal with volatile and dynamic information that is live on the wire.

- *Software Forensics* – a branch of digital forensic science that examines evidence found in malicious code and malware. I have seen people in this field reverse engineer malware payloads to understand how the criminal organizations responsible for their creation and deployment built them.

- *Live System Forensics* – a branch of digital forensic science that collects evidence on compromised systems that are currently live. Much of the evidence is from volatile memory. Powering down the compromised host erases the evidence.

- *Mobile Device Forensics* – a branch of digital forensic science that relates to collecting evidence from mobile devices that everyone in society uses today. Remember the famous case of the FBI conducting a terrorism investigation, and they needed to gather evidence from an encrypted iPhone. The use of mobile devices is accepted in business today, and I expect that the forensics required for these devices will grow and probably merge with the practitioners who conduct computer forensics.

- *IoT/ICS/SCADA Forensics* – a branch of digital forensic science that is about evidence collected from ICS and SCADA devices and a new class of industrial devices known as the "Internet of Things." As more devices connect to the internet, such as cars, refrigerators, homes, HVAC systems, and manufacturing plants, forensic investigations will utilize the devices' computing capabilities and data.

The CISO must also be aware that evidence collected for a digital forensic investigation can come from numerous types of media such as hard drives, removable media, network logs, application logs, email, server content (shares, data stores, databases, and logs), volatile memory, and network traffic. When you consider all of the possible sources for forensics data, it is quickly evident that there are many data sources and a significant amount of data that can be hard to acquire and also easy to damage if not collected correctly. What is driving the requirement for digital forensics in the business?

I believe the CISO will deal with both internal and external requirements for forensic services. The following conditions make a case for what business value they bring to the organization.

1. *Internal requirements* – These requirements are unique to each business and will typically be driven by corporate policies and meeting those recommended standards. Companies conduct internal audits and at times may have to investigate discovered anomalies or prove they are meeting current standards and both of these situations may call for forensic services. The organization's legal department may also need digital forensic services to fulfill e-discovery requests or to prove the business is complying with applicable laws and regulations.

   Another stakeholder that may require digital forensic services is the company's HR department. They may need forensic services during an employee misconduct investigation or in response to a previous employee's firing/termination.

   One last internal stakeholder group that may require digital forensic services is risk management. The risk management team is in the business of conducting assessments or audits and may need forensic services to ensure the organization is meeting specific security controls or framework standards. When looking at internal requirements, seek to understand the breadth and number of forensic services that internal stakeholders currently need and then decide whether to establish an internal digital forensic service or use a third-party service.

2. *External requirements* – These are requirements that push the organization to use digital forensic services due to the

regulated industries the organization operates in, e.g., healthcare, finance, insurance, and telecommunications. Other external factors that can influence the organization to use forensic services are industry, regional, and country-specific laws. Some of these laws may require the organization to have some forensic capability as evidence they are meeting requirements to protect sensitive data.

One last external factor that may inspire organizations to use forensic services is the desire to differentiate from competitors by adopting an industry best practice standard or framework certification such as NIST, ISO, or COBIT. Several of these best practice frameworks and certifications have security controls focused on incident response, and these controls typically include the requirement for forensic services to collect and analyze evidence.

Chapter 17 Key Point and Action Item 4

Though not necessarily in support of forensic activity, you will likely be asked to sequester evidence for civil litigation, regulatory enforcement, or internal investigation of potential employee misconduct.

You should review your tools for evidence collection and make sure adequate e-discovery capabilities are included to the extent needed.

As you can see, many factors will influence how an organization uses digital forensics. The business value of these services is evident in the business cases for digital forensics that I outlined above in my brief explanation of an organization's internal and external drivers for these services. I believe it is evident that there are numerous use cases for how digital forensics aides an organization's business operations. That leads us to our next question: *"What resources are required to develop a digital forensics lab and should the CISO build one?"*

Building a Forensics Capability

To establish a forensic capability for your organization, you will need to research current trends within the business units of your organization, trends in the cybersecurity industry for using digital forensics, and trends from both competitors and partners within your industry. Finally, I would suggest you reach out to peers in the cybersecurity community.

Two resources I would recommend are the American Society of Crime Laboratory Directors (ASCLD 2017) and the ANSI-ASQ National Accreditation Board (ANSI-ASQ 2017). Their websites cover requirements for both larger forensics labs and programs and the management of digital forensics laboratories. I have used them to read up on the ISO requirements for establishing a certified forensics lab and to better understand the training and resource management requirements to operate a digital forensics program.

As you can imagine, the resources and personnel required can be substantial, which is why it is critical that you establish what the scope of your forensic services capability is going to be before you commit any budget money. Determining the extent of your services will allow you to understand what resources you will need for this internal service and when you will need to contact a third party for assistance. Let's next discuss some of the requirements for fielding an operational internal digital forensics program.

As the CISO, you have decided to establish a forensics program for your organization, and you have done the research on which services and types of forensics your team will offer. Now, you need to look at where to locate the forensics program and how much space the team members will require. If there are plans to get the program certified, then the lab space for the program will need to be carefully reviewed. You will need to inspect the area to verify there is room for storage and evidence lockers.

Depending on the type of forensics services offered, there will need to be room for work benches, and there will need to be room for forensic workstations. This space will also need to be secured so that only authorized personnel can access it, and there will need to be an assessment of the types of network connectivity that will be required and of environmental controls and power requirements.

A digital forensics lab environment will need to have strict environmental controls so that equipment and evidence are not damaged. Install backup power and UPS devices so that forensic services will not be affected by a loss of power. Some other considerations that you will need to factor into building a lab for forensic services are that the flooring in the space should be made of an anti-static material, and the walls should be soundproofed to ensure sensitive discussions remain inside the work area.

Now you have an idea of the number and type of resources required to establish a forensic lab. However, we are not covering what an organization should do if they operate internationally. I bring this up because there may be different requirements for how to process the data and manage a forensic program. If an organization operates globally, then they may have a distributed forensic program with multiple labs. If this is the case, then the previous link I provided for the ANSI-ASQ National Accreditation Board is one I believe you should use. They use the ISO-based certifications, and that would help you if you are going to establish a digital forensics program that will have multiple labs in different countries.

You will also need to take into account the hardware and software your team members will need to provide forensic services. The equipment will be everything from evidence lockers and safes to forensic workstations that have unique hardware and software requirements. You will also need to look at how to store your forensic images and sensitive data/reports. For example, are you going to use data storage located on-premises or will you use a hosted cloud service?

Whichever one you select, you will need to verify that you have encryption and authentication mechanisms in place to ensure the collected forensic data is secure and you have the audit controls set up to prove that no data compromise took place and that you have maintained the chain of custody over this evidence. Along with these hardware and software requirements, you will also need specific tools. Some are open source software that is free, and some are from specific forensic software vendors that charge license fees that can go into the hundreds of thousands of dollars.

The scope of the services you have opted to provide will dictate what hardware, software, and tools you will purchase for the forensics program. For anything outside of this scope, you may want to have a third-party forensic partner who will provide specialized services that you deem are too expensive.

Chapter 17 Key Point and Action Item 5

Though we know some level of capability will be required for most organizations, due to the equipment and expertise required, forensics can be one of the most expensive services to provide. Using a third-party service provider to augment your capabilities will usually be necessary.

You should work with one or more third-party forensics companies to build a roadmap for creating your organization's forensic capability using the appropriate combination of in-house and outsourced services.

Staffing a Forensics Lab

There is still one more element to discuss for a forensics program, and this is the most expensive part. Namely, the trained personnel who will conduct the investigations, analyze the collected data and provide contextual reports on the findings of how an incident occurred and who may be responsible. Our final question is about the makeup of this last element: *"What roles and resources are needed to field a digital forensics team?"*

The objectives the CISO wishes to achieve with this program, and the scope of services the CISO plans to offer will dictate the requirements for the type of team, training, and policies. The program's objectives will give the team a strategic view of what services stakeholders' need, who their customers are, and the business value the forensics program is expected to provide the organization. Some of the first resources a CISO will need to acquire in developing a forensics team will be the people who will perform the services.

There are a few different approaches you can take, each with its pros and cons. I would look first at using personnel I already have in my security program and training them on the new forensics services I want to offer my stakeholders. If I am building a full forensics lab program, this would give me a security employee who already knows the corporate network environment and now has updated forensics training. I could later hire a replacement for that team member as they fully transition into the digital forensics role.

Trying this option first would allow a CISO to have team members trained in forensics and offer some essential digital forensics services, and then if given funding approval stand up a full lab environment. Personnel could transition to the new team as replacements are rotated in to fill the empty security positions. Using this approach gives you the ability to slowly implement a digital forensics program and establish the business value these services provide. Then, as stakeholders make more requests for these services, you can make a case for fully funding a digital forensics laboratory and team.

If this approach isn't feasible, I would recommend either finding a corporate partner that the organization could team with to establish a digital forensics lab to be used by both organizations or possibly joining an industry trade organization that has this capability for its members. One last option would be to train security team members on digital forensics "first responder" services, so they understand what data to collect and how to do it properly. Then have a trusted third party who is on retainer to provide the in-depth analysis and reporting on the data collected from intrusions and related cyber-criminal incidents.

I have seen the last option used by many of the CISOs that I know; and if you only require forensic services for the occasional request from HR or Legal, then it is honestly one of the better options to implement. Just remember, if you decide this is your path I would have your in-house legal counsel review your cyber-insurance policy to see if you have a rider to pay for these types of service and what triggers must occur before you can use them.

I hope I have provided some insight into why I believe digital forensics services have some relevant use cases that make them essential to the business. To me, these services are just part of the overall cybersecurity and risk management programs that the CISO provides their organization. How much digital forensics services an in-house team offers will depend on research the CISO and their staff conducts and on comparing the costs of using an external service versus building and maintaining an internal team.

Don't be surprised if the executive management team wants the CISO to provide forensic services, even though a managed service provider may be cheaper. The organization may have sensitive data and operations, or they may not be ready to allow someone outside the organization to assist with painful incidents, like a data breach. In the end, the CISO may propose a hybrid approach. Train some of your staff, get them some experience, and also have a partner you can rely on in the event of a full-blown business continuity event. As a CISO, sometimes you need to trust your inner paranoia and prepare for that breach, so when it comes, you will have the critical services you need to protect your organization.

Summary

In Chapter 17, we began our discussion by asking these three questions:

- What is digital forensics and what value does it bring to the business?
- What resources are required to develop a digital forensics lab and should the CISO build one?
- What roles and resources are needed to field a digital forensics team?

It is near certainty that your role as CISO will at various times require the collection and cataloging of evidence that will be used in some legal capacity. Even if your organization never presses charges against any individual or entity or initiates a single lawsuit, you will still likely need to preserve evidence and establish its validity and completeness. As the burden of fighting cybercrime continues to increase and the convergence of OT and IT continues to bring the physical and digital worlds closer together, our jobs will require us to stop time, even though it seems like we're moving at the speed of light.

While the expectations are very high, we've heard it said many times: "Rome wasn't built in a day." When something goes wrong, the key is to react with grace, learn from our mistakes and from the tactics used against us, build a better program, and come back strong. What we learn is more important than what we know.

In closing, we would like to leave you with these five key points and next steps:

1. The chain of custody for evidence must be established immediately. This is not something that can be done retroactively. Consequently, you need to know ahead of time the circumstances under which you must preserve evidence, the exact items to collect, and the appropriate handling procedures. **You should work with your legal team to establish criteria for sequestering assets and build a checklist of all the items to collect when the criteria have been met.**

2. Learning from failure is essential as the likelihood of being attacked again is near 100%. Asking ourselves what we could have done differently and what we experienced that we didn't expect are invaluable disciplines. **You should create your own**

template for conducting post-mortem reviews to answer the questions laid out in this section, incorporating additions and changes based on your internal review and your repetition of the post-mortem review process.

3. Our partners in law enforcement have lots of experience in collecting and preserving evidence. In addition, judges and prosecutors routinely make them aware of the requirements for what to collect and how to protect what has been gathered. **You should, along with your legal counsel, meet with appropriate law-enforcement departments and update your list from action #1 to include items requested by law enforcement and cleared by your legal group.**

4. Though not necessarily in support of forensic activity, you will likely be asked to sequester evidence for civil litigation, regulatory enforcement, or internal investigation of potential employee misconduct. **You should review your tools for evidence collection and make sure adequate e-discovery capabilities are included.**

5. Though we know some level of capability will be required for most organizations, due to the equipment and expertise required, forensics can be one of the most expensive services to provide. Using a third-party service provider to augment your capabilities will usually be necessary **You should work with one or more third-party forensics companies to build a roadmap for creating your organization's forensic capability using the appropriate combination of in-house and outsourced services.**

As our physical and digital worlds continue to converge and product liability becomes more real for both software and technical components, the burden of knowing what to collect, when to collect it, and how to handle it will continue to increase.

Chapter 18 – Building Your Strategic Plan

Introduction

While drafting and editing the material for this book, we thought we could offer additional value by providing an essay on each topic by all three authors, independently edited, to preserve their unique perspective and voice.

It is a technique that was intended to provide multiple viewpoints that would both explore the topics more thoroughly and provide options for readers to use these different viewpoints to help them solve different problems depending on their needs at the time.

We appreciate your tolerance with our construct, and hope we've achieved what we intended. In this final chapter, we've decided to stitch together our combined perspective and present an integrated essay on building your strategic plan.

Some of the questions the authors used to frame their thoughts for this chapter include:

- What components should the CISO use in developing their cybersecurity strategic plan?
- How should the CISO align their strategic plan to the organization's business objectives?
- What steps can the CISO use to leverage the cybersecurity strategic plan for future growth?

> "Your strategic plan should address your current state cybersecurity practices, near-term objectives to be addressed in the next 12 months, midterm objectives in the next 18-24 months, and long-term objectives over the next three years."

How Did I Get into This?

There are many ways you may have come into this responsibility. In larger companies, you may have been the subject of a recruiting process or an internal vetting process. You may be replacing someone or inheriting an issue with board visibility. In this case, you're probably going to have something in place. In the best case you can carry forward most of the existing plan, but you may be faced with a complete overhaul.

If you're coming into the position at a smaller company, you could still be subject to an internal vetting process, perhaps as the former "network" or "compliance" person. In this case, you're likely to have at most a bare skeleton of a plan. It might not be much more than a budget or an organization chart, possibly just a list of services the other IT managers are looking forward to getting off their plates.

We are drawing attention to the latter condition because as we mentioned in the preface to Volume 1, cybercrime will continue to move "down the food chain" as more relative economic value is managed via interconnected computer networks. As a result, many smaller to medium-sized organizations have requirements to have specific security practices and capabilities in place given regulatory obligations or increased diligence necessitated by the organization's customers and other stakeholders. CISOs hired or promoted by these companies will be scrambling to build security programs from scratch.

We'll cover the building blocks of a sound strategic plan, aligning the plan to the organization's business objectives, and using the strategic plan as a roadmap for the future of your cybersecurity function. While we walk through developing the plan, we'll continue to offer both a complete treatment grounded in best practice and reveal our thought process to maintain the instructional approach to ensure this is helpful to CISOs just stepping into the role.

Structure of Your Strategic Plan

The cybersecurity strategic plan needs to be concise and easy to understand and reflect realistic expectations for funding that are in line with what the organization can afford. The plan document is not the place to surface a 300% increase in funding. That is a discussion that should already have taken place between you and the management team and, as appropriate, the board. The document should be organized in a methodical manner that makes it easy for the stakeholders to read and its objectives should be aligned with current business functions and processes. We recommend the following structure:

1. Mission Statement – This is the declaration of the organization's core purpose that normally doesn't change over time.

   Example: Develop and execute a proactive, company-wide security program based on *Organization*'s strategic business objectives.

2. Vision Statement – An aspirational description of what the organization would like to achieve or accomplish in the mid-term or long-term future.

   Example: Incorporate a continuous security mindset into all aspects of our business functions.

3. Introduction – This is a statement describing the business and the environment in which the security program currently operates. The executive leadership team typically will use this section to communicate broad information about the cybersecurity program and its critical role in the strategic plan for the business and key stakeholders.

4. Governance – This portion of the document will explain how the strategic plan will be implemented, who will audit the process, and what committees or personnel will be part of the overall process of assessing its effectiveness and recommending changes to it over time. This is a long-term plan, and there should be a documented process of how this plan will be managed and audited and who will be responsible for it over time.

5. Strategic Objectives – The strategic objectives define how the cybersecurity organization should invest its time and resources to manage the security risks discovered in the assessment and SWOT data previously described. In

laying out the objectives, the CISO is assuming there will be sufficient resources for people, processes, and technology. The objectives typically are arrayed over a one- to a three-year timeline. Understand that timelines can be shortened with additional resources. Each objective will have several initiatives, derived from the analyzed security gap data, which need to be completed to achieve the objective.

Objective Examples:

- Improved Security of System and Network Services
- Proactive Risk Management
- Business Process Enablement
- Security Incident Management

Your objectives will typically mirror the gaps found in your assessment and the improvements or investments you want to make in currently effective processes that you want to continue to mature.

6. Key Initiatives – An initiative will state what objectives it satisfies when completed, it will have a description of the security/risk issues it will alleviate, and it should state the benefits it brings to the business when completed.

The following is an example of an initiative:

Initiative 1 – Security Policy, Standards, and Guidelines Framework

Enables Objectives – Improved security of system and network services, proactive risk management and crisis and security incident management.

Description - Develop, approve, and launch a suite of information security policies, standards, and guidelines based on the ISO/IEC27001 code of best practices for information security. These policies will formally establish the organization's Cybersecurity Program and set forth employee responsibility for information protection. The policy, standards, and guideline framework will also take into consideration the multitude of Federal, State, and Industry regulations that govern the use of personal, financial, customer, and vendor data managed by the business.

Key Benefits
- Clear security baselines for all departments
- Policy-based foundation to measure results
- Consistent application of security controls across the enterprise

Developing Your Plan

We've mentioned throughout these two volumes that how you approach any task is going to depend on the needs of the organization. Part of your value to the organization is that you bring your experience and your human network to help the organization assess and adjust to reality, and plan for the future. As with other divisions within your organization, your strategic plan should address your current state cybersecurity practices, near-term objectives to be addressed in the next 12 months, midterm objectives to be addressed in the next 18-24 months, and long-term objectives to be addressed over the next three years.

We've also mentioned that cybersecurity is not something you can do in a vacuum. It is very much a contact sport. Resist the temptation to hide away and work on your plan in isolation. Engage with your business partners and involve all of your stakeholders in the process of identifying the priorities for your strategic plan. The role of the CISO is to help the organization reduce the inherent risks of its business model and mitigate the residual risks that cannot be avoided. You exist to serve the business, not the other way around. Determine what the management teams need and what the board needs from your cybersecurity program and develop a strategic plan to deliver that.

Recognize, however, that these stakeholders may not be familiar with the more "formal" language of enterprise risk management (ERM) or other risk-management practices we've expounded on in the CISO Desk Reference Guide. The founder's family or close-knit executive teams often dominate many smaller to medium-sized organizations. They are confronting globalization, new competitors, enhanced regulatory oversight, and several other factors that strain their capabilities to understand what the risk environment is for the organization. Tailor your discovery to your audience. Your job is to help these stakeholders navigate this environment in a manner that is financially prudent for the organization, while also reflecting the security "debt" that you may have inherited.

In each of the previous chapters, we've given you a series of assignments that, taken together, should provide the bulk of your discovery. The next step is to determine how to apply this information and come up with a plan that emphasizes your strengths, shores up your weaknesses, and buys you the time you need to implement the program the organization needs. One tool you might consider using is a Strengths, Weaknesses, Opportunities, and Threats (SWOT) analysis. In figure 1 we show a typical set of definitions for a SWOT analysis that you can use to assess capabilities.

	STRENGTHS	WEAKNESSES
INTERNALLY	What do we want to **protect** that we have or are good at doing?	What do we want to **improve** that we have or are not good at doing?
	OPPORTUNITIES	**THREATS**
EXTERNALLY	What do we want to **take advantage** of to help our organization?	What do we want to **defend against** to help our organization?

Figure 18.1 SWOT Analysis

Conducting this SWOT analysis can provide you with a present-day strategic view of your security program and the value it provides. Some things you might consider when performing your SWOT analysis include:

- Your current capacity to deliver security services
- Your core competencies (what the security program is doing well)
- The business processes the security program supports
- The staffing roles, skills, and knowledge strengths and shortfalls
- The currently deployed security assets
- The effective and ineffective security controls
- The financial resources the program currently has available

It is also important to understand how the organization views the development of new competencies and capabilities. For some organizations, the preferred approach is to build these capabilities internally – effectively tooling up and staffing up to meet the challenge. Other organizations will look to third parties to address missing capabilities. In Chapter 10, we introduced you to Geoffrey Moore's model of mission-critical "core versus context" and provided a matrix to help you group your capabilities. We introduced this matrix initially as a tool for determining the approach to developing or acquiring talent, but you can easily adapt it to your full program. Here is that matrix again:

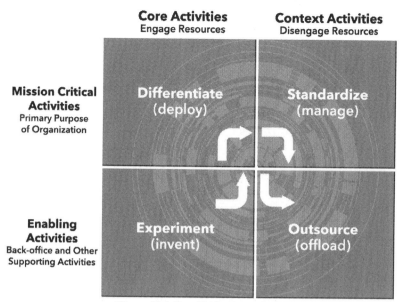

Figure 18.2 Core Vs Context Matrix

Knowing how the organization has traditionally addressed other challenges can offer important insights. If the executive team and the board have historically funded new initiatives with the desire to build these competencies internally, you'll know that you are in a building mode. You'll be thinking about what staffing levels and competencies will be necessary for your security program, what tools and applications you'll need, and start to develop a budget to build these capabilities.

If you are typically addressing the capabilities via contractors and outsourcing, your security program will need to focus on oversight capabilities. In this case, your vendor management and procurement teams will be key resources. There is also a hybrid approach in which the organization may leverage third-party providers to support objectives for some period as new competencies are developed internally or to cover requirements that simply cannot be developed based on budget or available resources.

In-source "Build from Scratch"

For many of us, assuming the budget was appropriate, this would be a blast. Building a security program from scratch offers professionally challenging and enjoyable projects that result in meaningful work. You will need to create an inventory of required security functions. You'll also use the tools you developed and complete the assignments from the previous 17 chapters. At that point, you'll have a nice inventory of what you need to protect and what you have on hand already.

If you are building a program from scratch and are in a position to start staffing up, you will have a couple of options to explore. Does the organization have overlooked talent internally that would be good additions to your team? Many systems and network administrators are chomping at the bit to move into cybersecurity. Do they have the requisite skills to make this transition? Do they have full-stack knowledge? Do they love to see how the technology works, how to exploit it, and how to defend it?

Meet with the existing team and see if there are individuals who could quickly be trained to join your security team. You will obviously need to coordinate with your colleagues in IT, notably the CIO, to ensure that you are not poaching key members of his or her team. Don't burn bridges. Human resources will also play a key role. If you are building a team from internal resources, you'll need HR to help facilitate training.

Equally important, you will need to look at your existing security architecture. Where are the blind spots? Are you able to meet regulatory and contractual obligations with your current security applications and processes? If not, surface this concern directly to your colleagues in the C-suite and get their acknowledgment that the organization has significant regulatory exposure and cannot meet contractual obligations. You should not try to resolve these issues in an isolated fashion. These are not your problems to solve alone. You will need executive support, funding, and organizational commitment to building the security program.

As it relates to your security infrastructure, there's a simple question that can help prioritize what you will need to deploy to facilitate better security – "What is it that I cannot see that I should see that will allow me to protect my organization better?" Take a full-stack, process-driven view. Leverage data flow diagrams for more material processes to understand where security controls should be deployed and evaluate the status of these controls.

Similar to the governance dynamics noted above, you will likely be in a position where key security capabilities may be simply missing (e.g., no SIEM, limited endpoint protection, little to no threat intelligence insights). You will need to prioritize where you implement new technologies and security applications. Knowing which business processes require the most protection and attention should inform this prioritization. You may not be in a position to resolve all issues immediately, so you will need guidance and insights from the executive team to ensure that your efforts are organizationally aligned.

When you are in a building from scratch mode, it's imperative that you have an appropriate cadence of program reviews with executive management and that the security metrics you use to evaluate progress are fundamentally tied to the business and linked to organizational initiatives. We recommend that you have the data reviewed by stakeholders and a trusted partner or peer to provide multiple perspectives into the possible critical gaps the data reveals. Having only one point of view is a risk unto itself, and it is essential for you to have several viewpoints to validate your data before you proceed with the next step in creating a long-term security strategy.

Out-source "Vendor and Supplier Due Diligence"

If you are the CISO for an organization that aggressively outsources non-core activity, you must become very adroit at understanding the dynamics of vendor risk management. You will also need to help your organization understand which services you can reasonably outsource to a third party and those that still require the direct engagement of the organization's internal resources.

We recommend that you begin with the business impact analysis (BIA). We introduced you to the BIA in Chapter 5 of Volume 1 when discussing metrics and reporting. We provided similar advice in Chapter 2 on regulatory and audit, Chapter 3 on data, and Chapter 4 on third-party risk. Learn as much as you can about the core processes that are material to the organization.

Speak with department heads and other line-of-business colleagues to start building an inventory of these processes, their dependencies (vendors, suppliers, staff, technology, etc.) and create a prioritized list of which processes should be evaluated first for their security impact. Here again, the core versus context matrix is invaluable as a tool to help you determine which security processes you can safely and effectively outsource.

As a CISO who works for an organization that has a proclivity to outsource, you will likely experience significant organizational momentum to outsource key elements of your security program (e.g., the use of a managed security services provider or an MSSP). Leveraging an MSSP can be a very prudent strategy when internal resources are limited, or there are budget constraints that preclude staffing up. You will need to invest extra diligence when selecting an MSSP.

Validate everything. Leave nothing to chance. The selected MSSP will have a huge impact on the credibility and effectiveness of your security program. Use good due diligence practices and invest the time necessary to ensure that the selection of the MSSP does not ultimately undermine your security program.

Work with your candidate MSSPs during the evaluation phase to review the security tools and services you need and review each service in detail. How will the service be staffed, what are the communications protocols, what are the measurements (measure every process you outsource)?

Remember a fundamental tenant of outsourcing – if it isn't spelled out in the service contract, it doesn't get done without a change order. Change orders are where service providers make their profit. Given this, it would be prudent to have a trusted third party review your service contract for anything you might have missed before you sign the contract. The review should be thorough for each process you are outsourcing.

To give an example, you may be with an organization where there is a requirement to have 7x24 security monitoring. If your organization cannot staff up to meet 7x24 requirements (which typically requires a minimum of 10 full-time employees), you'll need to find an MSSP that can provide this coverage in a cost-effective manner. You'll need to evaluate the appropriate scope of work, delineate appropriate roles and responsibilities, and define deliverables. If the services require 7x24 monitoring and support, validate services and capabilities by going to the MSSP's SOC after hours, preferably late at night or early in the morning.

Look for areas of potential conflict or ambiguity. Logs are an especially important topic. How long are logs retained, which systems are part of the logging environment, how are logs triaged, etc.? Know if there are systems that are multi-tenant and how multi-tenancy impacts service delivery. Validate the forensic and more technical security competencies of the provider.

For each process you'll be outsourcing, recognize that the devil is in the details and it's your job to sweat the details. Ask yourself two questions after you've reviewed the delivery for each process: How will I know they are delivering as contracted? And how can I take this process back in-house if I need to?

There is one more risk to look for that might not be obvious. In a scenario where outsourcing has been the primary modus operandi of the organization, you may also have inherited significant security debt – not necessarily internal – that is tied to immature vendor oversight and vendor risk management practices on other departments' outsourced business processes. You haven't been there to help them understand and account for the full spectrum of risks they have faced, and you may discover issues that you'll need to surface and, working together, resolve to an acceptable level of risk.

Work with your colleagues within the organization to create a model that defines the materiality of your vendors. You can base this on the type and volume of information shared (e.g., PHI, PII, or intellectual property) as well as the criticality of the vendors' services to your organization's operations.

CISO, Govern Thyself

The vision, goals, and objectives of your plan should be reviewed at least annually with senior leadership. This review will ensure that the plan's projects, policies, and roadmap are relevant, current, and applicable to the organization's current technology and application portfolios and strategic business objectives. The CISO's partnership with the organization's executive management team is vital to ensure the strategic plan for cybersecurity keeps pace with the changing business environment and is flexible enough to address any significant challenges. The continued commitment and a strong mandate from executive leadership and the cooperation of all stakeholders within the organization are required for the CISO to successfully achieve the objectives in this strategic plan.

Another critical aspect of governance is transparency, both from the perspective of creating visibility about the plan and the resources being assigned to achieve it. This is an essential driver for the engagement of the entire organization and the ability of everyone – you, your team, your management peers and the organization as a whole – to be held accountable for the outcomes you collectively agreed to achieve

It is primarily up to you to communicate the benefits of following this roadmap, and you need to show your team, your management peers, and your entire workforce how to turn it into a working strategy. Communicate the strategic objectives you developed from input provided by stakeholders, lines of business, and executive leadership. Explain how the SWOT analysis and security gap assessment discovered specific issues to address and how they were prioritized based on the impact to business operations. Outline how each of these security initiatives aligns with a specific security/business objective in the strategic plan and then explain the benefits to the organization of remediating these risks.

It also helps to look at the strategic plan and the resulting project schedule as the foundation for a discussion on remediating risk. You may not receive all of the funding to complete all of the initiatives you have set forth for each year, but that is why this is a living document and why you make adjustments. The point is to have your strategic committee for cybersecurity and your stakeholders review the strategic plan and project schedule.

Continuously assess the operating environment and adjust the project schedule initiatives based on any new risks and their potential impact on business operations. This strategic plan and the security project schedule will be core elements of your security program. You will then be able to point to these as proof of the business value your program brings to the company and how your teams are partnered to enable your organization to be successful.

Summary

In Chapter 18, we began our discussion by asking these three questions:

- What components should the CISO use in developing their cybersecurity strategic plan?
- How should the CISO align their strategic plan to the organization's business objectives?
- What steps can the CISO use to leverage the cybersecurity strategic plan for future growth?

In this chapter, we revisit several themes that we've touched on throughout these two books. The first is that there are many tools available to you as a CISO entering into a new role or even if you're an old hand looking to improve your program. With our footnotes, bibliography, and references to standards, we believe we've given you a combination of best practices along with an informative narrative that should allow you to benefit from the battles we've already fought. Please, use the resources we've pointed you to. They have been invaluable to us, and we think they'll help you as well.

The second theme is that almost every problem a CISO faces can be addressed by healthy amounts of preparation and critical thinking. Do your homework, dig in and learn everything you can about your organization, the industry you operate in, and your organization's goals. Apply that knowledge to your plans, your staffing, and where you put your time, attention, and money.

The third and final theme is that cybersecurity is a team sport, and to succeed, you'll need to build a world-class team. You'll do this by developing and then using your staff and your human network. For your human network to help you, communication is key. Get out into your organization and talk to your team, your peers, your management. Meet regularly with colleagues and vendors. Join local, regional, and industry groups. Share your knowledge and absorb what you learn in return.

Conclusion

With the second volume of the CISO Desk Reference Guide, we've attempted to provide the reader with guidance that will help them mature their cybersecurity program. We've addressed building and growth topics, such as talent management and education, as well as approaches to monitoring, threat intelligence and backups and planning. We concluded with discussions about programs for incident management, communications, recovery, and forensics.

The last key action for the reader to take is to build a strategic cybersecurity plan. We've emphasized that cybersecurity is a team sport, and we come back again to your human network.

We encourage you to continue to add energy to your human network, engage with your peers within your organization and with your colleagues in the broader cybersecurity community. Every industry and every region have ample opportunities to meet and form relationships with leaders and experts. Seek them out. It will be well worth your time.

Again, we welcome your feedback and invite you to visit our website: https://www.cisodrg.com or our LinkedIn company page: https://www.linkedin.com/company/ciso-desk-reference-guide.

Glossary
COMMON TERMS, DEFINITIONS, AND ACRONYMS

Insider Threat
The threat that an insider will use her/his authorized access, wittingly or unwittingly, to do harm to the security of their organization. This threat can include damage through industrial espionage, unauthorized disclosure, access or theft of company proprietary information, or through the loss or degradation of departmental resources or capabilities.

Adequate Security
Security commensurate with the risk resulting from the loss, misuse, or unauthorized access to or modification of information.

Advanced Persistent Threat (APT)
An adversary that possesses sophisticated levels of expertise and significant resources which allow it to create opportunities to achieve its objectives by using multiple attack vectors (e.g., cyber, physical, and deception). These objectives typically include establishing and extending footholds within the information technology infrastructure of the targeted organizations for purposes of exfiltrating information, undermining or impeding critical aspects of a mission, program, or organization; or positioning itself to carry out these objectives in the future.

API
Application Programming Interface

Appification
Applications are delivered using many more models than before, including more single-function applications, more interlaced single-function applications, and more reusable components and services that originate or are accessed both inside of and outside of your organization.

Assessment
See *Security Control Assessment.*

Assessor
See *Security Control Assessor.*

Attack Surface	The attack surface of an enterprise IT environment is the sum of the different points (the "attack vectors") where an unauthorized user (the "attacker") can try to enter data to or extract data from an environment.
Attack Vectors	An attack vector is a path or means by which a hacker (or cracker) can gain access to a computer or network server in order to deliver a payload or malicious outcome. Attack vectors enable hackers to exploit system vulnerabilities, including the human element.
Attribution	Cyber attribution is the process of tracking, identifying and laying blame on the perpetrator of a cyberattack or other hacking exploit.
Audit Log	A chronological record of information system activities, including records of system accesses and operations performed in a given period.
Audit Record	An individual entry in an audit log related to an audited event.
Audit Trail	A chronological record that reconstructs and examines the sequence of activities surrounding or leading to a specific operation, procedure, or event in a security-relevant transaction from inception to final result.
AUP	Acceptable Use Policy
Authentication	Verifying the identity of a user, process, or device, often as a prerequisite to allowing access to resources in an information system.
Authenticator	The means used to confirm the identity of a user, processor, or device (e.g., user password or token).
Authenticity	The property of being genuine and being able to be verified and trusted; confidence in the validity of a transmission, a message, or message originator. See *Authentication*.
BAA	Business Associate Agreement

Baseline Configuration	A documented set of specifications for an information system, or a configuration item within a system, that has been formally reviewed and agreed on at a given point in time, and which can be changed only through change control procedures.
Best Evidence	The best evidence rule is a legal principle that holds an original copy of a document as superior evidence. The rule specifies that secondary evidence, such as a copy or facsimile, will be not admissible if an original document exists and can be obtained.
Blacklisting	The process used to identify: (i) software programs that are not authorized to execute on an information system; or (ii) prohibited Universal Resource Locators (URL)/websites.
Blast Radius	Originally and most often used to denote the affected zone from a nuclear explosion, of late, the term is being used for impact analysis in technology parlance. For example, when a particular IT service fails, the users, customers, other dependent services that are affected, fall into Blast Radius.
BSIMM	Building Security Un Maturity Model
Business Continuity Plan (BCP)	An organization-wide collection of procedures that are managed by a coordinator. These procedures consist of actions to be taken by specific personnel and business units in the event of an emergency or disaster. This plan is activated by a senior member of the executive team who has specific authority during the event to take actions protecting the business.
Business Impact Analysis (BIA)	Information collected on the services and procedures the organization delivers to its customers. This analysis requires stakeholders from all business units to identify critical services that must be delivered even in the event of a disaster. It is also during this analysis that a risk assessment is conducted on

the impact to the business if these critical services were interrupted.

BYOD	Bring Your Own Device
CCOE	Cyber Center Of Excellence
Chain of Custody	Chain of custody (CoC), in legal contexts, refers to the chronological documentation or paper trail that records the sequence of custody, control, transfer, analysis, and disposition of physical or electronic evidence.
Change Management	Change management is a systematic approach to dealing with the transition or transformation of an organization's goals, processes or technologies. The purpose of change management is to implement strategies for effecting change, controlling change and helping people to adapt to change.
Chatham House Rule	When a meeting, or part thereof, is held under the Chatham House Rule, participants are free to use the information received, but neither the identity nor the affiliation of the speaker(s), nor that of any other participant, may be revealed.
Chief Information Security Officer	A chief information security officer (CISO) is the senior-level executive within an organization responsible for establishing and maintaining the enterprise vision, strategy, and program to ensure information assets and technologies are adequately protected. The CISO directs staff in identifying, developing, implementing, and maintaining processes across the enterprise to reduce information and information technology (IT) risks. They respond to incidents, establish appropriate standards and controls, manage security technologies, and direct the establishment and implementation of policies and procedures.

Chief Privacy Officer	A chief privacy officer (CPO) is a corporate executive charged with developing and implementing policies designed to protect employee and customer data from unauthorized access. Job includes maintaining a comprehensive and current knowledge of both corporate operations and privacy laws, as well as communicating details of the company's privacy policy to staff and customers alike.
CMM	Capability Maturity Model
CMMI	Capability Maturity Model Integration
COBIT	Control Objectives for Information and Related Technology
Compensating Security Controls	The security controls employed in lieu of the recommended controls in the security control baselines described in frameworks such as NIST Special Publication 800-53 or ISO 27001 that provide equivalent or comparable protection for an information system or organization.
Computer Forensics	Branch of digital forensic science that examines evidence found on computers, hard drives, and removable digital storage media.
Confidentiality	Preserving authorized restrictions on information access and disclosure, including means for protecting personal privacy and proprietary information.
Configuration Management	A collection of activities focused on establishing and maintaining the integrity of information technology products and information systems, through control of processes for initializing, changing, and monitoring the configurations of those products and systems throughout the system development life cycle.
Configuration Management Database (CMDB)	A configuration management database (CMDB) is a repository that holds data relating to a collection of IT assets (commonly referred to as configuration items (CI)), as well as to descriptive

relationships between such assets.

Configuration Settings	The set of parameters that can be changed in hardware, software, or firmware that affect the security posture and/or functionality of the information system.
Continuous Monitoring	Continuous monitoring is the process and technology used to detect compliance and risk issues associated with an organization's financial and operational environment. The financial and operational environment consists of people, processes, and systems working together to support efficient and effective operations.
Countermeasures	Actions, devices, procedures, techniques, or other measures that reduce the vulnerability of an information system. Synonymous with security controls and safeguards.
Customer Relationship Management (CRM)	Customer relationship management (CRM) is a technology for managing all your company's relationships and interactions with customers and potential customers.
Cyber Attack	An attack, via cyberspace, targeting an enterprise's use of cyberspace for the purpose of disrupting, disabling, destroying, or maliciously controlling a computing environment/infrastructure; or destroying the integrity of the data or stealing controlled information.
Cyber Desert	Term used to explain a geographic area where there is a need for talented workers with skills in cyber security but there are no applicants available.
Cyber Hygiene	Cyber hygiene is the establishment and maintenance of an individual's the daily routines, occasional checks and general behaviors required to maintain a user's online "health" (security). This would typically include (but is not limited to) using a firewall, updating virus definitions, running security scans, selecting and maintaining passwords (and other entry systems),

	updating software, backing-up data and securing personal data.
Cyber Kill Chain	A kill chain is used to describe the various stages of a cyber-attack as it pertains to network security. The actual model, the Cyber Kill Chain framework, was developed by Lockheed Martin and is used for identification and prevention of cyber intrusions.
Cyber Risk	'Cyber risk' means any risk of financial loss, disruption or damage to the reputation of an organization from some sort of failure of its information technology systems.
Cyber Threat Intelligence (CTI)	Threat intelligence, also known as cyber threat intelligence (CTI), is organized, analyzed and refined information about potential or current attacks that threaten an organization. The primary purpose of threat intelligence is helping organizations understand the risks of the most common and severe external threats.
Cybersecurity	The ability to protect or defend the use of cyberspace from cyber-attacks.
Cybersecurity Awareness	A security awareness program is the best solution that an organization can adopt to reduce the security threats caused by internal employees. A security awareness program helps employees to understand that the information security is not an individual's responsibility; it is the responsibility of everyone.
Cyberspace	A global domain within the information environment consisting of the interdependent network of information systems infrastructures including the Internet, telecommunications networks, computer systems, and embedded processors and controllers.
Dark Web	The dark web is the World Wide Web content that exists on darknets, overlay networks that use

	the Internet but require specific software, configurations or authorization to access.
Data Breach	Security incident in which sensitive, protected or confidential data is copied, transmitted, viewed, stolen or used by an individual or group that is unauthorized to do so.
Data Loss Prevention (DLP)	DLP systems detect and alert on sometimes block) data leaving the network.
Data Mining/Harvesting	An analytical process that attempts to find correlations or patterns in large data sets for the purpose of data or knowledge discovery.
DDoS	Distributed Denial of Service
Defense-in-Breadth	A planned, systematic set of multidisciplinary activities that seek to identify, manage, and reduce risk of exploitable vulnerabilities at every stage of the system, network, or subcomponent life cycle (system, network, or product design and development; manufacturing; packaging; assembly; system integration; distribution; operations; maintenance; and retirement).
Defense-in-Depth	Information security strategy integrating people, technology, and operations capabilities to establish variable barriers across multiple layers and missions of the organization.
DevOps	DevOps (development and operations) is an enterprise software development phrase used to mean a type of agile relationship between development and IT operations. The goal of DevOps is to change and improve the relationship by advocating better communication and collaboration between these two business units.
DevSecOps	DevSecOps strives to automate core security tasks by embedding security controls and processes into

the DevOps workflow. DevSecOps originally focused primarily on automating code security and testing, but now it also encompasses more operations-centric controls.

Digital Media   A form of electronic media where data are stored in digital (as opposed to analog) form.

Disaster Recovery Plan (DRP)   A collection of processes, plans, and procedures for restoring the company's IT operations or infrastructure to full functionality during and after the event. The DRP is usually an addendum to the BCP and many organizations use these names interchangeably to refer to similar processes.

DNS   Domain Name Server

Domain   An environment or context that includes a set of system resources and a set of system entities that have the right to access the resources as defined by a common security policy, security model, or security architecture. See *Security Domain*.

EMR   Electronic Medical Records System

Enterprise Architecture   A strategic information asset base, which defines the mission; the information necessary to perform the mission; the technologies necessary to perform the mission; and the transitional processes for implementing new technologies in response to changing mission needs; and includes a baseline architecture; a target architecture; and a sequencing plan.

Enterprise Risk Management (ERM)   Enterprise risk management (ERM) is the process of planning, organizing, leading, and controlling the activities of an organization in order to minimize the effects of risk on an organization's capital and earnings.

ERP	Enterprise Resource Planning
Event	Any observable occurrence in an information system.
Exfiltration	The unauthorized transfer of information from an information system.
External Threat Intelligence	Threat intelligence that is available from multiple sources outside the organization. These external sources can be subscriptions or "feeds." These feeds can be consumed directly by an installed security appliance for a monthly fee or used by a security analyst in a security portal.
F.U.D.	Fear, uncertainty and doubt (often shortened to FUD) is a disinformation strategy used in sales, marketing, public relations, talk radio, politics, religious organizations, and propaganda.
Failover	The capability to switch over automatically (typically without human intervention or warning) to a redundant or standby information system upon the failure or abnormal termination of the previously active system.
Fair Information Practice Principles	Principles that are widely accepted in the United States and internationally as a general framework for privacy and that are reflected in various federal and international laws and policies. In a number of organizations, the principles serve as the basis for analyzing privacy risks and determining appropriate mitigation strategies.
FIPS-Validated Cryptography	A cryptographic module validated by the Cryptographic Module Validation Program (CMVP) to meet requirements specified in FIPS Publication 140-2 (as amended). As a prerequisite to CMVP validation, the cryptographic module is required to employ a cryptographic algorithm implementation that has successfully passed validation testing by the Cryptographic Algorithm

Validation Program (CAVP). See *NSA-Approved Cryptography*.

Firmware	Computer programs and data stored in hardware - typically in read-only memory (ROM) or programmable read-only memory (PROM) - such that the programs and data cannot be dynamically written or modified during execution of the programs.
FISMA	The Federal Information Security Management Act (FISMA) is United States legislation that defines a comprehensive framework to protect government information, operations and assets against natural or man-made threats. FISMA was signed into law part of the Electronic Government Act of 2002.
Full Stack Knowledge	Full stack knowledge would include experience with applications, databases, operating systems, hypervisors, networks (LAN/WAN/IP), backup and storage services, cloud services, and coding. It is knowledge of the full enterprise network and its applications and by many is considered a prerequisite for those who work in cyber security.
GDPR	The General Data Protection Regulation (GDPR) is a legal framework that sets guidelines for the collection and processing of personal information of individuals within the European Union (EU).
GLBA	The Gramm-Leach-Bliley Act (GLB Act or GLBA), also known as the Financial Modernization Act of 1999, is a federal law enacted in the United States to control the ways that financial institutions deal with the private information of individuals.
Governance	All processes that coordinate and control an organization's resources and actions.

	Its scope includes ethics, resource-management processes, accountability and management controls.
GPS	Global Positioning System
GRC	Governance, risk management and compliance or GRC is the umbrella term covering an organization's approach across these three areas: Governance, risk management, and compliance.
Hardware	The physical components of an information system. See *Software* and *Firmware*.
HIPAA	HIPAA: Acronym that stands for the Health Insurance Portability and Accountability Act, a US law designed to provide privacy standards to protect patients' medical records and other health information provided to health plans, doctors, hospitals and other health care providers.
HITECH	The Health Information Technology for Economic and Clinical Health (HITECH) Act, enacted as part of the American Recovery and Reinvestment Act of 2009, was signed into law on February 17, 2009, to promote the adoption and meaningful use of health information technology.
Honeypot	A system (e.g., a web server) or system resource (e.g., a file on a server) that is designed to be attractive to potential crackers and intruders, like honey is attractive to bears.
Human Network	The network of peers, subject matter experts, law enforcement, vendors, and partners. It is recommended meeting regularly with these colleagues and building trust relationships with the people with whom you can effectively partner with.
Hybrid Security Control	A security control that is implemented in an information system in part as a common control and in part as a system-specific

control. See *Common Control* and *System-Specific Security Control.*

ICFR	The Guide to Internal Control Over Financial Reporting (ICFR) describes the process used by U.S. public companies to enhance the reliability of their financial statements by reducing the risk of material errors or misstatements.
IDS	Intrusion Detection System
Impact	The effect on organizational operations, organizational assets, individuals, other organizations, or the Nation (including the national security interests of the United States) of a loss of confidentiality, integrity, or availability of information or an information system.
Impact Value	The assessed potential impact resulting from a compromise of the confidentiality, integrity, or availability of information expressed as a value of low, moderate or high.
Incident	An occurrence that actually or potentially jeopardizes the confidentiality, integrity, or availability of an information system or the information the system processes, stores, or transmits or that constitutes a violation or imminent threat of violation of security policies, security procedures, or acceptable use policies.
Incident Response	Incident response is an organized approach to addressing and managing the aftermath of a security breach or cyberattack, also known as an IT incident, computer incident, or security incident. The goal is to handle the situation in a way that limits damage and reduces recovery time and costs.

Indicators of Compromise (IOCs)	In forensics an artifact observed on a network or in an operating system that with high confidence indicates a computer intrusion. Typical IOCs are virus signatures and IP addresses, MD5 hashes of malware files or URLs or domain names of botnet servers.
Industrial Control System (ICS)	An information system used to control industrial processes such as manufacturing, product handling, production, and distribution. Industrial control systems include supervisory control and data acquisition (SCADA) systems used to control geographically dispersed assets, as well as distributed control systems (DCSs) and smaller control systems using programmable logic controllers to control localized processes.
Information Leakage	The intentional or unintentional release of information to an untrusted environment.
Information Security	The protection of information and information systems from unauthorized access, use, disclosure, disruption, modification, or destruction in order to provide confidentiality, integrity, and availability.
Information Security Architecture	An embedded, integral part of the enterprise architecture that describes the structure and behavior for an enterprise's security processes, information security systems, personnel and organizational subunits, showing their alignment with the enterprise's mission and strategic plans.
Information Security Policy	Aggregate of directives, regulations, rules, and practices that prescribes how an organization manages, protects, and distributes information.
Information Security Program Plan	Formal document that provides an overview of the security requirements for an organization-wide information security program and describes the program

management controls and common controls in place or planned for meeting those requirements.

Information Security Risk	The risk to organizational operations (including mission, functions, image, reputation), organizational assets, individuals, other organizations, and the Nation due to the potential for unauthorized access, use, disclosure, disruption, modification, or destruction of information and/or information systems.
Information Steward	An organizational employee with statutory or operational authority for specified information and responsibility for establishing the controls for its generation, collection, processing, dissemination, and disposal.
Information System Owner	Individual responsible for the overall procurement, development, integration, modification, or operation and maintenance of an information system.
Information System Resilience	The ability of an information system to continue to: (i) operate under adverse conditions or stress, even if in a degraded or debilitated state, while maintaining essential operational capabilities; and (ii) recover to an effective operational posture in a time frame consistent with mission needs.
Information System Security Officer	Individual with assigned responsibility for maintaining the appropriate operational security posture for an information system or program.
Information System-Related Security Risks	Risks that arise through the loss of confidentiality, integrity, or availability of information or information systems and that considers impacts to the organization (including assets, mission, functions, image, or reputation), individuals, other organizations, and the Nation.

See *Risk.*

Information Technology	Any equipment or interconnected system or subsystem of equipment that is used in the automatic acquisition, storage, manipulation, management, movement, control, display, switching, interchange, transmission, or reception of data or information by the organization.
Information Technology Product	See *Information System Component.*
Information Type	A specific category of information (e.g., privacy, medical, proprietary, financial, investigative, contractor-sensitive, security management) defined by an organization or in some instances, by a specific law, directive, policy, or regulation.
Insider	Any person with authorized access to any internal organizational resource, to include personnel, facilities, information, equipment, networks, or systems.
Insider Threat Program	A coordinated group of capabilities under centralized management that is organized to detect and prevent the unauthorized disclosure of sensitive information.
Integrity	Guarding against improper information modification or destruction and includes ensuring information non-repudiation and authenticity.
Intellectual Property (IP)	Intellectual property (or "IP") is a category of property that includes intangible creations of the human intellect, and primarily encompasses copyrights, patents, and trademarks. It also includes other types of rights, such as trade secrets, publicity rights, moral rights, and rights against unfair competition.

Internal Network	A network where: (i) the establishment, maintenance, and provisioning of security controls are under the direct control of organizational employees or contractors; or (ii) cryptographic encapsulation or similar security technology implemented between organization-controlled endpoints, provides the same effect (at least with regard to confidentiality and integrity). An internal network is typically organization-owned yet may be organization-controlled while not being organization-owned.
Internal Threat Intelligence	Information that an organization's security and operations teams have from previous experiences with vulnerabilities, malware incidents, and data breaches. This information, if properly documented, can provide organizations with some meaningful insights into earlier compromises of their enterprise networks. It can also highlight recurring methodologies that worked against the security program and its implemented risk management controls.
Internet of Things (IoT)	The Internet of Things (IoT) is a system of interrelated computing devices, mechanical and digital machines, objects, animals or people that are provided with unique identifiers and the ability to transfer data over a network without requiring human-to-human or human-to-computer interaction.
Intrusion Detection Systems (IDS)	An intrusion detection system (IDS) is a type of security software designed to automatically alert administrators when someone or something is trying to compromise information system through malicious activities or through security policy violations.
Intrusion Prevention Systems (IPS)	An intrusion prevention system (IPS) is a system that monitors a network for malicious activities such as security threats or policy violations. The main function of an IPS is to identify

suspicious activity, and then log information, attempt to block the activity, and then finally to report it.

IR	Incident Response
IRP	Incident Response Plan
ISAC	Information Sharing and Analysis Center
ISC2	International Information System Security Certification Consortium
ISO	International Standards Organization
ISP	Internet Service Provider
ISSA	Information Systems Security Association
ITGC	IT general controls (ITGC) are controls that apply to all systems components, processes, and data for a given organization or information technology (IT) environment.
ITIL	ITIL, formally an acronym for Information Technology Infrastructure Library, is a set of detailed practices for IT service management (ITSM) that focuses on aligning IT services with the needs of business.
ITSM	Information Technology Service Management
Machine Learning (ML)	Machine learning is an application of artificial intelligence (AI) that provides systems the ability to automatically learn and improve from experience without being explicitly programmed. Machine learning focuses on the development of computer programs that can access data and use it learn for themselves.
MAD	Maximum Allowable Downtime
Malicious Code	Software or firmware intended to perform an unauthorized process that will have adverse impact on the confidentiality, integrity, or availability of an information system. A virus, worm, Trojan horse, or other code-based entity that infects a host. Spyware and some forms of adware are also examples of malicious code.

Malware	See *Malicious Code*.
Managed Interface	An interface within an information system that provides boundary protection capability using automated mechanisms or devices.
Managed Security Service Provider (MSSP)	An MSSP (managed security service provider) is an Internet service provider (ISP) that provides an organization with some amount of network security management, which may include virus blocking, spam blocking, intrusion detection, firewalls, and virtual private network (VPN) management.
Managed Service Provider (MSP)	A managed services provider (MSP) is most often an information technology (IT) services provider that manages and assumes responsibility for providing a defined set of services to its clients either proactively or as the MSP (not the client) determines that services are needed.
Media	Physical devices or writing surfaces including, but not limited to, magnetic tapes, optical disks, magnetic disks, Large-Scale Integration (LSI) memory chips, and printouts (but not including display media) onto which information is recorded, stored, or printed within an information system.
Metadata	Information describing the characteristics of data including, for example, structural metadata describing data structures (e.g., data format, syntax, and semantics) and descriptive metadata describing data contents (e.g., information security labels).
Multifactor Authentication	Authentication using two or more different factors to achieve authentication. Factors include: (i) something you know (e.g., password/PIN); (ii) something you have (e.g., cryptographic identification device, token); or (iii) something you are (e.g., biometric). See *Authenticator*.

National Institute of Standards and Technology (NIST)	The National Institute of Standards and Technology (NIST) was founded in 1901 and is now part of the U.S. Department of Commerce. NIST is one of the nation's oldest physical science laboratories. Congress established the agency to remove a major challenge to U.S. industrial competitiveness at the time—a second-rate measurement infrastructure that lagged behind the capabilities of the United Kingdom, Germany, and other economic rivals.
National Vulnerabilities Database (NVD)	The NVD is the U.S. government repository of standards-based vulnerability management data represented using the Security Content Automation Protocol (SCAP). This data enables automation of vulnerability management, security measurement, and compliance. The NVD includes databases of security checklist references, security-related software flaws, misconfigurations, product names, and impact metrics
Network Access Control (NAC)	A feature provided by some firewalls that allows access based on a user's credentials and the results of health checks performed on the telework client device.
Network Address Translation (NAT)	A mechanism for mapping addresses on one network to addresses on another network, typically private addresses to public addresses.
Network Based Intrusion Detection System	An intrusion detection and prevention system that monitors network traffic for particular network segments or devices and analyzes the network and application protocol activity to identify and stop suspicious activity.

Network Behavior Analysis	An intrusion detection and prevention system that examines network traffic to identify and stop threats that generate unusual traffic flows.
Network Discovery	The process of discovering active and responding hosts on a network, identifying weaknesses, and learning how the network operates.
Network Tap	A direct connection between a sensor and the physical network media itself, such as a fiber optic cable.
Network Vulnerability Scanner	See Vulnerability Scanner
NFCA	National Fusion Center Association
NIST	National Institute of Standards and Technology
Non-Repudiation	Assurance that the sender is provided with proof of delivery and that the recipient is provided with proof of the sender's identity so that neither can later deny having processed the data.
Open Source Security	Open-source software security is the measure of assurance or guarantee in the freedom from danger and risk inherent to an open-source software system. Working groups such as OWASP were started to address the issues of security in coding and open source software.
OPSEC	Systematic and proven process by which potential adversaries can be denied information about capabilities and intentions by identifying, controlling, and protecting generally unclassified evidence of the planning and execution of sensitive activities. The process involves five steps: identification of critical information, analysis of threats, analysis of vulnerabilities, assessment of risks, and application

of appropriate countermeasures.

OSINT	Open-Source Intelligence
OSTIP	Open-Source Threat Information Platform
OT	Operations Technology
OTX	Open Threat Exchange
OWASP	The Open Web Application Security Project (OWASP) is a 501(c)(3) worldwide not-for-profit charitable organization focused on improving the security of software. Our mission is to make software security visible, so that individuals and organizations are able to make informed decisions.
PaaS	Platform as a Service
Packet Filter	A routing device that provides access control functionality for host addresses and communication sessions.
Packet Filter Firewall	Packet filter firewalls are routing devices that include access control functionality for system addresses and communication sessions.
Packet Sniffer	Software that observes and records network traffic.
Password Cracking	The process of recovering secret passwords stored in a computer system or transmitted over a network.
Patch Management	The systematic notification, identification, deployment, installation, and verification of operating system and application software code revisions. These revisions are known as patches, hot fixes, and service packs.
Payment Card Industry Data Security Standard (PCI-DSS)	The Payment Card Industry Data Security Standard (PCI DSS) is an information security standard for

	organizations that handle branded credit cards from the major card schemes. The standard was created to increase controls around cardholder data to reduce credit card fraud.
PCAP	Packet Capture
Penetration Testing	Security testing in which evaluators mimic real-world attacks in an attempt to identify ways to circumvent the security features of an application, system, or network. Penetration testing often involves issuing real attacks on real systems and data, using the same tools and techniques used by actual attackers. Most penetration tests involve looking for combinations of vulnerabilities on a single system or multiple systems that can be used to gain more access than could be achieved through a single vulnerability.
Personally-Identifiable Information (PII)	Information that can be used to distinguish or trace an individual's identity, such as name, social security number, biometric records, etc. alone, or when combined with other personal or identifying information that is linked or linkable to a specific individual, such as date and place of birth, mother's maiden name, etc.
Pharming	Using technical means to redirect users into accessing a fake Web site masquerading as a legitimate one and divulging personal information.
Phishing	A technique for attempting to acquire sensitive data, such as bank account numbers, through a fraudulent solicitation in email or on a web site, in which the perpetrator masquerades as a legitimate business or reputable person.

Physical Controls & Safeguards	Physical measures, policies, and procedures to protect a covered entity's electronic information systems and related buildings and equipment from natural and environmental hazards, and unauthorized intrusion.
PIPEDA	Personal Information Protection and Electronic Documents Act (Canada)
Plain Text	Intelligible data that has meaning and can be read or acted upon without the application of decryption. Also known as clear text.
Platform as a Service (PaaS)	A model of service delivery whereby the computing platform is provided as an on-demand service upon which applications can be developed and deployed. Its main purpose is to reduce the cost and complexity of buying, housing, and managing the underlying hardware and software components of the platform, including any needed program and database development tools. The development environment is typically special purpose, determined by the cloud provider and tailored to the design and architecture of its platform. The cloud consumer has control over applications and application environment settings of the platform. Security provisions are split between the cloud provider and the cloud consumer.
PMI	Program Management Institute
Polymorphic	The feature pertaining to the dynamic treatment of data elements based on their type, allowing for an instance of a method to have several definitions. Polymorphic malware or polymorphic viruses change attributes specifically to evade malware detection tools.
Polymorphism	The feature pertaining to the dynamic treatment of data elements based on

	their type, allowing for an instance of a method to have several definitions. Malware exists in a state of polymorphism if it is able to alter its attributes to avoid detection.
Port Scan	A technique that sends client requests to a range of service port addresses on a host.
Port Scanner	A program that can remotely determine which ports on a system are open (e.g., whether systems allow connections through those ports).
Process Hijacking	A process checkpoint and migration technique that uses dynamic program re-writing techniques to add a checkpointing capability to a running program. Process hijacking makes it possible to checkpoint and migrate proprietary applications that cannot be re-linked with a checkpoint library allowing dynamic hand off of an ordinary running process to a distributed resource management system (e.g., the ability to trick or bypass the firewall allowing the server component to take over processes and gain rights for accessing the internet).
Programmable Logic Controller (PLC)	A small industrial computer originally designed to perform the logic functions executed by electrical hardware (relays, switches, and mechanical timer/counters). PLCs have evolved into controllers with the capability of controlling complex processes, and they are used substantially in SCADA systems and DCS. PLCs are also used as the primary controller in smaller system configurations. PLCs are used extensively in almost all industrial processes.

Proprietary Information (PI)	Top Secret (TS) information, COMSEC information excluding controlled cryptographic items when unkeyed and utilized with unclassified keys, restricted data (RD), special access program (SAP) information, or sensitive compartmented information (SCI).
Protected Health Information (PHI)	Individually identifiable health information:
	(1) Except as provided in paragraph (2) of this definition, that is:
	(i) Transmitted by electronic media;
	(ii) Maintained in electronic media; or
	(iii) Transmitted or maintained in any other form or medium. (2) Protected health information excludes individually identifiable health information in:
	(i) Education records covered by the Family Educational Rights and Privacy Act, as amended, 20 U.S.C. 1232g;
	(ii) Records described at 20 U.S.C. 1232g(a)(4)(B)(iv); and
	(iii) Employment records held by a covered entity in its role as employer.
Protocol	A set of rules (i.e., formats and procedures) to implement and control some type of association (e.g., communication) between systems.
Protocol Analyzer	A device or software application that enables the user to analyze the performance of network data so as to ensure that the network and its associated hardware/software are operating within network specifications.
Proxy	An application that "breaks" the connection between client and server. The proxy accepts certain types of traffic entering or leaving a

network and processes it and forwards it.

Public Key Certificate   A set of data that uniquely identifies an entity, contains the entity's public key, and is digitally signed by a trusted party, thereby binding the public key to the entity.

Public Key Infrastructure   A support service to the PIV system that provides the cryptographic keys needed to perform digital signature-based identity verification and to protect communications and storage of sensitive verification system data within identity cards and the verification system.

Public Key Infrastructure (PKI)   A support service to the PIV system that provides the cryptographic keys needed to perform digital signature-based identity verification and to protect communications and storage of sensitive verification system data within identity cards and the verification system.

Quantitative Assessment   Use of a set of methods, principles, or rules for assessing risks based on the use of numbers where the meanings and proportionality of values are maintained inside and outside the context of the assessment.

Quarantine   To store files containing malware in isolation for future disinfection or examination.

RACI   Responsible Accountable Consulted and Informed

Recovery Point Objective (RPO)   The point in time to which data must be recovered after an outage.

Recovery Time Objective (RTO)   The overall length of time an information system's components can be in the recovery phase before negatively impacting the organization's mission or mission/business processes.

Remediation	The act of mitigating a vulnerability or a threat.
Replay Attack	An attack that involves the capture of transmitted authentication or access control information and its subsequent retransmission with the intent of producing an unauthorized effect or gaining unauthorized access.
Reproducibility	The ability of different experts to produce the same results from the same data.
Residual Risk	The potential for the occurrence of an adverse event after adjusting for the impact of all in-place safeguards. (See Total Risk, Acceptable Risk, and Minimum Level of Protection.).
Resilience	The ability to prepare for and adapt to changing conditions and withstand and recover rapidly from disruptions. Resilience includes the ability to withstand and recover from deliberate attacks, accidents, or naturally occurring threats or incidents.
Restoration	The process of changing the status of a suspended (i.e., temporarily invalid) certificate to valid.
Revocation	The process of permanently ending the binding between a certificate and the identity asserted in the certificate from a specified time forward.
Risk	The level of impact on organizational operations (including mission, functions, image, or reputation), organizational assets, or individuals resulting from the operation of an information system given the potential impact of a threat and the likelihood of that threat occurring.

Risk Analysis	The process of identifying the risks to system security and determining the likelihood of occurrence, the resulting impact, and the additional safeguards that mitigate this impact. Part of risk management and synonymous with risk assessment.
Risk Assessment	The process of identifying risks to organizational operations (including mission, functions, image, reputation), organizational assets, individuals, other organizations, and the Nation, resulting from the operation of an information system. Part of risk management, incorporates threat and vulnerability analyses, and considers mitigations provided by security controls planned or in place.
Risk Management	The process of managing risks to organizational operations (including mission, functions, image, or reputation), organizational assets, or individuals resulting from the operation of an information system, and includes: (i) the conduct of a risk assessment; (ii) the implementation of a risk mitigation strategy; and (iii) employment of techniques and procedures for the continuous monitoring of the security state of the information system.
Risk Management Framework (RMF)	The Risk Management Framework (RMF), presented in NIST SP 800-37, provides a disciplined and structured process that integrates information security and risk management activities into the system development life cycle.
Risk Mitigation	Prioritizing, evaluating, and implementing the appropriate risk-reducing controls/countermeasures recommended from the risk

management process. A subset of Risk Response.

Risk Tolerance	The level of risk an entity is willing to assume in order to achieve a potential desired result.
Roles & Responsibilities	Functions performed by someone in a specific situation and obligations to tasks or duties for which that person is accountable.
Roles Based Access Control (RBAC)	A model for controlling access to resources where permitted actions on resources are identified with roles rather than with individual subject identities.
Root Cause Analysis (RCA)	A principle-based, systems approach for the identification of underlying causes associated with a particular set of risks.
Root Certificate Authority	In a hierarchical public key infrastructure (PKI), the certification authority (CA) whose public key serves as the most trusted datum (i.e., the beginning of trust paths) for a security domain.
Rootkit	A set of tools used by an attacker after gaining root-level access to a host to conceal the attacker's activities on the host and permit the attacker to maintain root-level access to the host through covert means.
RPO	Recovery Point Objective
RTO	Recovery Time Objective
SaaS	Software as a Service
Sandbox	A system that allows an untrusted application to run in a highly controlled environment where the application's permissions are restricted to an essential set of computer permissions. In particular, an application in a sandbox is usually restricted from accessing the file system or the network. A widely used example of

applications running inside a sandbox is a Java applet.

Sandboxing

A restricted, controlled execution environment that prevents potentially malicious software, such as mobile code, from accessing any system resources except those for which the software is authorized.

SANS

The SANS Institute was established in 1989 as a cooperative research and education organization. Its programs now reach more than 165,000 security professionals around the world. A range of individuals from auditors and network administrators, to chief information security officers are sharing the lessons they learn and are jointly finding solutions to the challenges they face.

Sarbanes-Oxley Act (SOX)

The Sarbanes-Oxley Act of 2002 (SOX) is an act passed by U.S. Congress in 2002 to protect investors from the possibility of fraudulent accounting activities by corporations. The SOX Act mandated strict reforms to improve financial disclosures from corporations and prevent accounting fraud.

Scalability

The ability of a system to handle a growing amount of work in a capable manner or its ability to be enlarged to accommodate that growth.

Script

A sequence of instructions, ranging from a simple list of operating system commands to full-blown programming language statements, which can be executed automatically by an interpreter.

Secret Key

A cryptographic key that is uniquely associated with one or more entities. The use of the term "secret" in this context does not

	imply a classification level; rather the term implies the need to protect the key from disclosure or substitution.
Security Administrator	A person dedicated to performing information security functions for servers and other hosts, as well as networks.
Security Assessment	The testing and/or evaluation of the management, operational, and technical security controls in an information system to determine the extent to which the controls are implemented correctly, operating as intended, and producing the desired outcome with respect to meeting the security requirements for the system.
Security Awareness Training	Security awareness training is a formal process for educating employees about computer security. A good security awareness program should educate employees about corporate policies and procedures for working with information technology (IT).
Security Configuration Management	The management and control of configurations for an information system to enable security and facilitate the management of risk.
Security Control	A safeguard or countermeasure prescribed for an information system or an organization designed to protect the confidentiality, integrity, and availability of its information and to meet a set of defined security requirements.
Security Control Assessment	The testing and/or evaluation of the management, operational, and technical security controls in an information system to determine the extent to which the controls are implemented correctly, operating as intended, and producing the desired outcome with respect to meeting the security requirements for the system.

Security Control Baseline	The set of minimum security controls defined for a low-impact, moderate-impact, or high-impact information system.
Security Event Management	Software that imports security event information from multiple data sources, normalizes the data, and correlates events among the data sources.
Security Incident	An occurrence that actually or potentially jeopardizes the confidentiality, integrity, or availability of an information system or the information the system processes, stores, or transmits or that constitutes a violation or imminent threat of violation of security policies, security procedures, or acceptable use policies.
Security Information and Event Management	A program that provides centralized logging capabilities for a variety of log types.
Security Perimeter	A physical or logical boundary that is defined for a system, domain, or enclave; within which a particular security policy or security architecture is applied.
Security Plan	Formal document that provides an overview of the security requirements for an information system or an information security program and describes the security controls in place or planned for meeting those requirements.
	See system security plan or information security program plan.
Security Policy	The rules and requirements established by an organization that governs the acceptable use of its information and services, and the level and means for protecting the confidentiality, integrity, and availability of its information.

Security Requirements	Requirements levied on an information system that are derived from applicable laws, Executive Orders, directives, policies, standards, instructions, regulations, or procedures, or organizational mission/business case needs to ensure the confidentiality, integrity, and availability of the information being processed, stored, or transmitted.
Security Technical Implementation Guide (STIG)	Based on Department of Defense (DoD) policy and security controls. Implementation guide geared to a specific product and version. Contains all requirements that have been flagged as applicable for the product which have been selected on a DoD baseline.
Security Testing	Testing that attempts to verify that an implementation protects data and maintains functionality as intended.
Security Tokens	Security tokens are used to allow access first to a computer and then to a network. Tokens come in various forms - for example, Personal Computer Memory Card International Association (PCMCIA) cards, flash memory, USB tokens, smart cards, and software.
Segregation of Duties / Separation of Duties (SOD)	A security principle that divides critical functions among different staff members in an attempt to ensure that no one individual has enough information or access privilege to perpetrate damaging fraud.
Session Hijack Attack	An attack in which the Attacker is able to insert himself or herself between a Claimant and a Verifier subsequent to a successful authentication exchange between the latter two parties. The Attacker is able to pose as a Subscriber to the

Verifier or vice versa to control session data exchange. Sessions between the Claimant and the Relying Party can also be similarly compromised.

SIEM	Security Incident and Event Management
Sniffer	A network monitoring tool, usually a software tool running on a PC.
SOC	Security Operations Center
Social Engineering	An attempt to trick someone into revealing information (e.g., a password) that can be used to attack systems or networks.
Software as a Service (SaaS)	The capability provided to the consumer is to use the provider's applications running on a cloud infrastructure2. The applications are accessible from various client devices through either a thin client interface, such as a web browser (e.g., web-based email), or a program interface. The consumer does not manage or control the underlying cloud infrastructure including network, servers, operating systems, storage, or even individual application capabilities, with the possible exception of limited user-specific application configuration settings.
SOP	Standard Operating Procedures
SPAM	Electronic junk mail or the abuse of electronic messaging systems to indiscriminately send unsolicited bulk messages.
Spanning Port	A switch port that can see all network traffic going through the switch.
Spear Phishing	A colloquial term that can be used to describe any highly targeted phishing attack.

Spoofing	The deliberate inducement of a user or resource to take incorrect action. Note: Impersonating, masquerading, piggybacking, and mimicking are forms of spoofing.
Spyware	Software that is secretly or surreptitiously installed into an information system to gather information on individuals or organizations without their knowledge; a type of malicious code.
SSL	Secure Socket Layer
	A method of interviewing that requires candidates to relate experiences within the framework of Situation, Task, Action,
STAR	and Results
Static Analysis	Detecting software vulnerabilities by examining the app source code and binary and attempting to reason over all possible behaviors that might arise at runtime.
	Structured Threat Information
STIX	Expression
Strong Authentication	A method used to secure computer systems and/or networks by verifying a user's identity by requiring two-factors in order to authenticate (something you know, something you are, or something you have).
Supervisory Control And Data Acquisition (SCADA)	A generic name for a computerized system that is capable of gathering and processing data and applying operational controls over long distances. Typical uses include power transmission and distribution and pipeline systems. SCADA was designed for the unique communication challenges (e.g., delays, data integrity) posed by the various media that must be used, such as phone lines, microwave, and satellite. Usually shared rather than dedicated.

SWOT	Strengths, Weaknesses, Opportunities, Threats
Syslog	A protocol that specifies a general log entry format and a log entry transport mechanism.
System Administrator	A person who manages a computer system, including its operating system and applications. A system administrator's responsibilities are similar to that of a network administrator.
System Development Life Cycle (SDLC)	The scope of activities associated with a system, encompassing the system's initiation, development and acquisition, implementation, operation and maintenance, and ultimately its disposal.
System of Records	A group of any records under the control of any agency from which information is retrieved by the name of the individual or by some identifying number, symbol, or other identifying particular assigned to the individual.
Tabletop Exercise	A discussion-based exercise where personnel with roles and responsibilities in a particular IT plan meet in a classroom setting or in breakout groups to validate the content of the plan by discussing their roles during an emergency and their responses to a particular emergency situation. A facilitator initiates the discussion by presenting a scenario and asking questions based on the scenario.
Tampering	An intentional but unauthorized act resulting in the modification of a system, components of systems, its intended behavior, or data.
TAP	Test Access Point
TAXII	Trusted Automated eXchange of Indicator Information
Threat Agent	The term Threat Agent is used to indicate an individual or group that can manifest a threat. It is fundamental to identify who

	would want to exploit the assets of a company, and how they might use them against the company.
Threat Modeling	Threat modeling is a procedure for optimizing network security by identifying objectives and vulnerabilities, and then defining countermeasures to prevent, or mitigate the effects of, threats to the system.
Threat Monitoring	Analysis, assessment, and review of audit trails and other information collected for the purpose of searching out system events that may constitute violations of system security.
Trust	A characteristic of an entity that indicates its ability to perform certain functions or services correctly, fairly, and impartially, along with assurance that the entity and its identifier are genuine.
TSA	Transportation Security Administration
TTP	Tactics, Techniques and Procedures
Unauthorized Access	Any access that violates the stated security policy.
Unauthorized Disclosure	An event involving the exposure of information to entities not authorized access to the information.
US CERT	United States Computer Emergency Readiness Team
USCG	United Stated Coast Guard
User Activity Monitoring	The technical capability to observe and record the actions and activities of an individual, at any time, on any device accessing U.S. Government information in order to detect insider threat and to support authorized investigations.
USSS	United Stated Secret Service
Virtual Private Network (VPN)	A virtual network built on top of existing networks that can provide a secure communications

	mechanism for data and IP information transmitted between networks.
Virus	A computer program that can copy itself and infect a computer without permission or knowledge of the user. A virus might corrupt or delete data on a computer, use e-mail programs to spread itself to other computers, or even erase everything on a hard disk. See malicious code.
Virus Definitions	Predefined signatures for known malware used by antivirus detection algorithms.
Volatile Data	Data on a live system that is lost after a computer is powered down.
Volatile Memory	Memory that loses its content when power is turned off or lost.
Vulnerability	Weakness in an information system, system security procedures, internal controls, or implementation that could be exploited or triggered by a threat source.
Vulnerability Assessment	Systematic examination of an information system or product to determine the adequacy of security measures, identify security deficiencies, provide data from which to predict the effectiveness of proposed security measures, and confirm the adequacy of such measures after implementation.
Vulnerability Scanning	A technique used to identify hosts/host attributes and associated vulnerabilities.
Warm Site	An environmentally conditioned work space that is partially equipped with information systems and telecommunications equipment to support relocated operations in the event of a significant disruption.

Watering Hole Attack	In a watering hole attack, the attacker compromises a site likely to be visited by a particular target group, rather than attacking the target group directly.
Web Service	A software component or system designed to support interoperable machine- or application-oriented interaction over a network. A Web service has an interface described in a machine-processable format (specifically WSDL). Other systems interact with the Web service in a manner prescribed by its description using SOAP messages, typically conveyed using HTTP with an XML serialization in conjunction with other Web-related standards.
Whaling	A specific kind of phishing that targets high-ranking members of organizations.
White List	A list of discrete entities, such as hosts or applications that are known to be benign and are approved for use within an organization and/or information system.
XML	eXtensible Markup Language
Zero-Day Attack	An attack that exploits a previously unknown hardware, firmware, or software vulnerability.

Bibliography

ACF. 2015. "Administration for Children and Families." *U.S. DEPARTMENT OF HEALTH AND HUMAN SERVICES.* July 1. https://www.acf.hhs.gov/sites/default/files/cb/im 1504.pdf.

Adler, Steven. 2007. "CIO Magazine." *CIO Magazine Website.* May 31. http://www.cio.com/article/2438861/enterprise-architecture/six-steps-to-data-governance-success.html.

Ambrose, Christopher. 2014. "Gartner Vendor Management." *Gartner.* October 31. https://www.gartner.com/doc/2894817/monitor-key-risk-criteria-mitigate.

ANSI-ASQ. 2017. *ANAB.* http://www.anab.org/forensic-accreditation.

ASCLD. 2017. *ASCLD.* http://www.ascld.org/.

AT&T Network Security. 2014. "Business Section: AT&T Security." *An AT&T Web site, Network Security.* December 12. https://www.business.att.com/content/src/csi/dec odingtheadversary.pdf.

Atkinson, Joyceline R. Davis and Tom. 2010. "Need Speed? Slow Down." *hbr.org.* Harvard Business Review. May. Accessed March 2016. https://hbr.org/2010/05/need-speed-slow-down.

Beard, Charles, Kevin Mickelberg, Emily Stapf, and Don Ulsch. 2015. "US cybersecurity: Progress stalled, Key findings from the 2015 US State of Cybercrime Survey." *PWC.* July 24. http://www.pwc.com/us/en/increasing-it-effectiveness/publications/assets/2015-us-cybercrime-survey.pdf.

BISSON, DAVID. 2015. *The State of Security.* September 23. http://www.tripwire.com/state-of-security/risk-based-security-for-executives/connecting-security-

to-the-business/the-top-10-tips-for-building-an-
effective-security-dashboard/.

Bonney, Bill. 2015. *Users Have a Duty Too.* February 6.
Accessed January 5, 2017.
https://www.linkedin.com/pulse/users-have-duty-
too-bill-bonney.

Bromiley, Matt. 2016. "Reading Room - Whitepapers."
SANS. June. https://www.sans.org/reading-
room/whitepapers/incident/incident-response-
capabilities-2016-2016-incident-response-survey-
37047.

Building Security In Maturity Model (BSIMM). 2017. *BSIMM
Framework.* January 11.
https://www.bsimm.com/framework/.

Caldwell, French. 2009. "Assess Vendor Risks." *Gartner.*
September 10.
http://www.gartner.com/document/1175014/gart
ners-simple-vendor-risk-management.

2003. *Carnegie Mellon University.* April.
http://resources.sei.cmu.edu/asset_files/Handbook
/2003_002_001_14102.pdf.

Center for Internet Security. 2016. "CIS SECURITY
BENCHMARKS." *Security Benchmarks.*
https://benchmarks.cisecurity.org/.

—. 2015. "CIS SECURITY CONTROLS LIBRARY." *CIS - Center
for Internet Security.*
https://www.cisecurity.org/critical-
controls/Library.cfm.

Chickowski, Ericka. 2016. "Dark Reading: Analytics."
Information Week, DarkReading website. March 16.
http://www.darkreading.com/analytics/10-ways-
to-measure-it-security-program-effectiveness/d/d-
id/1319494.

Cichonski, Paul, Tom Millar, Tim Grance, and Karen
Scarfone. 2012. "NIST SP800-61 rev2." *NIST Special
Publications.* August.
http://nvlpubs.nist.gov/nistpubs/SpecialPublicatio
ns/NIST.SP.800-61r2.pdf.

—. 2012. "Special Publications: NIST Pubs." *National Institute of Standards and Technology web site.* August 23. http://nvlpubs.nist.gov/nistpubs/SpecialPublicatio ns/NIST.SP.800-61r2.pdf.

CIS. 2010. "CIS Consensus Information Security Metrics." *Center for Internet Security.* Center for Internet Security. November 11. Accessed June 11, 2016. https://benchmarks.cisecurity.org/downloads/metr ics/#progress.

—. 2016. "CIS CONSENSUS INFORMATION SECURITY METRICS." *Center for Internet Security.* 04 12. https://benchmarks.cisecurity.org/downloads/metr ics/index.cfm#progress.

—. 2015. "CIS Controls for Effective Cyber Defense ver 6.0." *Center for Internet Security, CIS Critical Controls.* Center for Internet Security. October 15. Accessed June 11, 2016. https://www.cisecurity.org/critical-controls/.

—. 2000. *CIS Critical Security Controls.* http://www.sans.org/critical-security-controls/.

—. 2015. "CIS Cyber Hygiene Tool Kit." *Center for Internet Security.* 04 12. https://www.cisecurity.org/cyber-pledge/tools/.

CISCO Security. 2016. "Cisco 2016 Annual Security Report." *Cisco.* January 30. http://www.cisco.com/c/m/en_us/offers/sc04/201 6-annual-security-report/index.html.

CISO Executive Network. 2010. http://www.cisoexecnet.com/sites/default/files/Da ta%20Breach%20Response%20Plan%20Checklist.p df.

Cloud Security Alliance. 2017. *Introduction to the Cloud Controls Matrix Working Group.* January 18. https://cloudsecurityalliance.org/group/cloud-controls-matrix/.

CMMI Institute. 2002. *About CMMI Institute.* Accessed June 10, 2016. http://cmmiinstitute.com/about-cmmi-institute.

Cooper, Price Waterhouse. 2014. *Price Waterhouse Cooper.* 12 31. http://www.pwchk.com/home/eng/rcs_info_security_2014.html.

CSO. 2017. "IDG Presentation." *CSO Online.* July. https://images.idgesg.net/assets/2017/09/idg_presentation_07202017.pdf.

Deloitte Development, LLC. 2015. "Cybersecurity and the role of internal audit: An urgent call to action." *Deloitte University Press.* Deloitte University Press. Accessed March 2016. http://www2.deloitte.com/content/dam/Deloitte/us/Documents/risk/us-risk-cyber-ia-urgent-call-to-action.pdf.

Department of Homeland Security. 2017. *Workforce Development Library.* May 22. https://niccs.us-cert.gov/workforce-development/workforce-development-library.

Department of Justice. 2015. "Best Practices for Victim Response and." *Computer Crime & Intellectual Property Section.* April. https://www.justice.gov/sites/default/files/opa/speeches/attachments/2015/04/29/criminal_division_guidance_on_best_practices_for_victim_response_and_reporting_cyber_incidents.pdf.

DISA. 2016. *DoD 8570 Information Assurance Workforce Improvement Program.* 11 24. http://iase.disa.mil/iawip/Pages/index.aspx.

Economic Espionage Act, 18 U.S.C. Ch. 90 § 1839. 1996. *United States Code Title 18 Chapter 90 Section 1839, Economic Espionage Act of 1996.* Edited by Office of the Law Revision. Washington, DC: Government Printing Office.

Eric M. Hutchins, Michael J, Cloppert, Rohan M. Amin, Ph.D. 2011. "Intelligence-Driven Computer Network

Defense Informed by Analysis of Adversary
Campaigns and Intrusion Kill Chains." *Lockheed
Martin*. Lockheed martin. Accessed September 4,
2017. https:..www.lockheedmartin.com.

ESG & ISSA. 2016. "ESG & ISSA Research Report on The
State of Cyber Security Professional Careers Part 1."
Enterprise Strategy Group (ESG) website. October 1.
http://www.esg-global.com/hubfs/issa/ESG-ISSA-
Research-Report-State-of-Cybersecurity-
Professional-Careers-Oct-2016.pdf.

FDIC. 2008. *Guidance For Managing Third-Party Risk*. June
6. Accessed June 10, 2016.
https://www.fdic.gov/news/news/financial/2008/f
il08044a.html.

FFIEC. 2015. "Responsibility And Accountability." *FFIEC
Online IT Examination Handbook*. FFIEC. November
10. Accessed June 8, 2016.
http://ithandbook.ffiec.gov/it-
booklets/information-security/security-
process/governance/responsibility-and-
accountability.aspx.

Fogerty, Kevin. 2015. "Reading Room." *SANS; Cleaning up
after a Breach*. December.
https://www.sans.org/reading-
room/whitepapers/analyst/cleaning-breach-post-
breach-impact-cost-compendium-36517.

Foley & Lardner LLP. . 2015. "Intelligence: Taking Control
of Cyber Security." *Foley & Lardner LLP* . March 11.
Accessed June 11, 2016.
https://www.foley.com/taking-control-of-
cybersecurity-a-practical-guide-for-officers-and-
directors-03-11-2015/.

Greenwald, Judy. 2014. *Home Depot has $105 million in
cyber insurance to cover data breach*. September 14.
http://www.businessinsurance.com/article/20140
914/NEWS07/309149975.

Gunter K. Stahl, et al. 2012. "Six Principles of Effective
Global Talent Management." *MIT Sloan Management
review*, 10.

Harris, Kamala D. 2016. "California Data Breach Report."
Office of the Attorney General for State of California.
February 10. https://oag.ca.gov/breachreport2016.

Hayslip, Gary. 2015. "LinkedIn: Pulse "Good Resources for
the CISO"." *LinkedIn.com for Professionals.* 12 15.
https://app.box.com/v/CISO-Team-Resources .

—. 2015. "Pulse, Articles by Gary Hayslip." *LinkedIn.* July 30.
https://www.linkedin.com/pulse/cyber-security-
continuous-life-cycle-part-ii-gary-hayslip.

IBM & Ponemon. 2015. "NH Learning Solutions Document
Portal." *NH Learning Solutions Website.* March 15.
https://nhlearningsolutions.com/Portals/0/Docum
ents/2015-Cost-of-Data-Breach-Study.PDF.

Ide, R. William, and Amanda Leech. 2015. "tcbblogs.org."
The Conference Board Governance Center Blog. July
27. http://tcbblogs.org/governance/2015/07/27/a-
cybersecurity-guide-for-directors/.

International Organization for Standardization. 2016.
"Information security incident management."
Information technology -- Security techniques. 11.
http://www.iso.org/iso/catalogue_detail.htm?csnu
mber=62071.

ISACA. 1996. *COBIT 4.1: Framework for IT Governance and
Control.* Accessed June 1, 2016.
http://www.isaca.org/Knowledge-
Center/COBIT/Pages/Overview.aspx.

—. 2007. *COBIT Mapping: Mapping of CMMI for
Development V1.2 With COBIT.* Accessed 2016.
http://www.isaca.org/Knowledge-
Center/Research/ResearchDeliverables/Pages/COB
IT-Mapping-Mapping-of-CMMI-for-Development-
V1-2-With-COBIT.aspx.

—. 2015. "ISACA Knowledge Center, State of Cybersecurity
2016." *ISACA - CYBER.* December 31.

http://www.isaca.org/cyber/Documents/state-of-cybersecurity_res_eng_0316.pdf.

ISO. 2015. "Information security management. Retrieved from International Organization for Standardization (ISO)." *ISO/IEC 27001 - Information security management.* ISO/IEC 27001. December 31. Accessed June 11, 2016. http://www.iso.org/iso/home/standards/management-standards/iso27001.htm.

—. 2016. "ISO/IEC 27035-2:2016." February. https://www.iso.org/standard/62071.html.

ISO/IEC. 2008. "Information Classification Policy (ISO/IEC 27001:2005 A.7.2.1)." *Information Security Standards.* July 9. Accessed June 11, 2016. http://iso27001security.com/ISO27k_Model_policy_on_information_classification.pdf.

ITIL. 1988. *ITIL Open Guide.* Accessed 2016. http://itlibrary.org/.

Johnston, Ronald, Alicia Jones, Kelley Dempsey, Nirali Chawla, Alicia Jones, Angela Orebaugh, Matthew Scholl, and Kevin Stine. 2011. "NIST: Special Publications ." *NIST, U.S. Department of Commerce Website.* September 30. http://nvlpubs.nist.gov/nistpubs/Legacy/SP/nistspecialpublication800-137.pdf.

KPMG. 2013. "KPMG ." *KPMG.* 12 31. https://www.kpmg.com/US/en/IssuesAndInsights/ArticlesPublications/Documents/vendor-risk-management.pdf.

Kristina Dorville. 2014. "Cybersecurity Workforce Planning Capability Maturity Model (CMM)." *NATIONAL INITIATIVE FOR CYBERSECURITY CAREERS AND STUDIES.* August 4. https://niccs.us-cert.gov/sites/default/files/Capability%20Maturity%20Model%20White%20Paper.pdf?trackDocs=Capability%20Maturity%20Model%20White%20Paper.pdf.

Lockton Affinity. 2015. "2015 MSPAlliance-Cyber-Coverage." *MSPAlliance Cloud Insurance Program.* March 20. http://mspalliance.com/wp-content/uploads/2008/11/2015-MSPAlliance-Cyber-Coverage-10-Reasons-White-Paper-3-15.pdf.

Masters, Greg. 2017. "SC Cyber-Crime." *SC Media.* June 26. https://www.scmagazine.com/loss-from-cybercrime-exceeded-13b-in-2016-fbi-report/article/671047/.

McMillan, Jeffrey Wheatman & Rob. 2015. "Business, Not Bytes - A Practical View of Security Metrics." *Gartner Security & Risk Management Summit.* Washington D.C.: Gartner. 22.

Mohamed, Arif. 2013. "Data classification: why it is important and how to do it." *ComputerWeekly.* http://www.computerweekly.com/feature/Data-classification-why-it-is-important-and-how-to-do-it.

Moore, Geoffrey A. 2005. *Dealing with Darwin: How Great Companies Innovate at Every Phase of Their Evolution.* New York, NY: Penguin Books.

National Institute of Standards and Technology. 2014. "Framework for Improving Critical Infrastructure Cybersecurity." *National Institute of Standards and Technology.* February 12. Accessed June 11, 2016. http://www.nist.gov/cyberframework/upload/cybersecurity-framework-021214.pdf.

National Institute of Standards and Technology SP800-61. 2012. "Computer Security Incident Handling." *NIST Publications - Special Publications.* August. http://nvlpubs.nist.gov/nistpubs/SpecialPublications/NIST.SP.800-61r2.pdf.

NIST 800-30 r1. 2012. "Guide for Conducting Risk Assessments." *NVLPUBS.NIST.GOV.* September. Accessed June 2016. http://nvlpubs.nist.gov/nistpubs/Legacy/SP/nistspecialpublication800-30r1.pdf.

NIST. 2015. "Cybersecurity Framework Frequently Asked Questions." *National Institute of Science and*

Technology - Cybersecurity Framework. National Institute of Science and Technology. December 31. Accessed June 11, 2016. http://www.nist.gov/cyberframework/cybersecurity-framework-faqs.cfm.

NIST. 2004. "FIPS PUB 199." *Standards for Security Categorization of Federal Information and Information Systems.* Prod. Information Technology Laboratory Computer Security Division. Gaithersburg, MD: National Institute of Standards and Technology, February.

—. 2014. *Framework for Improving Critical Infrastructure Cybersecurity.* February 12. http://www.nist.gov/cyberframework/upload/cybersecurity-framework-021214.pdf.

—. 2011. "NIST Special Publication 800-137." *NIST Pubs Legacy.* September. http://nvlpubs.nist.gov/nistpubs/Legacy/SP/nistspecialpublication800-137.pdf.

—. 2010. "SP 800-34 rev.1." *NIST Contingency Planning.* May. http://nvlpubs.nist.gov/nistpubs/Legacy/SP/nistspecialpublication800-34r1.pdf.

—. 2012. "Special Publications." *Computer Security Incident Handling Guide.* Aug. http://nvlpubs.nist.gov/nistpubs/SpecialPublications/NIST.SP.800-61r2.pdf.

Open Web Application Security Project (OWASP). 2016. *Category:OWASP Enterprise Security API.* December 16. https://www.owasp.org/index.php/ESAPI.

—. 2016. *OWASP Top Ten Project.* December 16. https://www.owasp.org/index.php/Category:OWASP_Top_Ten_Project.

—. 2016. *Welcome to OWASP.* December 08. https://www.owasp.org/index.php/Main_Page.

OWASP. 2017. *Threat Risk Modeling.* January. https://www.owasp.org/index.php/Threat_Risk_Modeling.

Paul E. Proctor, Jeffrey Wheatman, Rob McMillan. 2016. "How to Build an Effective Cybersecurity and Technology Risk Presentation for Your Board of Directors." *Gartner Website.* March 03. http://www.gartner.com/document/3238219.

PCI Security Standards Council. 2014. "Best Practices for Implementing a Security Awareness Program." *PCI Security Awareness Program Special Interest Group.* October. https://www.pcisecuritystandards.org/documents/PCI_DSS_V1.0_Best_Practices_for_Implementing_Security_Awareness_Program.pdf.

PCI-DSS. 2006. *Payment Card Industry Data Security Standards.* Accessed June 2016. https://www.pcisecuritystandards.org/.

Pink, Daniel H. 2009. *Drive: The Surprising Truth About What Motivates Us.* New York, NY: Riverhead Hardcover.

PMI. 2017. *Project Management Institute.* https://www.pmi.org/pmbok-guide-standards.

Porath, Tony Schwartz and Christine. 2014. "Why You Hate Work." *New Your Times*, May 30: 5.

Raptis, Steve. 2015. "Cyber Risk: Analyzing Cyber Risk Coverage." *Risk and Insurance.* March 13. http://www.riskandinsurance.com/analyzing-cyber-risk-coverage/.

Restuccia, Dan. 2015. "Burning Glass Technologies Research, Cybersecurity Jobs 2015." *Burning Glass Technologies Research.* December 13. http://burning-glass.com/wp-content/uploads/Cybersecurity_Jobs_Report_2015.pdf.

Ryan Stark, Doug Wolfberg. 2015. "The Anthem Breach: 5 Disturbing Facts You Need to Know." *IH Executive.com.* June 30. http://www.ihexecutive.com/insights/article/12077442/the-anthem-breach-5-disturbing-facts-you-need-to-know.

Scholtz, Tom, and Rob McMillan. 2014. "Tips and Guidelines for Sizing Your Information Security Organization." *Gartner.* April 24. http://www.gartner.com/document/2718319?ref= TypeAheadSearch&qid=c0a5b37bd85c58a1a5eafcc 60c0fdce8.

Security, Center for Internet. 2016. *CIS CONSENSUS INFORMATION SECURITY METRICS.* March 01. https://benchmarks.cisecurity.org/downloads/metr ics/.

Security, ThreatTrack. 2014. *ThreatTrack Whitepapers.* December 13. http://www.threattracksecurity.com/resources/wh ite-papers/chief-information-security-officers-misunderstood.aspx.

Seiner, Robert S. 2014. *Non-Invasive Data Governance, The Path of Least Resistance and Great Sucess.* Basking Ridge, NJ: Technics Publications.

State of New York, Office of Information Technology Services. 2016. "Cyber Incident Response Standard." *Enterprise Information Security.* May 04. https://its.ny.gov/document/cyber-incident-response-standard.

The Santa Fe Strategy Center LTD. 2016. *Standardized Information Gathering Questionnaire.* Accessed June 13, 2016. https://sharedassessments.org/.

Tucker Bailey, Josh Brandley, and James Kaplan. 2013. "Business Functions: McKinsey&Company." *McKinsey&Company Website.* December. http://www.mckinsey.com/business-functions/business-technology/our-insights/how-good-is-your-cyberincident-response-plan.

UCF. 2004. *Unified Compliance Framework.* Accessed 2016. https://www.unifiedcompliance.com/.

Verizon. 2016. "Verizon's 2016 Data Breach Investigations Report." *Verizon Labs.* http://www.verizonenterprise.com/verizon-insights-lab/dbir/2016/.

Wikipedia 2. 2016. *ITIL security management.* March 19.
Accessed June 12, 2016.
https://en.wikipedia.org/wiki/ITIL_security_manag
ement.

Wikipedia. 2016. *Application Security.* August.
https://en.wikipedia.org/wiki/Application_security.

—. 2016. *Capability Maturity Model Integration.* March 31.
Accessed June 10, 2016.
https://en.wikipedia.org/wiki/Capability_Maturity_
Model_Integration.

—. 2016. *ITIL.* May 31. Accessed June 12, 2016.
https://en.wikipedia.org/wiki/ITIL.

Wilson, Mark, and Hash, Joan. 2003. "NIST Special
Publication 800-50." *NIST - National Institute of
Standards and Technologies .* October.
http://nvlpubs.nist.gov/nistpubs/Legacy/SP/nistsp
ecialpublication800-50.pdf.

Wright, Craig. 2011. "The Incident Handlers Handbook."
SAN's Reading Room. December 5.
https://www.sans.org/reading-
room/whitepapers/incident/incident-handlers-
handbook-33901.

Index

FISMA, 64
Fusion Center, 135, 136, 260

G

Gaps
    Applications, 120
    Security, 77, 100, 108, 115,
        150, 153, 155, 205, 207, 283,
        308
    Skills, 25, 35, 46, 52
Geoffrey Moore
    Dealing with Darwin, 32

H

Hygiene (Cyber), 26, 63, 64, 67,
    71, 75, 76, 78, 79, 80, 81, 82, 83,
    86, 89, 105, 122, 146, 155, 176,
    196, 227, 238, 254, 267

I

Identity and Access, 67, 185, 254,
    294, 375
Indicator of Threat or
    Compromise, 106, 129, 138,
    152, 159, 160, 166, 214, 215,
    220, 244, 254, 255, 267, 273
InfraGard, 66, 135, 139, 146, 260
Infrastructure
    Critical, 26, 57, 66, 135, 136,
        154, 204, 260, 292
    Network, xvii, 37, 50, 100, 142,
        147, 149, 165, 181, 193, 290
    Security, 109, 160, 216, 312
Integrity (Data), 52
Isolation (Tactic), 215, 262

L

Lab (Forensic), 300
Landscape (Threat), xviii, 71, 80,
    82, 98, 142, 150, 178
Lateral Movement, 176, 276, 279,
    281
Law Enforcement, 43, 131, 134,
    135, 136, 139, 154, 164, 165,

200, 202, 203, 212, 215, 232,
    238, 239, 245, 260, 263, 272,
    273, 275, 278, 283, 288, 289,
    291, 292, 294, 304
Law Enforcement Coordination
    Center, 136, 139
Legal
    Counsel, 107, 142, 203, 213,
        218, 243, 245, 246, 250, 251,
        253, 255, 259, 261, 272, 273,
        278, 279, 287, 288, 292, 302,
        303, 304
    Liability, 203, 243
    Remedy, 203
legislation, 194
Lessons Learned (Discipline and
    Process), 76, 77, 79, 80, 87, 89,
    92, 233, 249, 264, 266, 267, 294

M

Managed Security Service
    Provider, 127, 222, 226, 313
Materiality, 68, 69, 72, 74, 108,
    144, 145, 147, 179, 211, 216,
    217, 247, 252, 312, 315
Maturity
    Organizational, 39, 114, 170
    Process, 122, 128
    Skills, 55, 81
Mission (Organization or Group),
    32, 33, 41, 50, 53, 64, 71, 87, 88,
    113, 170, 180, 231, 294, 307,
    310, 376
Mission-Critical, 32, 33, 310
Moore, Geoffrey (Dealing with
    Darwin), 32, 33, 310

N

Negligence, 208
NFCA, 135, 136
Notification
    Breach, 145, 202, 213, 243,
        251, 263, 264, 271, 283
    Customers, 213, 245
    Law Enforcement, 203, 283
    Regulators, 202, 212, 213, 250,
        251, 264

236, 248, 252, 253, 258, 262,
271, 295

About the Authors

Bill Bonney (CISA) is a security evangelist, author and consultant. Most recently, Bill was Vice President of Product Marketing and Chief Strategist at FHOOSH, a maker of high-speed encryption software. Prior to FHOOSH, Bill was Vice President of Product Marketing and Principal Consulting Analyst at TechVision Research with specialties in information security, Internet of Things (IoT) security and identity management. Before joining TechVision Research, he held numerous senior information security roles in various industries, including financial services, software and manufacturing.

Bill holds multiple patents in data protection, access and classification, is a member of the Board of Advisors for CyberTECH, a San Diego incubator, and is on the board of directors for the San Diego CISO Roundtable, a professional group focused on building relationships and fostering collaboration in information security management. Bill is a highly regarded speaker and panelist addressing technology and security concerns. He holds a Bachelor of Science degree in Computer Science and Applied Mathematics from Albany University.

LinkedIn Profile: https://www.linkedin.com/in/billbonney

Matt Stamper, CISA, CIPP-US. As both a Certified Information Systems Auditor (CISA) and a Certified Information Privacy Professional (CIPP-US) with both public and early-stage company experience, Matt brings a broad, multi-disciplinary understanding to cybersecurity best practices to his clients. His diverse domain knowledge spans IT service management (ITSM), cybersecurity, cloud services, control design and assessment (Sarbanes-Oxley, HIPAA-HITECH), privacy (GDPR), governance, enterprise risk and IT risk management (ERM/ITRM). Matt's diverse experience also includes sales management & individual revenue contribution, new product & service development as well as international experience in both Latin America and China. Matt excels at conveying complex cybersecurity and IT concepts to

boards of directors, executive management, as well as professional service providers. His executive-level experience with managed services, cybersecurity, data centers, networks services, and ITSM provides a unique perspective on the fast-changing world of enterprise IT, IoT, and cloud services.

Matt received a Bachelor of Arts from the University of California at San Diego, where he graduated Cum Laude and with Honors and Distinction in Political Science. His graduate studies include a Master of Arts in Pacific International Affairs from the University of California at San Diego and a Master of Science degree in Telecommunications sponsored by AT&T. He is fluent in Spanish and has worked in executive roles in Latin America.

LinkedIn Profile: https://www.linkedin.com/in/stamper

Gary R. Hayslip, CISSP, CISA, Chief Information Security Officer, Webroot Inc.

As Chief Information Security Officer (CISO) for Webroot, Gary advises executive leadership on protecting critical information resources and oversees enterprise cybersecurity strategy. As CISO, his mission includes creating a "risk aware" culture that places a high value on  securing and protecting customer information entrusted to Webroot. Gary is a proven cybersecurity professional, his previous information security roles include multiple CISO, Deputy Director of IT and Senior Network Architect roles for the City of San Diego, the U.S. Navy (Active Duty) and as a U.S. Federal Government employee.

Gary is involved in the cybersecurity and technology start-up communities in San Diego. He is an advisory board member for CyberTECH, the parent organization for the Cyber incubator CyberHive and the Internet of Things incubator iHive. He also serves as a member of the EvoNexus Selection Committee where he reviews and mentors Cybersecurity and Internet of Things startups, and he is a member of the board of directors for the Cyber Center of Excellence. Gary holds numerous professional certifications including CISSP, CISA, and CRISC, and holds a Bachelor of Science in Information Systems Management from University of Maryland University College & Masters in Business Administration from San Diego State University.

LinkedIn Profile: http://www.linkedin.com/in/ghayslip
Twitter: @ghayslip

Made in the USA
Lexington, KY
05 August 2019